D1560043

*Kinship and Neighborhood
in a Southern Community*

Kinship and Neighborhood in a Southern Community

Orange County, North Carolina, 1849–1881

Robert C. Kenzer

The University of Tennessee Press

KNOXVILLE

A portion of this book was originally published in a somewhat different form as "Family, Kinship, and Neighborhood in an Antebellum Southern Community," in William J. Cooper, Jr. et al., eds., *A Master's Due: Essays in Honor of David Herbert Donald* (Baton Rouge: Louisiana State University Press, 1985). It is reprinted here with the gracious permission of Louisiana State University Press.

The paper in this book meets the minimum requirements of the American National Standard for Permanence of Paper for Printed Library Materials. ∞ The binding materials have been chosen for strength and durability.

Library of Congress Cataloging in Publication Data

Kenzer, Robert C., 1955–
    Kinship and neighborhood in a southern community.

    Bibliography: p.
    Includes index.
    1. Orange County (N.C.)—Social conditions.
2. Neighborhood—North Carolina—Orange County—History—19th century. 3. Kinship—North Carolina—Orange County—History—19th century. I. Title.
HN79.N82Q734   1987   306'.09756'565   87-13869
ISBN 0-87049-542-9 (alk. paper)

For Carol

Acknowledgments

In researching and writing this book I have incurred a number of debts. The original research was aided by very generous funding from both the Department of History and the Charles Warren Center for Studies in American History of Harvard University. During subsequent revisions I have received financial assistance from both the Center for Family and Community History and the Department of History of Brigham Young University.

One of the most enjoyable aspects of the research was the opportunity to work in a number of excellent archives, staffed with most capable and extremely kind individuals. These include the Southern Historical Collection and the North Carolina Collection in the library of the University of North Carolina, Chapel Hill, the Manuscript Department of William R. Perkins Library at Duke University, the North Carolina Division of Archives and History, and the Baker Library of the Harvard University Graduate School of Business Administration. Robert L. Byrd of the Manuscript Department of Duke University and Richard Shrader of the Southern Historical Collection were especially helpful.

A number of individuals have assisted me in the research, organization, and writing of this book. While working on my dissertation I received especially useful suggestions from Professors William L. Barney, Sydney Nathans, and Otto H. Olsen. Jean B. Anderson introduced me to many Orange County sources and provided me with copies of numerous genealogies. Betty June Hayes, the Register of Deeds for Orange County, helped me with the records in the

Orange County Courthouse. Neil L. York, my colleague at BYU, not only provided a number of excellent suggestions on how to revise my manuscript but constantly sustained my spirit through the long process of revisions.

Stephan Thernstrom was a most valuable second reader of my original dissertation at Harvard. His insight into how the methodology of urban historians could be adapted to a rural setting was quite helpful.

I am indebted to David Herbert Donald for his assistance during the research and writing of my dissertation and his repeated encouragement during the many revisions of the manuscript. He has been most generous with his time and energy in reading numerous drafts of my chapters and, through what I am sure was sometimes an ordeal for him, showed more patience than I could ever have expected. His kindness and warmth will remain the most fond memory of my graduate school years.

From the University of Tennessee Press I have benefited from the valuable insights of three readers, Orville Vernon Burton, Don Harrison Doyle, and James A. Ward, and received many excellent suggestions from acquisitions editor Cynthia Maude-Gembler, copyeditor Lee Campbell Sioles, and designer Dariel Mayer.

Although I note my wife Carol last in order, her role in my writing this book is first in importance. Her greatest contribution was not toiling over the manuscript census, copying thousands of marriage bonds, or taking photographs of tombstones on the most sultry of North Carolina summer days, though she did all of this and much more. Rather, it was her constant encouragement and companionship which helped this study reach its conclusion and gave it a far greater meaning for me than the story it may tell.

Contents

Illustrations

MAPS

CHARTS

Tables

Kinship and Neighborhood
in a Southern Community

Introduction

Previous examinations of southern culture have approached the region from a wide variety of perspectives, focusing variously on multiple or single states, collections of counties or specific ones, classes, races, institutions, or individuals. Although each of these approaches has provided valuable insights, none has been able to describe a fundamental unit which not only governed the daily lives of southerners but which tied generations of them together over time. By identifying a basic unit of southern culture—the rural neighborhood—this book advances a new framework for addressing some of the central issues of nineteenth-century southern history. These include the relations between classes, the role of families in shaping southern culture, and, most important, the continuities that persisted in southern life before, during, and after the Civil War.

Because this work's scope is confined to a single community—Orange County, North Carolina—rather than the entire region, it is possible to analyze in extensive detail southern social life, economic structure, government, and politics. There is no claim, however, at least in a statistical sense, that Orange County was typical of the entire South. Before the Civil War, slaveholding and cotton production in Orange County clearly resembled that in counties of the upper, rather than the lower, South. This investigation's emphasis on broad patterns, nevertheless, paints a portrait of a regional culture that negates the significant variations that others have noted were present in the South.

Recreating another community in detail or tracing the history of a

single community is not this study's purpose. Two general histories
of Orange County already exist. Further, in order to provide broad
interpretation in defining the role of rural neighborhoods, some
peripheral questions about demography, economic structure, and
politics must remain unanswered, particularly when the available
sources can provide at most only very sketchy conclusions.

This study starts with the basic observation that on the eve of the
Civil War, more than a century after Orange County was established, many of the descendants of the first white settlers were still
residing on their ancestors' original landholdings. Geography, the
means of transportation, secular and religious institutions, and, most
importantly, marriage patterns had created eight isolated, self-
contained, tightly knit, rural neighborhoods in the county. These
neighborhoods not only provided a source of security and continuity
for their inhabitants, but they were also the basis of social existence.
Even former residents of the neighborhoods who had moved to other
parts of the South felt their control. Further, their impact was so
pervasive that it crossed racial lines and had parallel effects on whites
and blacks.

The rural neighborhood's role was especially important in regard
to the community's antebellum economic and social structure. Historians who have been intrigued by the lack of social conflict in the
South should be interested in the way the rural neighborhoods in
Orange County defined social status not in strict economic terms but
through family and kinship ties. Ownership of land and slaves was
never the sole measurement of social status; the residents of these
rural neighborhoods had a more complex sense of time and place.
People of average or even no means could perceive wealthy planters
in familial rather than class terms, because they often possessed common ancestors.

The role of rural neighborhoods extended beyond economic and
social areas to touch numerous aspects of the community's administrative and political structure. Although historians have identified
the county court as the center of southern local administration, they
have devoted little attention to its role on an area smaller than the
county itself. In Orange County the antebellum county court served
as a representative, although undemocratic, body of the rural neighborhoods. If the court's members, the magistrates, were neither
elected nor were typical of the people of the neighborhoods they

represented, they nevertheless exerted their efforts in a direct manner to serve the kin network of their respective rural neighborhoods.

Politics also was shaped by the system of rural neighborhoods. Although historians have often emphasized the role of ideology in party politics before the Civil War, by the 1850s ideology had taken a back seat to kinship ties in Orange County in the forming of political allegiances. Party affiliation had become an inheritance bestowed upon young men, who received the traditional party orientation of their rural neighborhood. The parties had in fact institutionalized the rural neighborhood by informally recognizing it as the basic unit of party activity.

When the war came in 1861, the people of Orange County, like the people of the South as a whole, were prepared, because antebellum militia companies had for years been active in the rural neighborhoods. These units quickly were transformed into an army that retained both the rural neighborhood leadership and membership. Hence, what some have termed a "rich man's war, but a poor man's fight," was not actually a matter of the "poor man" being deceived by the "rich man." Once the fighting began, the "poor man" recognized that he was fighting to defend his neighborhood, which was literally represented by the composition of his military company. Further, it should not be surprising that southern military reversals coincided with the attrition of the rural neighborhood orientation of the military companies. Equally significant, as the war eroded the rural neighborhood's important role in the military, it also slowly destroyed the traditional self-sufficiency of the rural neighborhoods for civilians.

Although the war compelled both the soldiers and civilians of Orange County to abandon their traditionally isolated life patterns and become part of a larger world, the rural neighborhood was revived within a few years after the end of the conflict. If their attempt to maintain a traditional culture was defeated on the battlefield, the soldiers upon returning to Orange County reasserted the former basis of their society—the dominance of their rural neighborhoods and kinship ties. Even the freedmen, although searching for a new way of life, were influenced by the rural neighborhood.

Any new economic system that developed in the postwar years was bound to have roots in the antebellum rural neighborhood. Therefore, the often-cited primary rural institution of the New

South, the general store, and its leading actor, the credit-lending merchant, were both extensions of the prewar, rural neighborhood. Even the exploited tenant farmer, whose status declined under the new system of agriculture, was in fact a carryover from the prewar era.

Nor was significant change to be found even as a result of the new manufacturing enterprises that developed after the war. The tobacco manufacturing industry that sprang up during the 1870s in Orange County's flourishing town, Durham, had a traditional basis. Both the men who owned the new businesses and achieved previously unknown degrees of prominence and power from them and the workers who earned their livelihood within them were actually playing out antebellum roles. Most of the leaders of Durham's tobacco industry were not only natives of Orange County, but had been, or held close ties with, the antebellum planter elite. Therefore, if this new industry did not threaten the antebellum social structure of the county, neither did it endanger the traditional rural neighborhood orientation. In fact, by providing new opportunity, Durham and its industry reinforced traditional social and economic arrangements.

Perhaps it was only in the area of administration and politics that the role of the rural neighborhood was questioned during the postwar years. Even in this regard, however, tradition—in this case racial attitudes—still played a central role. Although many in Orange County desired to preserve the representative nature of the county administrative body, which by 1869 had been transformed from the county court to the county commission, it was impossible. If the county commission retained the practice of using the rural neighborhoods as a unit of administration, the antebellum notion of this body representing the neighborhoods could not be maintained in a society where nearly one-third of the population was black. To bypass the racial problem, traditional racial attitudes dictated that a new system had to be devised, even if it were neither representative nor democratic.

In order to meet the challenge of the new black voter, it was necessary for whites to abandon their antebellum rural neighborhood party orientation. The result was not only a new party system based primarily on race, but one that could easily justify turning its back on the common white man's vote. In addition, rather than developing a competitive, county-wide, two-party system, such as had existed before the war, the new political system and its machinery redefined the basic meaning of politics.

Orange County is the logical candidate for a study that would provide a new perspective on southern history because an unusually large number of its public and private records have survived. The Southern Historical Collection of the University of North Carolina and the Duke University Archives, two of the largest southern manuscript collections—both located within the nineteenth-century borders of Orange County—contain the papers of many of the county's residents and institutions. Additionally, the nearby North Carolina State Archives in Raleigh have preserved the public documents for the county. Supplementing these records and providing a week-by-week account of events in Orange County was the excellent newspaper, the *Hillsborough Recorder*.

Although others have drawn upon the same types of sources as those used in this study—the federal manuscript census, private correspondence, diaries, marriage records, wills, estate inventories, church minutes, mercantile ledgers, election returns, credit ratings, and especially genealogies—this study utilizes all of these sources simultaneously in an attempt to discover as much as possible about every inhabitant who lived in the county for three decades. Only after these sources are used collectively in the context of the rural neighborhood do they take on a meaning that offers us a new perspective on southern culture.

CHAPTER I

"We Are Well Blessed With Kin"

Family, Kinship, and Neighborhood in an Antebellum Southern Community

The history of Orange County, North Carolina, is a history not of individuals but of families. During the 1740s and 1750s the first permanent settlers came to Orange, primarily from Pennsylvania and Virginia. Their descendants were still residing in the same settlements a century later. By 1850 these settlements had evolved into tightly knit rural neighborhoods. Each neighborhood was tied together by an extensive network of kinship. This pattern of family structure was not confined to the white community: blacks developed a separate but parallel network of families. In Orange County, families lived close to each other, and people looked to their relatives and neighbors for assistance and security. This interlocking kinship network gave the county a remarkably stable social order prior to the Civil War.

I

Orange County was established as a political unit in 1752 in response to the needs of the growing population of North Carolina's piedmont. When formed, the county was rectangular in shape and stretched south from the Virginia border. It encompassed an enormous area, approximately 3500 square miles, that within a century was carved into ten other counties. (see Map 1).

Although some white settlers had come to this area of North Carolina as early as 1740, it was not until the early 1750s that the population began to grow rapidly. Only 20 residents paid taxes in

1748; 1113 paid in 1752. By 1767 Orange had the largest population of any county in North Carolina.[1]

Most of the settlers were Scotch-Irish and German immigrants from Pennsylvania who came to North Carolina's piedmont in search of less expensive land.[2] Many of them shared not only the common experience of migration but also a common ancestry. Often groups of them had lived in the same village in Europe and crossed the Atlantic on the same vessel. Once they settled on the Carolina frontier these families quickly forged their lives together. For instance, to the Hawfields settlement, located along the Haw River in the center of what would become Orange County, came the Blackwoods, Craigs, Freelands, Kirklands, Johnstons, and Strayhorns (see Map 1). Four of these families—the Blackwoods, Craigs, Freelands, and Kirklands—may have lived near one another in County Londonderry in northern Ireland before moving to the colonies in the same vessel.[3] These families arrived in America around 1741 and settled in Paxtang Township, along the Susquehannah River in Dauphin County, Pennsylvania. Here they probably met the Johnston family who, after coming from Ireland in 1732, had also settled in Dauphin.[4] Sometime between 1743 and 1745 these five families and Gilbert Strayhorn, who had just returned from North Carolina, made the trip down the Shenandoah Valley on what was known as the "Great Wagon Road" and settled near the Haw River.[5]

The land these people settled was composed of gently rolling hills and valleys. The area generally ranged from only 250 to 600 feet above sea level. The most fertile soil was in the bottomlands. Most of the land was blanketed by huge pine and hardwood forests. These trees served as an excellent building material for cabins and fences and as a source of fuel, but they also necessitated painstaking work, since there could be no farming until the land was cleared. The numerous rivers and creeks furnished the settlers with water for themselves and their livestock, but they also isolated groups of settlers from one another.

Intending to stay, the settlers promptly established a Presbyterian church, which they called "Hawfields." But within a few years rumors began to spread about the validity of the land titles they had received from the agents of the Earl of Granville, the Lord Proprietor of the land. Rather than defending their titles, all six of the original families of Hawfields moved about ten miles to the east, settled along a creek of the Haw River, and purchased this new land directly from the Earl of Granville (see Map 1). Trusting that their difficulties were past and their future secure at last, they named the creek "New Hope" and established another Presbyterian church there in 1756.[6]

In 1754 the county seat of Orange was located on four hundred acres five miles north of the New Hope Presbyterian church. First named "Corbin Town" and then "Childsburg," the town's name was changed in 1756 for a final time to "Hillsborough," to honor the Earl of Hillsborough.[7]

Hillsborough was the commercial as well as the administrative and judicial center for Orange County for over a century. By the 1770s the town, an observer recalled, "was a small village, which contained thirty or forty inhabitants, with two or three small stores and two or three ordinary taverns, but it was an improving village."[8] Although the town grew over the the next eighty years, it remained quite modest in size.

Other rural settlements similar to New Hope began to dot the countryside as the appeal of cheap and abundant land attracted other people to Orange. Eight miles northwest of Hillsborough another group of Scotch-Irish from the counties west of Philadelphia established themselves on the Eno River in 1755 and organized the Eno Presbyterian Church. Within six years some members from this settlement founded a new settlement and church a few miles to the east on the Little River.[9]

Such settlements never developed into villages or towns. Nor were they ever formally recognized as administrative, civil, or judicial districts. Rather, they were rural settlements that were largely self-sufficient: from birth to death most residents rarely found it necessary to leave the settlement's borders. But borders of settlements often overlapped, and residents living near the edge of one settlement might have a close relationship with those living nearby in the neighboring settlement.

At the same time the Scotch-Irish were settling the lands south and north of Hillsborough, Virginians were migrating to the lands east of the county seat.[10] Coming from the area between the Potomac and James rivers, their soil exhausted from over a century of cultivation, these Virginians chose the land along the Flat River about fifteen miles northeast of Hillsborough and along the New Hope and its tributaries. With the passing of time, these settlements became known as "Flat River" and "Patterson," the latter in honor of John T. Patterson, the first man to build a mill on the lower New Hope Creek.[11]

Not all settlers had such distinctive ethnic or geographic origins. Some Quakers came to Orange in these early years, probably from both Pennsylvania and eastern North Carolina. Rather than forming a distinct settlement, these Quakers lived in a diffused band stretching from Cane Creek to northeast of Hillsborough. But many of the Quakers moved west to Guilford County when it was formed in 1770; others who resided in the vicinity of the Eno and Little River settlements joined the Presbyterian churches there; and by the midnineteenth century, the Quakers' influence had disappeared.[12]

Another settlement grew up on the Cane Creek. The most prominent family in this area, the Cates, were probably Germans from Pennsylvania. Some of the other families had German surnames, but this settlement was not distinctly composed of Germans. Rather, what seems to have united these people was the establishment of the Cane Creek Baptist Church in 1789.[13]

Another settlement without a distinct ethnic background sprang up southwest of the New Hope and southeast of the Cane Creek settlements. Dominated by its largest family, the Lloyds, by the midnineteenth century this settlement was called "White Cross."

Still other settlers lived between the Flat River and the Patterson settlements, a fairly level area with few rivers or creeks to impede movement, so that its residents had a great deal of contact with their neighbors to the north, south, and west. This openness made this the least distinctive of all the settlements. The small village of Durham emerged there in the area during the 1850s.

II

By 1850 Orange County had been settled for more than a century, during which time many families had moved into the county, and others had left. Despite these changes, however, the basic pattern of Orange County settlements remained very much the same.

Judging from the surnames of the males who headed households in 1850, many of the residents by the mid-nineteenth century were descendants of the families who had settled the county during its early years. Specifically, forty-nine of the sixty most common surnames in 1850 were recorded on the county's 1779 tax list.[14] Because the county lost four-fifths of its area through five divisions—the last taking place in 1849—and because a substantial number of people moved west, some of these families were more numerous at one time or another. Nevertheless, what stands out is the continuity of surnames over a century.

There are no maps of Orange County from the 1850s to indicate where these families resided. Further, because this was a rural society, families had no street addresses. The only sources that provide a hint of where the families resided are the ledgers of the federal manuscript census, in which census takers recorded in handwriting their tabulations. Every ten years one or two census takers would travel across the county and record the names of all the free inhabitants. Hence, a general picture of residential patterns can be reconstructed by numbering the households in the same order that the census takers recorded them generally assuming that they numbered the families in the order they visited them and that, therefore, consecutive or nearly consecutive numbers suggest that families lived adjoining or near each other.[15] The manuscript census reveals that by 1850 the descendants of the original settlers were residing in the same eight settlements—which by then should be termed "rural neighborhoods"—that their ancestors had established (see Map 2). Each of these neighborhoods contained approximately 250 households and covered 80 square miles (see Appendix 1-A to B).[16] There were about three households to a square mile. Therefore, there was one family for every 200 acres, although residents of the neighborhood lived much closer than these figures might suggest because a large number tended to cluster along creeks and rivers.

Since these neighborhoods were neither recognized as civil divisions nor mentioned in any public records, their borders were never legally defined. For the residents of these neighborhoods, however, no formal definition was necessary. If a stranger were to ask them to indicate on a map of Orange County where their neighborhood was located, like the historian, they probably would have drawn a circle on the map. Nevertheless, they constantly showed in their writing and actions that their neighborhood was the focal point of their family, as well as the primary force shaping their community's social, economic, political, and administrative structure. For these people, therefore, the rural neighborhood was not only a place where they lived, but a way of life.

The Lloyds, residents of the White Cross neighborhood, are representative inhabitants of a neighborhood.[17] Thomas Lloyd, the founder of the Lloyd family in Orange, came from Virginia in the 1750s. Settling between nine and ten miles south of Hillsborough, Lloyd was appointed a justice of the peace in 1757 and served as a member of the North Carolina General Assembly for a number of terms between 1761 and 1768. Lloyd fathered three sons, two of whom remained in Orange for the remainder of their lives. These sons in turn produced more children, almost all of whom remained in the county. By 1850 there were nineteen grandsons and great-grandsons of Thomas Lloyd in Orange who bore his surname, headed households, and lived in close proximity to where he originally settled. After Thomas Lloyd's land was divided among his children, they tended to live quite near one another, often on adjacent land. In turn, when this property was inherited by his grandchildren, they continued to live side by side. Cousins also resided in the same general area, though they lived further apart.[18]

This pattern of close kin residences in rural neighborhoods was partly an outgrowth of geography and the lack of transportation. In 1772 Governor Josiah Martin commented to the Earl of Hillsborough on the "extreme badness of the roads" in Orange; eighty years later they were not much better.[19] Until 1855, when the North Carolina Central Railroad linked Hillsborough and Durham, a horse or carriage hobbled along the thirteen miles of dirt path between the two points "at a rate of not much better than three miles per hour."[20] Other roads in the county were similarly jolting and slow—and well near impassable following rain or snow.[21]

Residents of one neighborhood consequently had little social or commercial intercourse with those of another. Children grew up acquainted with only a limited number of nearby residents. Even after the beginning of a common school system in 1839, the pattern of local isolation was unbroken. School district borders were drawn to prevent children from facing the dangers of crossing creeks or rivers, which were quite often already the borders of neighborhoods.[22]

The church, probably the most important social institution in the lives of Orange's families, also seems to have been affected by these residential patterns. For instance, between 1823 and 1860 the Little River Presbyterian Church had a large number of members, but about one-third of the members' surnames accounted for three-fourths of the membership.[23] The families with the most common surnames in the church—the Woods, Halls, Allisons, and Rays—all could trace their ancestry in Orange as far back as 1761, when both the Little River settlement and church were established.

The church, which had strong disciplinary power, played an important role in preserving the bonds between families and promoting cohesion in the neighborhood. For example, two sisters-in-law in the Little River Presbyterian Church were called before the church elders for "living a very unhappy life" because they "had a fight" with one another. Apparently the elders soothed the women's differences, for the church's records note the two "agreed to become reconciled to each other & to endeavor to live in the future as Christians should do."[24]

The church regulated behavior and promoted conformity to the norms of morality of the neighborhood. One scholar of southern evangelicalism has given this process the appropriate title, "To Set In Order the Things that are Wanting."[25] Between 1823 and 1860 the Little River Presbyterian Church called members before the elders fourteen times for such infractions as intoxication, gambling, and profanity. Only in three cases did the elders find it necessary to excommunicate members.[26] In all of these cases the excommunication resulted from the member's continual refusal, often over a period of a year, to come before the elders, answer the charges, and show signs of repentance. By their defiance of church authority, these three members had in fact removed themselves from the church, and the excommunication merely acknowledged this situation. This defiance could not have been the result of fear of punishment. The elders, realizing that severe punishment might force the relatives of guilty members into an uncomfortable position, demonstrated a high degree of tolerance. They even permitted a fellow elder charged with swindling and forgery to be readmitted into the church once he displayed repentance. That so many did agree to display such repentance demonstrates the powerful role that the church must have played in their lives.[27]

These isolated, self-contained, rural neighborhoods were cemented by a distinctive pattern of marriages. Since family connections were

MAP 1   *Orange County, ca. 1752*

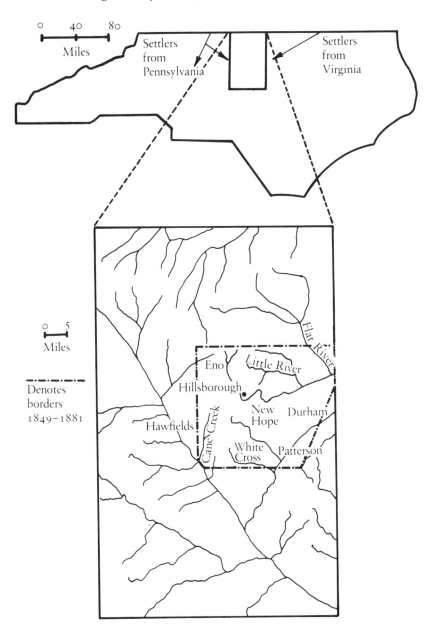

so intimate and so important, young people contemplating marriage had to consider not only their own preferences but also the wishes of their relatives and friends in the neighborhood. Writing in 1857, Lambert Hall of the Little River neighborhood cautioned his bride-to-be, Frances Bennett, that "before matters go too far with us, I would like us to consult some of our nearest and dearest friends relative to the subject [marriage] between us to see if it would be agreeable or not with the majority of them."[28] He later suggested that a grandmother who favored the marriage might help secure parental consent. "You stated," he acknowledged to his fiancée, "that you had talked to your grandma about it and that she seemed very willing to it. . . . She also told you that she talked to your parents about [it]—but seems as if they had not desided [sic] yet."[29]

If couples received parental consent and got married, as newly-weds they still sought the blessings of other relatives. They would spend days, as one groom termed it, "visiting *kinfolks*." The round of visits might go on some time, he predicted: "I think it will take us [from summer] until Christmas to get around seeing all; we are well blessed with kin."[30]

Ordinarily young people found their spouses among nearby neighbors. Half the brides and grooms lived less than one hundred households apart—about one to three miles—before their marriages (see Table 1 and Appendix 1-A to C). In only a few cases did spouses come from households listed in the census as over five hundred households apart, or from two different neighborhoods.[31]

No neighborhood better represented the pattern of marriages between nearby residents than New Hope. The marriage between John Kirkland and Mary Jane Strayhorn in 1851 illustrates how, during four generations, marriages had united the families that originally settled New Hope (see Chart 1). Both John and Mary Jane had strong connections with the Blackwoods, Craigs, and Johnstons. Further enhancing their common ancestry was the fact that, through sibling exchange, William Craig's sister Elizabeth had married William Blackwood and William Blackwood's sister Margaret had married William Craig. The only one of the six original New Hope families not represented in their genealogy is the Freelands; but, in fact, both John and Mary Jane had numerous ties with the Freelands through marriages of their aunts, uncles, and siblings.[32]

Marriages further unified the neighborhoods because the newly-

The tombstone of Lambert W. and Frances Bennett Hall. This Little River neighborhood couple felt it important to consult the feelings of their friends and relatives before they married. (Photograph by the author.)

weds established their new households near their parents (see Table 2 and Appendix 1-D). In nearly six out of ten marriages the bride and groom established their new household less than one hundred houses —under three miles—from one or the other's parents. This close residence of parents and children was clearly dictated by the agrarian nature of the economy.[33] Therefore, for both spouses, marriage meant not a dramatic separation from but continued close association with both sets of parents.

This pattern of marriage and residence bonded together a number of households in the neighborhood which, even though headed by people with different surnames, nevertheless had a common ancestry. For example, a list of the households from the manuscript census for the White Cross neighborhood immediately bordering the household

CHART 1 *Genealogy of John Kirkland and Mary Strayhorn of New Hope*

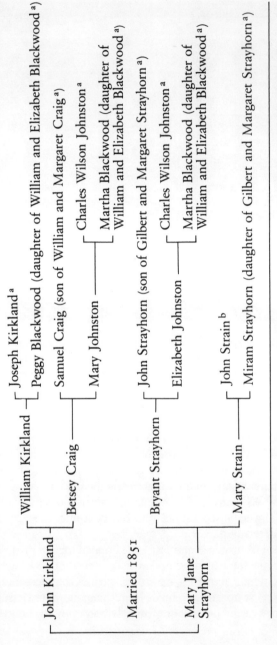

SOURCES: David I. Craig, *A Historical Sketch of the New Hope Church, in Orange County, North Carolina* (Reidsville: N.C.: S. W. Paisley, 1886.) 12–19; Luther M. Sharpe Genealogy, Luther M. Sharpe Papers, William R. Perkins Library, Duke University, Durham, N.C.: Henry Poellnitz Johnston, *The Gentle Johnstons and Their Kin* (Birmingham: The Featon Press, 1966).
[a]Denotes an original settler of New Hope.
[b]Henry Poellnitz Johnston explains that the names "Strain" and Strayhorn refer to the same family.

The tombstones of John and Mary Jane Strayhorn Kirkland. Their marriage in 1851 symbolized more than a century of kinship marriages between the descendants of the founders of the New Hope neighborhood. (Photograph by the author.)

of Stephen Lloyd II, one of Thomas Lloyd's grandsons, demonstrates the bonds of kinship shared by neighbors in 1850 and 1860 (see Chart 2). Within the neighborhoods, children in one family frequently married siblings in another family. Thus two of the six sons and three of the five daughters of Henry Lloyd (Stephen II's cousin and another of Thomas's grandsons) chose spouses with the surname "King." Forms of leviratic marriage, though not common, strengthened these neighborhood bonds. For example, William Brewer, following the death of his wife, Nancy Lloyd Brewer, married her sister, Sally. He had two sons by each sister.

III
The diary of Adolphus Williamson Mangum gives us some insight into what it was like to reside in these isolated, self-contained, inter-

CHART 2 *Relationship of Head of Household to Stephen Lloyd II*

Household Number in 1850 Census	Name of Household Head	Relationship to Stephen Lloyd II
542	Lloyd, Stephen III	son
543	Lloyd, Henry B.	son
544	Lloyd, Manly	son
545	Lloyd, Stephen II	
546	Lloyd, Chesley	son
547	Andrews, Henry C.	grandson
548	Suit, Jourdan	unidentifiable [a]
549	Reeves, John	unidentifiable
550	Poe, Hasting	cousin's husband
551	Durham, Mebane	niece's husband
552	Lloyd, William	cousin
553	Brewer, William	son-in-law
554	Lloyd, Dilly	sister-in-law
in 1860 Census		
1576	Andrews, William	cousin's husband
1577	McCauley, Elizabeth	cousin
1578	Poe, William	unidentifiable
1579	King, Matthew	niece's husband
1580	Pearson, Presley	unidentifiable
1581	Brewer, Merideth	grandson
1582	Brewer, William	son-in-law
1583	Lloyd, Stephen III	son
1584	Andrews, George	son-in-law
1585	Lloyd, Stephen II	
1586	Lloyd, Manly	son
1587	Lloyd, Henry B.	son
1588	Strowd, Andrew	unidentifiable
1589	Lloyd, Chesley	son
1590	Lloyd, Sidney	cousin
1591	Strowd, Alfred P.	niece's husband's brother

SOURCES: U.S. Census MS., Orange County, 1850. 1860, Schedule 1; Thomas Lloyd Papers, Duke University Library, Durham, N.C.; Eugene Suggs, "Sketches of Major General Thomas Lloyd of Orange County, North Carolina, " North Carolina Collection, University of North Carolina Library, Chapel Hill, N.C. For a discussion of the census taker's route and an explanation why households are not always listed as neighbors in consecutive censuses, see Appendix 1-A.
[a] Many of those who are listed as unidentifiable were probably related to Stephen, but the exact relationship cannot be determined.

MAP 2   *The Rural Neighborhoods of Orange County, 1850s*

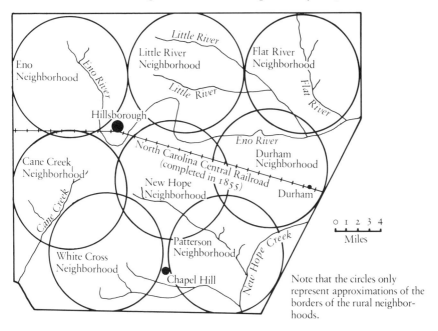

Eno
Neighborhood

Little River

Little River
Neighborhood

Little River

Flat River
Neighborhood

Flat River

Eno River

Hillsborough

Eno River
Durham
Neighborhood

Cane Creek
Neighborhood

North Carolina Central Railroad
(completed in 1855)

New Hope
Neighborhood

Durham

Cane Creek

0 1 2 3 4

Miles

White Cross
Neighborhood

Patterson
Neighborhood

New Hope Creek

Chapel Hill

Note that the circles only
represent approximations of the
borders of the rural neighborhoods.

married neighborhoods in Orange County during the 1850s.[34] Adolphus proved to be a very careful observer of his neighborhood, Flat
River. On one walk through the neighborhood, he explored his feelings about the area, which were linked to his childhood experience:

> . . . I passed my childhood scenes & had my reminiscences of child-
> hood recalled to my view. . . . I crossed the fence below the old school-
> house spring & here . . . were the trees that I used to climb with my
> supposed agility, the old spring around which we used to meet &
> indulge in mirthful glee; and at which I used to slake my "often-
> returning thirst." . . .
> . . . I passed by the old steep bank higher up old Dials [Creek] to the
> washing hole where the striplings of the neighborhood used to meet on
> Sunday mornings & play & wash in the water. So pleasant were the
> hours that I spent there that I never shall forget the spot while I walk
> these mortal shores. The sandybank, the old oak logs, the peculiar shape
> of the hole of water & the overshadowing trees strange as it may seem
> have an unchanging home in the memory. Oh scenes of my childhood,
> how dear, how unequalled, how long remembered!!![35]

For Adolphus and for many others like him who could trace their ancestry back for a century in the neighborhood, time, place, and person were interwoven and could never be separated.[36]

Adolphus also described the neighborhood general store, which rivaled the church as an important focal point for the neighborhood's residents. They would gather at the store not only to purchase those goods—such as salt, sugar, cloth, and gunpowder—that could not be produced in the neighborhood, but to meet their friends and relatives. At the store of Adolphus's father, where he frequently found himself "*pro tem*" clerk, often he and "several others had a long 'chat' on matters and things in general. . . . "[37] At the general store, which served as a post office, neighbors read copies of such local, state, and national publications as the *Hillsborough Recorder*, *The Christian Advocate*, and *The National Intelligencer*.[38] Political meetings and temperance society gatherings also took place at the store.[39] The general store, therefore, not only united the neighborhood people, but it also provided them contact with the outside world.

Much of Adolphus's diary is primarily a log of his and his relatives' visits with each other. His cousins—the Parkers, Laws, Cozarts, Moizes, Carringtons, Lockharts, Harrises, and Mangums —frequently came to his home for conversation and stayed to share meals. Although these kinsmen lived a very short distance away, often after an evening of socializing they would chose to stay overnight at the Mangums' house.[40]

One series of visits that Adolphus made was to his great aunt, Dicey Mangum, who, though in her seventies, lived alone.[41] On one occasion he brought her some game he had hunted. Such assistance between the generations of families was particularly important in Orange, where in 1860 more than 80 percent of the men aged seventy or older still continued to head their own households. Support of family and relatives was also very important for the almost 17 percent of the households in Orange that were headed by women.[42] Twenty-four percent of the elderly men and 17 percent of the women who headed households resided just next door to someone with the same surname as their own.[43] Many more of them lived equally close to kin with a different surname.

Relatives assumed a high degree of responsibility for each other not only out of love but because of fear of what neighbors would

Adolphus Williamson Mangum, Sr. (1834–90). His diary elo-
quently described the role of family and kinship ties in the Flat
River neighborhood. (Photograph courtesy of North Carolina
Collection, UNC Library at Chapel Hill.)

think or say about intentional maltreatment or even neglect. When a
seventy-eight-year-old mother insisted on heading her own household, her sons worried. "She might fall & be seriously hurt for life,"
one brother warned another. Further, he explained, "Is it not a duty
we owe ourselves & our mother[?] . . . heretofore we have held our
peace, let anything happen to her & we will be held responsible, let
us therefore advise her, if she does not choose to act upon the advise
[sic] given, we are to some extent clear." [44] The mother seems to have

had the final word in the matter, for seven years later, while she lived next door to one son, she still continued to head her own household. Protection and assistance to kin extended to children in this era when disease often swept through the region and struck down parents. In nearly half the cases when both parents were lost, the court awarded custody of the orphan to a relative with whom the child shared a surname. In a large number of other cases the aid was provided by a relative in the neighborhood with a different surname. For instance, in 1852 Bryant Strayhorn of New Hope became the guardian for his niece and nephew, Elizabeth and Joseph Craig.[45]

Such kinship ties bound the neighborhoods together. From birth to death, residents' lives were shaped not only by the households in which they lived but also by the kin network of the neighborhood.

IV

Residents of these closely knit, intermarried neighborhoods rarely moved elsewhere. Demographers, in dealing with the highly fluid population of the United States in this era, often speak of the "rate of persistence"—the percentage of the population that remained in the same locality from one decennial census to another. In several southern and western communities only 30 to 40 percent of the population stayed on through the 1850s.[46] But in Orange County the rate of persistence was higher (see Table 3.A). Fifty percent of the white men living in Orange in 1850 still resided in the county ten years later.

The rate of persistence varied with age. Men in their twenties were the least persistent; as a man grew older and approached middle age, he became more likely to remain in Orange. It is harder to calculate how many older men stayed in the county because, during a decade, death would remove their names from the census ledgers. Still it is evident that the vast majority of elderly men stayed in Orange for a decade.[47]

Whether or not a man was a household head also affected his decision to stay in the county or to move elsewhere. At all age levels men who did not head households—who therefore probably were not married—were less persistent than those who did (see Table 3.B). The emigration of young men in their twenties produced less social disruption in the neighborhoods than the removal of middle-aged men who had families.

Men who had kinsmen in the neighborhood were also less likely to emigrate than those who had none. Indeed, the more relatives a man had, the more likely he was to remain in the county (see Table 3.C); number of relatives was a stronger factor in persistence than even extent of property or slave ownership.[48]

In Orange County as a whole during the 1850s there was a much higher rate of persistence than in other American communities. This can be explained in part by Orange's predominantly rural population; farmers were less likely to emigrate than city dwellers.[49] An equally important factor was the fact that the overwhelming majority of the population was native born. By 1860 almost every head of household in Orange was native not only to the United States but to North Carolina. By contrast, in the northern states, recently arrived Irish and German immigrants, who moved more frequently, lowered the rate of persistence.[50]

This higher rate of persistence in Orange County also suggests that the few newcomers to the area were assimilated into the rural neighborhoods. A man who moved into a neighborhood, purchased property, joined the local church, and married a woman with one of the common surnames, was likely to remain in Orange. His children would be even more likely to stay, since through their mother's family they had a number of kin connections in the neighborhood.

The higher rate of persistence in Orange County needs to be placed in the wider perspective of North Carolina and the community's history. Being a seaboard state with virtually no immigration, beginning in the early nineteenth century North Carolina experienced a much slower rate of population growth than the other states, as many of its citizens migrated west in search of greater economic opportunity. As a result, the state's population dropped in national rank from fifth in 1820 to twelfth in 1860. By the latter date, 405,621 North Carolina natives resided outside of the state, compared to a total population in North Carolina of 992,622.[51] Indicative of this long-term demographic pattern, Orange County's population remained fairly stable during the 1850s; indeed, where there were 11,330 whites in 1850, there were but 11,311 in 1860. Already a significant disparity had developed in the adult sex ratio, as the number of women aged twenty to thirty-nine began to surpass men of the same age who, as has been shown, were very likely to migrate.[52] Hence, by the 1850s a selective process already may have been in place for a number of decades, as those who were most likely to leave the community had already left it. Consequently, those men who remained in the county during the 1850s formed a highly stable core who, despite the catastrophic impact of the Civil War, would still be residing in the community in 1870. What makes this stable core particularly noteworthy was that it included an unusually large number of young men. Orange County's rate of persistence nearly matched that of Chelsea Township, Vermont—a community that has been identified as having probably the highest rate of persistence in the nation during this era—despite Orange County's having a much larger share of men between the ages of twenty and thirty-nine.[53]

Though most inhabitants remained in Orange, something needs to be said about those who left. The federal manuscript census provides information only on those who stayed in the same county for a decade, but family genealogies tell something of the lives of those who left Orange. These genealogies do not present the traditional picture of people forced to break off family ties as they migrated to the frontier.[54] Rather, those who left Orange seem to have been fairly successful in transplanting the kinship network established in Orange to their new frontier locations.

One of the best examples of this transplantation can be found among the descendants of the Johnston family of the New Hope neighborhood. Three of the seven children of George Johnston, son of Charles Wilson Johnston, an original settler of New Hope, left Orange and migrated during the 1830s to Greene County, Alabama. In addition, three of George's married granddaughters, children of the four siblings who remained in Orange, made their way to Greene. A son of George's sister, Mary, who married a Samuel Craig, also migrated to Greene. In Greene County these emigrant families from Orange continued to intermarry.[55] In so doing they were only repeating the actions of their ancestors who had left Ireland with their relatives and neighbors, initially settled in Pennsylvania, and then moved to Orange.[56]

Kinship thus played an important role in promoting continuity. Within Orange this continuity was expressed by high rates of persistence. The kin network, however, was not limited to Orange's borders but extended beyond them to the frontier, where it encouraged a more stable transition from the older communities of the East to the younger communities of the West.

V

Orange County was not simply a white community: one-third of its population consisted of blacks, the vast majority being slaves. The same forces that so significantly shaped the relations among whites also affected those among blacks.

The first tax list for Orange in 1755 recorded that 8 percent of the white families owned slaves. During the second half of the eighteenth century the number of slaves grew at a rate similar to that of the white population, and by 1790 blacks composed 17 percent of the county's population. Throughout the first half of the nineteenth century, the slave population grew at an even faster rate than the white population and stood by 1860 near 33 percent.[57]

The experiences of slaves in Orange County varied. Some masters were protective and lenient; others were careless and harsh. One former slave from Orange County remembered spartan conditions: "We did not know nothin' 'bout feather beds. Slaves like dat had bunks an' some slept on de floor. We went barefooted most of the time."[58] In contrast, another slave fondly recalled: "When any of us niggers got sick Mis' Annie would come down to de cabin to see us. She brung de best wine, good chicken an' chicken soup an' everything else she had at de big house dat she thought we would like, an' she done everything else she could to get us well again."[59]

Slaves' perceptions of slavery differed depending on the size of their masters' holdings. In 1860, Paul C. Cameron, the owner of nearly five hundred slaves, was the largest slaveholder in Orange.[60] Although his slaves were generally well treated, their sheer numbers forced them to live fairly regimented lives that included little contact with their master. This fact was noted by one of Cameron's former slaves who stated, "Marse Paul had a heap of nigrahs. . . . When he met dem in de road he wouldn' know dem an' when he axed who dey wus an' who dey belonged to, dey tell him dey belonged to Marse Paul Cameron an' den he would say dat wus all right for dem to go right on."[61] The majority of slaveholders owned few slaves, however, and these masters not only lived in close proximity to their slaves but often worked alongside them in the fields.

Stagville Plantation slave quarters. The barracks-like housing in which some of Paul C. Cameron's slaves lived. (Photograph courtesy of North Carolina Division of Archives and History.)

As slave marriages were not recognized by law, families always faced the danger of separation.[62] A former slave from Orange sadly recalled the difficulties and pains of the slave family: "I belonged to a man named Bob Hall. . . . He died when I was eight years old and I was put on the block and sold in Nelson Hall's yard by the son of Bob Hall. I saw my brother and sister sold on this same plantation. My mother belonged to the Halls, and father belonged to the Glenns. They sold me away from my father and mother and I was carried to the state of Kentucky."[63] It is not surprising then that another former slave concluded that marriage and family life was "a joke in the days of slavery." He remembered: "the main thing in allowing any form of matrimony among the slaves was to raise slaves in the same sense and for the same purpose as stock raisers raise horses and mules, that is for work. A woman who could produce fast was in great demand. . . ."[64] Despite all these problems, slaves sought to establish and preserve their families. Evidence of their success in maintaining stability in slave family relations comes from a questionnaire many completed after the Civil War. When required by law between 1866 and 1868 to declare how long they had lived together, black couples in Orange reported marital relations spanning a long period. Two-thirds said they had been married before the war.[65]

Just as geography limited the number of potential spouses for whites, the boundaries of even the largest plantation in the county severely restricted the choices for slaves. A slave could marry either another slave who also resided on the plantation, or, if the master permitted it, one from a nearby plantation. The slaves of small slaveholders, like their masters, rarely left the neighborhood. Therefore, for these slaves, selection of spouses was even more restricted. These restrictions resulted in the creation of a black community bonded together by a century of intermarriage in a manner quite similar to that of the white neighborhoods.[66]

Like Orange County whites, slaves mostly lived and died within the same community. When a master died, there was always a possibility that his slaves could be sold to an owner outside of the county, but in most cases they were parceled out among the master's children, nearly all of whom lived in the same rural neighborhood.[67] The kin-oriented structure of the white rural neighborhood, therefore, generally allowed the slaves to preserve their own network of kinship.

VI

The isolation after initial settlement in Orange County, together with the continued rural nature of the region, the lack of foreign immigration, and the limited means of transportation—all fostered a life largely shaped by the primary relations among kinfolk. Although close family residences did not always guarantee absolute harmony, they did encourage stability. By promoting cohesion and order, the network of kinship in Orange not only shaped the county's antebellum economic, social, administrative, and political structure, it also later defined the character of both the community's participation in the Civil War and the impact of that conflict on the community.

CHAPTER 2

Kin over Class

The Antebellum Economic
and Social Structure

Antebellum Orange County had a fairly simple economic structure. Most of the people were farmers, and even those who did not farm were closely tied to the county's agrarian economy. Although the few towns had a more diverse occupational composition than the countryside, they failed to provide an alternative source of employment for the county's farmers. Most of the county's farmers grew enough food on their farms to meet their needs. For those products that could not be produced locally, a farmer did not need to look further than the rural general store in his neighborhood. Therefore, the farmers' economic contacts with the outer world were few and occurred through local intermediaries.

The social structure of this agricultural economy was marked first by a caste line that separated all blacks (mostly slaves) from all whites. Whites, in turn, belonged to one of two groups: planter families who owned huge plantations and large numbers of slaves, and farmer families who made their living on small plots of land. Such vast disparities in wealth held the potential for creating intense class conflict among whites, but in Orange County the caste division based on race, together with the network of kinship, prevented class antagonism and promoted social cohesion.

I

Before the Civil War, Orange County was an agricultural society with three-fourths of all white men reporting that farming was their primary occupation (see Table 4). Further, a number of men, especially older ones, who had other occupations, also operated farms.[1]

Even the small segment of the population employed in manufacturing was still linked to agriculture. In 1860 nearly half of the county's manufacturing firms were mills that ground the locally grown corn and wheat. These were not factories that employed large numbers of laborers; indeed, rarely did more than two men work in a mill.[2] Most of the other manufacturing firms were blacksmiths, tanners, wool carders, wagon makers, and carriage builders, all of whom produced for the limited market created by Orange County farmers. The average amount of capital invested in these firms did not exceed the value of a medium-sized farm.[3]

There were only two true manufacturing establishments. The first of these was the "Orange Factory Cotton Mill," which manufactured cotton yarn. The second was the "Webb and Whitted Tobacco Factory," which produced plug tobacco. The cotton mill employed fifty and the tobacco factory nineteen workers. Since the tobacco factory was located in Hillsborough, its workers probably resided in the town; however, the cotton mill's location on the Flat River compelled the mill's owners to construct houses for their employees. Because of its location, "Orange Factory" became a very tiny community unto itself, with its own post office and store. Many of its employees were young women for whom mill work was but temporary employment before marriage.[4] Though larger, these firms, like the other manufacturing enterprises in Orange, relied totally on local agricultural products for their raw materials.[5]

II

In addition to the rural neighborhoods, the county contained one hamlet (Durham), one village (Chapel Hill), and one town (Hillsborough). None of the three provided farmers in the county with alternative employment.

In the early 1850s "Durhamville"—or, as it later was called, "Durham,"—was merely a post office named after a nearby resident, Dr. Bartlett Durham. In 1854, however, because of Dr. Durham's donation of four acres, the North Carolina Central Railroad decided to establish a depot on the site. Within the next six years, three stores, two barrooms, one hotel, a church, and close to thirty dwellings surrounded the depot. In 1858 Robert F. Morris moved to Durham and established a tobacco manufacturing firm in one

The University of North Carolina on the eve of the Civil War. (Photograph courtesy of North Carolina Collection, UNC Library at Chapel Hill.)

of these small houses. The hamlet had only about a hundred inhabitants.[6]

The village of Chapel Hill was founded in 1793, the year after the trustees of the University of North Carolina decided to construct the new state university on a site twelve miles south of Hillsborough. Over the next sixty years the village and the university grew together. By 1860, to meet the needs of a permanent population of about 250 people, there were the expected number of merchants and craftsmen. In addition, to cater to the special interests of the university's faculty and students, there were a number of boarding houses, three restaurants, two tailors, a bookseller, and even a florist.[7] One professor's wife found the village "a pleasant place to live" in which the "society cannot be surpassed."[8]

The university also provided Chapel Hill with a most diverse population. Faculty members hailed not only from North Carolina and other southern states, but from such northern states as New York, New Jersey, and New Hampshire. The student body, which tripled in size between 1840 and 1860 (when it stood at 460 scholars), matched the diversity of the faculty. Although intended originally as a state university, the University of North Carolina became a southern institution; in 1860 only about 60 percent of the students were natives of North Carolina. The rest represented almost every southern and occasionally a northern state.[9]

Once they collected in Chapel Hill, some students demonstrated little interest in scholarship. "This is a good place for a boy to get an education," one student informed his sister, "but I think Chapel Hill makes more fools than wise men." The university's officials had to deal with students who often "engaged in carousing" and on one occasion accidentally burned the university belfry. In 1858 some students, who had formed a "lawless club," intentionally started a bonfire with benches and blackboards they had removed from recitation rooms. Leaders of the movement were expelled and forced to reimburse the university. By 1860 the university had sent some distinguished alumni to the political arena: one president, one vice-president, ten United States senators, and fifty members of the House of Representatives.[10]

Hillsborough was the only true town in Orange. However, even it remained modest in size because it failed to become either a major trade or manufacturing center. By 1860 there were a number of merchants and craftsmen in the town, but the market for their goods and services was quite limited.[11] Unlike Durham, the county seat was unaffected by the construction of the North Carolina Central Railroad in the 1850s; from 1850 to 1860 the town's population rose from 917 to only 942 inhabitants.[12]

The presence of a number of lawyers shaped the town's economic structure. Hillsborough was the residence of such noted North Carolina jurists as Frederick Nash and Thomas Ruffin. Because lawyers were trained through apprenticeships in this era, the presence of these lawyers attracted other would-be lawyers to the town. Graduates of the state university flocked from Chapel Hill to Hillsborough to study law. For example, after his graduation from the university in 1824, William A. Graham of Lincoln County, North Carolina, who would later be the state's governor, moved to Hillsborough to study law under Thomas Ruffin. Once his apprenticeship ended, Graham, like many others, decided to remain in the town.[13]

With the earnings from their law practices these lawyers purchased land and slaves, and, although they could have moved out into the country, many continued to reside in Hillsborough. To meet the needs and tastes of these affluent men and their families, educators and other professionals also moved into Hillsborough. For example, in 1837 the Rev. and Mrs. Robert Burwell moved from Virginia to Hillsborough to establish a female academy for girls. Over the next twenty years the Burwell Academy educated not only Hillsborough's wealthy daughters, but girls from the best families of North Carolina. Similarly, in 1858, when Colonel Charles C. Tew, a native of Charleston, South Carolina, looked for a site on which to establish a military academy for boys in North Carolina, he chose Hillsborough.[14] John Berry, a resident of the town and one of North Carolina's most gifted architects, spent most of his life designing the homes for the best of Hillsborough society. By 1860 the town had five carpenters, three coach and carriage makers, two tailors, one jeweler, and one gardener—all of whom primarily served the needs of the wealthy.[15]

III

Most Orange County residents had little to do with these townsmen. The self-sufficiency of their farms reinforced the self-contained character of the rural neighborhoods.

MAP 3   *A Soil Survey of Orange County, ca. 1860*

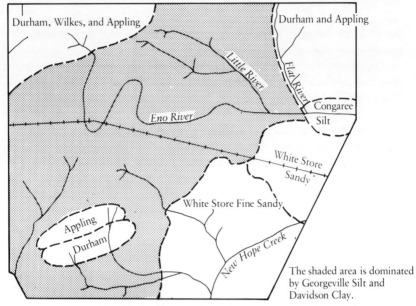

Durham, Wilkes, and Appling

Durham and Appling

Little River

Flat River

Congaree
Silt

Eno River

White Store
Sandy

White Store Fine Sandy

Appling
Durham

New Hope Creek

The shaded area is dominated
by Georgeville Silt and
Davidson Clay.

SOURCES: E.S. Vanatta et. al., *Soil Survey of Orange County* (Washington, D.C.: U.S. Department of Agriculture, 1921); S.O. Perkins et al., *Soil Map of Durham County* (Washington, D.C.: U.S. Department of Agriculture, 1920).

The geography of the county helps to explain the type of farming they practiced. Although there are over twenty different types of soil in Orange County, most of the land belongs to one of a few predominant types (see Map 3).[16] In nearly half the county the soil is a mixture of both Georgeville silt and Davidson clay loams, which run in a broad band from the southwest to the northeast. The next most prevalent soil type, White Store fine sandy loam, is confined to the Patterson neighborhood in the southeastern corner of the county. In the Durham neighborhood, directly to the northeast, much of the soil is of the White Store sandy variety. The northeast and northwest corners of the county and patches of the White Cross neighborhood consist primarily of Durham, Wilkes, and Appling loams. Finally, one last important soil type—Congaree silt loam—is found along the rivers and creeks of the entire county and is present in large quantities along the Eno River east of the point at which it meets the Flat River.

All of the soil in Orange, to varying degrees, is suitable for corn and wheat production, and in 1860 nearly all farmers, both north and south of the North Carolina Central Railroad, grew corn and wheat.[17] Since the Georgeville silt and Davidson clay loams generally produced low yields of such crops as tobacco and cotton, this great central swath, stretching diagonally from southwest to northeast, was used primarily for growing grains.

In 1860 the production of cotton was confined to the White Store fine sandy soil in the southeast and the Congaree silt loam along the the lower New Hope Creek and the Eno River. As a listing of the order in which the federal census taker visited these farms indicates, the thirty-eight farmers who grew cotton lived close to each other. Although most farmers produced three bales of cotton or less, had small amounts of improved acreage, and owned few, if any, slaves, three planters—Paul Cameron, John Lipscomb, and Fendal Souther-land—all with large amounts of improved land and large numbers of slaves, alone produced more than 90 percent of all the county's cotton.

Before the Civil War, farmers in Orange grew tobacco on a much wider scale than cotton. Tobacco grew best on Durham, Wilkes, and Appling loam, most of which was found north of the railroad. Small amounts of tobacco were produced south of the railroad in the White Cross neighborhood, on its patches of Appling and Durham loam, and in the Durham neighborhood, on the coarse variety of White Store loam.[18]

The new "bright" tobacco, which in the 1850s was beginning to replace the "dark" variety traditionally grown in Maryland and Virginia, grew best on the siliceous soil found on the "gently rolling divides between the streams" prevalent in the northern half of the county.[19] Strips of this type of soil were so small that few farmers possessed enough of it to produce tobacco on a large scale. Because few tobacco producers had more than three to four acres under cultivation, they could not grow more than two thousand pounds of the crop.[20]

Tobacco was a labor-intensive crop that required care for the entire year.[21] From January through March a farmer would prepare the soil to produce tobacco beds by burning the ground to kill all grass and weed seeds, pulverizing the soil, and planting the tobacco seeds, which were so tiny that one hundred square yards of beds would be planted with only four tablespoons of seed. From April to May the farmer prepared the hills or furrows where his young tobacco plants would be transplanted from their beds. If the plants survived the transplanting in June, the farmer's work had really only begun. In July and August he had before him the painstaking tasks termed "laying," "topping," "worming," and "suckering," which involved his extracting excess stem, leaves, and sprouts as well as removing by hand the green horn-worm from each plant. In September and October the plants were cut and housed for curing. The curing process was done by air, fire, and flue. In November the leaves were stripped with great care from the stalks, sorted by quality, and rehung to achieve the proper amount of moisture. The final stages before marketing consisted of tying the leaves in bundles and packing (termed "prizing") them in hogsheads under pressure. Marketing did not occur until late spring or early summer. From seed bed to final sale, a year and a half passed.

Though most tobacco was grown on a small scale, planters who owned large numbers of slaves produced big crops. One-half of the farmers who owned slaves produced more than two thousand pounds of tobacco; only one-fourth of the nonslaveholding farmers did so. Only a few slaveholders produced more than five thousand pounds of tobacco, but these few accounted for nearly one-third of the entire crop.[22]

Even when producing cotton or tobacco, nearly all farmers raised enough food on their land to meet the needs of their households. Even north of the railroad, where three-fourths of the farmers grew tobacco, the overwhelming majority produced enough corn—the major foodstuff for southerners—to meet the needs of both the free and slave inhabitants of their households. Most of those who did not produce enough corn grew wheat.[23]

Since Orange County residents lived on self-sufficient farms, there were few destitute persons in the county. The county poorhouse took care of very young children, mostly orphans, and some very aged adults, especially those who were mentally deficient; the county lacked an orphanage or asylum. If others in the county needed assis-

The remains of the Little River neighborhood general store.
(Photograph by the author.)

tance, they generally obtained it from relatives who resided close to them, as when Adolphus Mangum of Flat River brought game he had hunted to his elderly great aunt Dicey Mangum.[24]

Because they grew their own food, Orange County farmers never went to the rural general stores to buy corn, rarely to purchase bacon. Although the goods purchased in these stores ranged from raisins to ribbons, pills to pitchers, and silk to soap, the items bought most often were sugar and coffee—neither of which could be produced locally. Other goods frequently purchased included such necessities as gloves, knives, and boots.[25]

Farmers did not venture beyond their local general stores to make purchases. For example, the customers at a general store in the southwestern section of the Cane Creek neighborhood in 1850 were mostly farmers who resided within a short distance of the establishment (see Map 4).[26] None of these customers made purchases at one of the larger general stores about ten miles to the northeast in Hillsborough. Most of the customers at the general stores in Hillsborough lived in the town or no more than one to two miles from its borders.[27]

Geography, credit, and social function—all determined that farmers made purchases only at their local general store. First, for a farmer in the Cane Creek neighborhood to travel the twenty miles round trip to shop at Hillsborough would have taken a needless six to eight hours. The ability to buy on credit was equally important; a farmer could not make purchases on credit from a town merchant who was unlikely to know him.[28] In addition, the rural general store served a social function. It was at the neighborhood store that one heard the local news and gossip. The rural merchant often was a relative of many of the inhabitants of the neighborhood. Failure to patronize such a relative, particularly one who provided easy credit, would not only be considered foolish but possibly insulting. Therefore, although a farmer could not be completely independent, his contacts with the outer world were primarily accomplished through such local intermediaries as neighborhood merchants.

IV

What made Orange County's agrarian economy distinctly southern was its foundation in slaveholding. But, as in the rest of the South, slave ownership was far from universal (see Table 5). In both 1850 and 1860, only a minority of all white male household heads owned slaves; even among the farmers, only about one-third were slaveholders.[29] Few owned many slaves. On the other hand, a small number of owners had a great many slaves; 10 percent of the household heads owned more than 70 percent of all the slaves in both 1850 and 1860 (see Table 6).[30]

Ownership of real estate was also highly concentrated. Two-fifths of the household heads—and about the same proportion for farmers—owned no land (see Table 7).[31] In addition, a small number of men owned a large amount of valuable land (see Table 8). Finally, among farmers alone, the degree of concentration of total acreage also remained stable for the decade (see Table 9).[32]

Many whites in Orange owned neither land nor slaves; some owned small to medium quantities of one, the other, or both; and a few owned a large quantity of both. Although in such a generally prosperous, largely isolated agricultural society a high degree of class tension would have been unusual, it would be reasonable to anticipate some degree of social antagonism among the inhabitants, whose economic status ranged from apparent poverty to extreme affluence.

MAP 4   *Residences of Customers at Cane Creek General Store,*
          1850

Customer's Household Number in 1850 Census

414	1827
478	1831
536	1851
538	1867
567	1869
569	1876
572	1880
1807	1885
1809	1893
1810	1907
1812	1909
1817	1911
1823	1913
1825	1929

Route of Census Taker in 1850

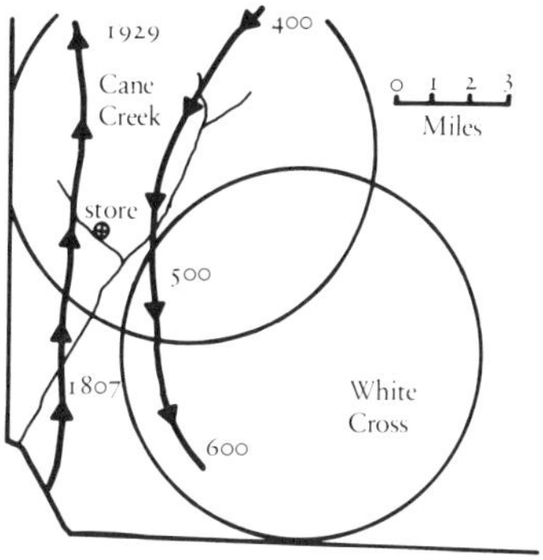

SOURCES: Long, Webb & Co., Account Book, June 17 to Nov. 17, 1848, Richard D. White Collection, North Carolina Division of Archives and History, Raleigh, North Carolina; U.S. Census MS., Orange County, 1850, Schedule I.

In the more urbanized and industrialized North, where wealth was also unequally distributed, the high degree of transiency has been used to explain why workers failed to develop what one writer calls, "a common consciousness necessary to transform an economic group into a social class." [33] But geographic mobility was not responsible for the absence of class tensions in Orange because, as was previously noted, the community had an unusually stable population. Further, in Orange there was at most only a minor link between wealth and the rate of persistence. [34]

Nor does economic mobility explain the absence of social tension. Only a few of those who remained through a decade succeeded in advancing themselves. Fewer than 10 percent of the male household heads who did not own slaves in 1850 had acquired any by 1860. Nearly 20 percent of those who owned slaves in 1850 had none ten years later.[35] During the decade some men did increase the total acreage they farmed, but most gains were small, and substantial advances usually were the result of inheritance (see Table 10). Further, when only the cases of those who were at risk to rise or fall are examined, there seems to be a trend toward downward mobility. Most outstanding is the fact that nearly 60 percent of the farmers with no land in 1850 persisted for the decade despite their failure to acquire any acreage. It is conceivable of course that there was just enough upward mobility for people to believe that economic advancement was possible.

A better explanation for the absence of social tension lies in the caste and neighborhood structure of Orange County. No matter how poor a white man was, socially he stood above all blacks. The racial or caste division, therefore, helped create homogeneity and unity among all whites. Further, southern society was not divided into clearly demarcated groups of slaveholders and nonslaveholders; nor were large landowners in some way aligned in opposition to small farmers and those who had no land at all.[36] In the rural neighborhoods, where all white families—rich and poor, slaveowners and nonslaveowners—were tightly knit by geography, religion, and kinship, there could be little class consciousness.

Among the descendants of Thomas Lloyd, for example, there were no clear social or economic distinctions between families that owned slaves and those that did not. Of the households headed by descendants of Thomas Lloyd's first son, Stephen, about one-third— approximately the average for Orange—owned slaves in either 1850 or 1860 (see Chart 3). But every one of these heads of household had either a grandparent, parent, sibling, or cousin who owned slaves.

Slaveholders and nonslaveholders frequently married. During the 1850s more than 25 percent of the brides and grooms from households with no slaves chose mates from households with slaves (see Table 11). For example, on March 13, 1852, in the Eno neighborhood, John H. Breeze married Ann Eliza Jordan. They had lived just six households apart. John's father, Richard, owned seven slaves. Ann's father, John, owned no slaves. By 1860 John and Ann owned one slave and resided five households away from Richard Breeze, now the owner of five slaves. Such marriages must have produced a ripple effect throughout the entire neighborhood. The children of such marriages had slaveowning grandparents who later bequeathed their grandchildren these slaves.[37] In addition, the bride and groom who did not make such a fortunate marriage often had a brother or a sister who did belong to a slaveholding family.

Slaveholding, then, was not a clear test for distinguishing class. If a man did not own a slave, there was nonetheless a great likelihood that he had grown up in a family where there were slaves. Through both of his parents, he might be related to a number of slaveowners in the neighborhood. Therefore, for many nonslaveholders, slavery was a basic feature of their neighborhood's culture, not an institution that separated social classes.

Nor did landholding create a significant barrier between classes. In a study of the Georgia upcountry one scholar has found that most antebellum landless farmers were renters who, he claims, "seemed to share the culture and outlook of yeomen."[38] Given Orange's rural neighborhood orientation and the close residential proximity of kin, most renters worked on their relatives' property. Although they owned no land, bonds of kinship linked them with the landowners.

The frequency of marriages between landowners' and nonlandowners' children indicates the absence of sharp social distinctions between these two groups. During the 1850s, half the grooms from households with no real estate married brides from households that owned property, and a slightly lower proportion of brides from poor families married husbands whose parents owned land (see Table 12). For example, on September 11, 1858, in the Little River neighborhood, William Woods married Demarius Roberts. In 1850 William's father, Henderson, owned no land and Demarius's father, James, owned $400 worth. They resided only nine households apart. By 1860 William and Demarius lived just next door to James Roberts. Both households owned farm land. William Woods, who resided nearby, was still a landless farmer. As with slaves, this land, along with household utensils, furniture, and farming equipment, was passed from one generation to the next and from one family to another. Therefore, when Dilly Lloyd, the widow of Thomas Lloyd, died in 1852, her property, valued at $1700 in 1850, was acquired not only by her sons, Thomas, Sorren, and Atlas, but also by her sons-in-law, Mebane Durham and H.M. Cave Strowd.[39]

V

The possibility still exists that the very large landowners and slaveholders—planters—did compose a distinct social group. In Orange County, owners of twenty or more slaves (the common historical designation of a planter) fell into two categories: first, those whose kinship ties encouraged them to maintain relationships with residents of the rural neighborhoods; second, those who were separated from the rest of society by both their ancestry and their perception of the community.[40]

The first group of planters were the descendants of the county's original settlers, none of whom originally had more than six slaves.[41] For three generations, spanning a century, some members of these families had gradually accumulated land and slaves. By 1850 their descendants included some men who owned large quantities of land and slaves, some who owned a small or medium quantity of both, and some who owned neither.

The Barbees of the Patterson neighborhood are representative. In 1850, with 41 slaves, William Barbee, a descendant of the original settlers of the Patterson neighborhood, was the largest slaveholder of his extended family. His children were also substantial slaveholders: his son, Willis, owned 14 slaves; his two daughters had married men owning 13 and 16 slaves. His third daughter, Mary, had made a most favorable marriage to her cousin, James N. Patterson, the second largest slaveholder in Orange County, who owned 65 slaves in 1850 and 106 slaves in 1860. Most of the other Barbees and their in-laws, however, were not so fortunate; while some also were planters, most owned fewer than five slaves or none at all. For example, in 1850 William Barbee's male cousins with the Barbee surname had the following number of slaves: Young Barbee, 0; George W. Barbee, 0; George Barbee, 0; Gray Barbee, Jr., 3; John Barbee, 3; Bartlett Barbee, 5; Gabriel Barbee, 11; Gray Barbee, 21.[42]

William Barbee continued to live in his rural neighborhood close to his less affluent relatives. Though he was rich and some of them were poor, he continued, as did all the Barbees, to be a member of the Patterson neighborhood church, Mount Moriah Baptist.[43]

At the same time, a planter like William Barbee had economic interests and social contacts that reached beyond his neighborhood. Many of these planters had extensive interests in transportation and

CHART 3 *Slaveholding among the Descendents of Thomas Lloyd:*
1850 and 1860

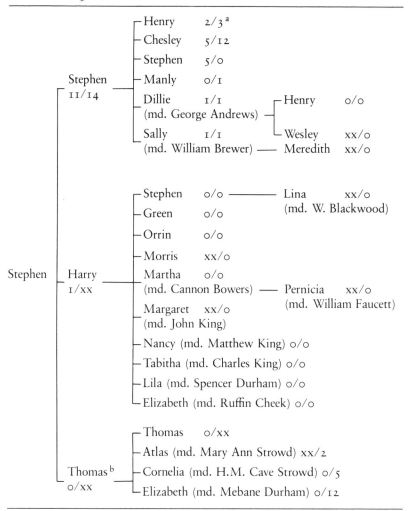

Stephen ┬ Stephen ┬ Henry   2/3[a]
        │ 11/14   ├ Chesley   5/12
        │   ├ Stephen   5/0
        │   ├ Manly   0/1
        │   ├ Dillie   1/1   ┬ Henry   0/0
        │   │ (md. George Andrews) │
        │   └ Sally   1/1   └ Wesley   xx/0
        │   (md. William Brewer) ── Meredith xx/0
        │
        ├ Harry ┬ Stephen   0/0 ────── Lina   xx/0
        │ 1/xx   │   (md. W. Blackwood)
        │   ├ Green   0/0
        │   ├ Orrin   0/0
        │   ├ Morris   xx/0
        │   ├ Martha   0/0
        │   │ (md. Cannon Bowers) ── Pernicia   xx/0
        │   ├ Margaret   xx/0   (md. William Faucett)
        │   │ (md. John King)
        │   ├ Nancy (md. Matthew King) 0/0
        │   ├ Tabitha (md. Charles King) 0/0
        │   ├ Lila (md. Spencer Durham) 0/0
        │   └ Elizabeth (md. Ruffin Cheek) 0/0
        │
        └ Thomas[b] ┬ Thomas   0/xx
          0/xx   ├ Atlas (md. Mary Ann Strowd) xx/2
                    ├ Cornelia (md. H.M. Cave Strowd) 0/5
                    └ Elizabeth (md. Mebane Durham) 0/12

SOURCES: U.S. Census MS., Orange County, 1850, 1860, Schedules 1 and 2; Thomas
Lloyd Papers, Perkins Library, Duke University, Eugene Suggs, "Sketches of Major
General Thomas Lloyd of Orange County, North Carolina Collection.
[a]number of slaves owned in 1850/number owned in 1860
[b]By 1850 Thomas had died and his wife Dilly headed the household.
xx Denotes either not a household head, left Orange County, or deceased.

banking.[44] Children of these planters sometimes married into other planter families from different neighborhoods.[45]

A second group of settlers were not the descendants of the county's original settlers. Paul C. Cameron, the largest planter in the county on the eve of the Civil War, was the grandson of Richard Bennehan, who came to Orange from Petersburg, Virginia, in 1768, nearly twenty years after the original settlers. Bennehan began not by farming but by managing a store. With his earnings from this store he made his first purchase of land, 893 acres, in 1776. By 1803, when his daughter Rebecca married Duncan Cameron of Mecklenburg County, Virginia, Bennehan owned 4500 acres and 41 slaves. His descendants were equally successful in acquiring wealth. His grandson, Paul C. Cameron, who in 1860 owned 12,675 acres and 470 slaves in Orange County in addition to plantations in Alabama and Mississippi, was one of the wealthiest men in the South.[46]

Another planter who was a latecomer to Orange was William A. Graham, a native of Lincoln County, North Carolina, over one hundred miles west of Orange. Graham did not come to Orange until 1820, when he began to attend the University of North Carolina. After his graduation in 1824, he studied and then practiced law in Hillsborough. Beginning in 1833, Graham represented Orange in the North Carolina Assembly for three terms—twice as Speaker of the House—served as governor and United States senator, and became secretary of the navy under President Millard Fillmore. In 1852, Graham reached the zenith of his antebellum political career when he received the Whig party's nomination for vice-president. With this illustrious career and his ownership of 67 slaves in 1860, he could bestow upon his son, John, sufficient credentials to enable him to marry Paul C. Cameron's daughter Rebecca shortly after the Civil War.[47]

The result of such marriages was the formation of an extensive network of planter families (see Chart 4). Paul C. Cameron married Anne Ruffin, the daughter of another latecomer to Orange, Thomas Ruffin, who served as the chief justice of the North Carolina Supreme Court. Justice Ruffin was married to Anne Kirkland, the daughter of William Kirkland, a merchant from Scotland who came to Orange in 1790. Ruffin's sister Mary was married to William Cain II, another substantial planter in Orange who also was the

Fairntosh. One of Paul C. Cameron's plantation homes in northeastern Orange County. (Photograph courtesy of North Carolina Division of Archives and History.)

descendant of a merchant. This marriage produced a daughter, Mary Clark, who married her first cousin, Thomas Ruffin, Jr. The Cain's other daughter, Martha Ann, married Pride Jones, the son of another recently arrived planter from Virginia, Cadwallader Jones.

These wealthy families were related to other planters who lived in other parts of North Carolina and the South. For example, Pride Jones's sister Sally married Josiah Collins, Jr., the son of one of eastern North Carolina's wealthiest planters. Josiah's brother George in turn married Paul Cameron's daughter Anne.

The connections among these planter families were complex. They shared not merely wealth but interests. They banded together to promote railroads, to act as directors of banks, and to serve in government.[48] Many of these planters were members of the Episcopal Church. Membership in this denomination—whose membership was small and whose churches were located only in Chapel Hill and Hillsborough—symbolized the separation of these planters from the rest of society.[49]

Time of settlement in Orange, marriage patterns, and participation in common economic, social, and political pursuits—all differentiated these planters from society in general. Where the vast majority of Orange's citizens resided in self-contained, rural neighborhoods that fostered a provincial outlook, these planters, many of whom owned land in the country but resided in Chapel Hill or Hillsborough, shared a far more cosmopolitan perspective.[50] They could look beyond Orange's borders and see others who had similar interests, concerns, and beliefs.

That the planter class in Orange was not monolithic had important implications for the county's social structure.[51] Those planters who were descended from families long settled in the neighborhoods served as intermediaries between their nonlandowning and small landholding relatives and the second group of planters. They shared a common ancestry with the former and similar economic interests with the latter. Through them their less affluent relatives could view wealth in terms not of class but of kin; through them planters appeared not as an abstract social group but as intimate neighbors.

VI

As in many communities throughout the nation during the antebellum period, there were a number of voluntary associations in

St. Matthew's Episcopal Church in Hillsborough. The church and denomination attended by many of the planters who were not part of the rural neighborhood system. (Photograph courtesy of North Carolina Collection, UNC Library at Chapel Hill.)

CHART 4 *Network of Planter Marriages in Orange County*

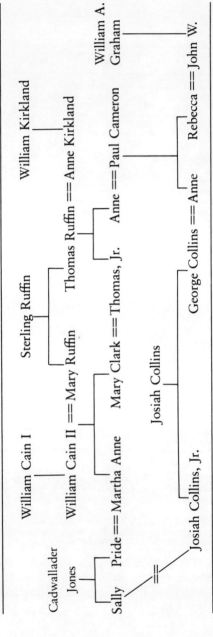

SOURCES: William S. Powell, "Dictionary of Orange County Biography," in Hugh Lefler and Paul Wager, eds., *Orange County, 1752–1952* (Chapel Hill, N.C. The Orange Printshop, 1953), 322–40; Jean Bradley Anderson, *Piedmont Plantation: The Bennehan Cameron-Plantation Lands in North Carolina* (Durham, N.C.: The Historic Preservation Society of Durham, 1985), frontispiece; Hugh Conway Browning, comp., "Orange County and Hillsborough Items of History: The Families of Hugh and James Caine," (n.d.), a genealogy given to me by Jean Bradley Anderson; Colonel Cadwallader Jones, *A Genealogical History* (Columbia, S.C.: Ye Bryan Printing Company, 1899), 42–59.
== Denotes marriage.

Orange County.[52] Reflective of the county's social and economic structure, however, these associations were insignificant in the rural neighborhoods. Their primary influence was felt by the county's towns, and they were dominated by the slaveholding elite.

The oldest voluntary association in Orange County, the Masons, held their first meeting in the county in 1788 and chartered their first lodge in Hillsborough, Eagle Lodge, in 1791.[53] Chapel Hill gained its first Masonic Lodge charter in 1824 with University Lodge. Because this lodge ceased to function in 1849, the village received a new charter for Caldwell Lodge in 1855. By 1860 there were seventy-six members in the Eagle Lodge and twenty-eight in the Caldwell Lodge.[54]

Like the Masons nationally, the Eagle and Caldwell lodges were involved in a number of benevolent activities. These included contributing funds both to build a male academy in Hillsborough as well as to construct a state seminary for the children of deceased lodge members. In addition, the lodges offered their members such occasional social activities as parades, dances, and annual events like the Anniversary of St. John the Baptist.[55]

The Masons' influence never extended into the county's rural neighborhoods. Its members, who were generally quite affluent, lived overwhelmingly either within or near the borders of Hillsborough or Chapel Hill. Its few rural members were either slaveholders or substantial landowners who felt comfortable with the more cosmopolitan social atmosphere of the county seat and university village.[56]

One voluntary association that may have had a more substantial impact on the community's rural neighborhoods was the Orange County Agricultural Society. Established in 1853, the Society was dedicated, as its President Paul C. Cameron noted, to "improving and advancing the husbandry of Orange." The Society annually held a county fair where it presented awards for the best displays of crops, livestock, agricultural implements, crafts, and household manufacturing. Although membership in the Society was open to anyone who was willing to pay one dollar, in fact from the outset its membership, which never reached two hundred, was dominated by residents of Hillsborough and Chapel Hill and by slaveholders. Not only was Cameron, the owner of hundreds of slaves, annually elected

The Eagle Masonic Lodge in Hillsborough. The voluntary association whose members were largely affluent town dwellers. (From copy in North Carolina Collection, UNC Library at Chapel Hill.)

president, but the largest planters in the county continually controlled the Society's offices.[57]

Voluntary associations played an insignificant role in the lives of residents of Orange County's rural neighborhoods because they simply were unnecessary. In communities of the Northeast and Midwest during this era, voluntary associations seemed to thrive because of the high degree of mobility and dislocation.[58] By contrast, in Orange County's rural neighborhoods, stability and continuity were the rule. Ties of kinship and institutions such as the rural church which reflected those ties obviated the need for people to look elsewhere to find meaning in their lives.

VII

In these ways the antebellum Orange County kinship systems and the economic and social structure mutually reinforced one another.

The type of farming practiced in this agricultural county sustained the self-contained, kin-oriented character of the rural neighborhoods. In turn, the kin-oriented character of the rural neighborhoods prevented the unequal distribution of wealth from producing intense social tension.

CHAPTER 3

"The Leopard's Spots and a Democrat's Principles"

The Antebellum Administrative and Political Structure

The neighborhoods in Orange were central to the county's administrative and political structure. The primary administrative body in the county, the county court, was composed of magistrates who represented the interests of the neighborhoods in which they resided. Further, it was in the neighborhoods that the political process was initiated, the campaigns were waged, and party affiliations were both formed and sustained.

I

The most important level of government for the people of Orange was the county government. Even on those rare occasions when it was necessary for them to deal with either the North Carolina or federal government, their contact occurred through such local intermediaries as the postmaster, usually a neighborhood storekeeper, or the sheriff.

The primary institution of county government was the county court. This body had nearly exclusive administrative and judicial authority. The court's administrative duties were very extensive: they included levying the county taxes, maintaining the county property, and appointing the county trustee, coroner, overseers of the roads, wardens of the poor, and superintendent of schools. The county court had jurisdiction in civil suits for the imposition of penalties over a hundred dollars. In addition, it served as an orphans' court to manage orphans' estates and award guardianship. In criminal cases the court had jurisdiction over sixty-two types of misdemeanors. It was restricted only from cases where conviction would result in death or dismemberment.[1]

The county court's members were the justices of the peace. These justices, or magistrates, were commissioned by the governor upon the recommendation of the county's representatives in the legislature.[2] They held their office for life, so long as they demonstrated good behavior. Because of its large population, Orange had many magistrates—seventy-seven in 1850. Death and resignations created a high rate of turnover among the justices: there were forty-six new appointments between 1850 and 1859.[3]

On the eve of the Civil War, North Carolina had probably the least democratic form of county government of any southern state.[4] The members of the county court, which had a near monopoly over the control of county affairs, were not elected. If these magistrates, like most of Orange's citizens, were farmers, they were far more likely to own slaves and a large amount of property than was the average citizen (see Table 13).[5]

Though undemocratic, the county court was rarely criticized. This silence may in part have reflected a recognition that there were disadvantages to holding a magistrate's office.[6] The compensation for his services was very small, less than three dollars a day. There were no privileges attached to the position until 1848, when the magistrates were freed from the road duty. A justice was restricted from holding any of the more lucrative county offices, such as sheriff. Further, a justice who was an attorney could not practice in the county in which he served as a magistrate.

The manner in which the court functioned also guarded it from criticism. Apparently a bastion of power, the court in reality was a weak institution. It convened for only four sessions annually. These sessions rarely lasted more than six days, and justices were obligated to attend only two sessions—and only one day of each session.[7]

The limited scope of the court's fiscal responsibilities also silenced detractors. The annual county taxes were so small, about two dollars per capita, and expenditures were so restricted that there was little room for corruption. Except for an increase in the aid to the poor in 1858 and 1859, probably a result of the nationwide depression beginning in 1857, the distribution of expenditures from 1856—the first year they were recorded—to 1859 remained fairly constant.[8]

The court's strongest bulwark against criticism, however, was the

Drawing of Orange County Courthouse, where the members of the antebellum county court assembled and represented the interests of their rural
neighborhoods. (Photograph courtesy of North Carolina Division of
Archives and History.)

fact that it was a representative body. Although the justices were
very wealthy, nearly all of them were farmers like the rest of the
population, and they were fairly equally divided in their membership
between the two political parties. Further, because of its large size—
there was one justice for every 28.6 white households in 1850—and
constant turnover, the court was not a small oligarchy. Finally, and
most important, the magistrates resided not in one locality or town,
but throughout the county. A listing of the household numbers of
the justices, as the census takers recorded them, reveals that magistrates could be found in all of the county's neighborhoods.[9]

The wide geographical distribution in magistrates' residences was
essential for enabling the county court to perform its administrative

duties. The court appointed magistrates to deal with the needs of the neighborhoods in which they resided. For example, the magistrates formed the tax lists and inspected elections in their own neighborhoods. The system of administration promoted harmonious court-neighborhood relations; rather than dealing with the court as a remote institution, the residents of the neighborhoods had contact with the body through well-known and respected neighbors and relatives.

The system of neighborhood representation extended beyond the court's regular functions. For example, the court was responsible for the construction and repair of bridges, an essential task in an agricultural society. In May 1850, when the court needed to contract with someone to repair a bridge over the Flat River, it left the decision to three magistrates who resided in the Flat River neighborhood: William Lipscomb, Richard Holeman, and William Duke.[10] These magistrates had knowledge of the river and could best judge the extent of necessary repairs. It was not surprising that these magistrates chose as contractor a resident of the neighborhood because he too knew the area well. The compensation for these projects, often hundreds of dollars, went not only to the contractor but also to the many residents of the neighborhood, often relatives of the magistrates, who assisted him.[11] This form of administration and patronage explains why the people tolerated a nondemocratic court. Residents permitted the unelected wealthy members of their neighborhood to represent them on the court so long as these justices truly represented the interests of the neighborhood.

II

The neighborhood was also the basic political unit in Orange County. The political process began in the neighborhood, and the campaigns were waged there.

Between late March and early May during even-numbered years of the 1850s, an announcement would appear in the county newspaper, the *Hillsborough Recorder*, informing the public that caucuses of the two political parties, Democratic and Whig, would occur that week in the neighborhood.[12] These meetings were held at the same location where elections would take place later in the year. For example, the Flat River Whigs always gathered at Ellison Mangum's general store, the polling place for the Flat River neighborhood. The announcements of these meetings often were accompanied by a letter from a member of the party, usually signed with a pseudonym, stressing the need for the complete participation of all the neighborhoods. For instance, in 1850 "Orange," the spokesman for the Whigs, emphasized the need for "full attendance" at all meetings so that all men could "speak to the wishes of their neighbors as to who shall be our candidates." [13]

All of these meetings followed a similar pattern. Initially, those in attendance would elect a chairman, usually a justice of the peace from the neighborhood. Next, two committees, consisting of three to five men each, would be chosen. One committee would write resolutions, and the other would appoint delegates to represent the neighborhood at the party's county convention. The resolutions rarely included a discussion of issues or endorsed particular candidates. Rather, they expressed confidence in the party's incumbents at all levels of the government and encouraged the party members throughout the county to participate in the nominating process. In May 1852 the Cane Creek Whigs drafted a typical neighborhood resolution: "That we deem it a duty of the Whigs in each neighborhood to meet in convention to bring out their strongest men as candidates for the Legislature, and use every effort to secure their election." [14]

The most important function performed by the neighborhood caucus was to select delegates to attend the party's county convention. The committee on delegate selection would choose, depending on the number of men who voted at the neighborhood precinct, ten to twenty delegates. The committee attempted to select as delegates men who represented the largest families in the neighborhood. This task was simple to perform because nearly all the men at the caucus were relatives. Often a number of delegates came from the same family: of the fourteen delegates chosen at the Flat River Whig's caucus in May 1852, three were Mangums, three were Tilleys, and three were Robertses. Likewise, at the White Cross neighborhood Democrat's caucus in May 1860, two of the fifteen delegates were Lloyds, and seven others were men who had married or were sons of women whose maiden name was Lloyd. [15]

Two or three weeks after the neighborhood caucuses, the delegates selected in the neighborhoods would meet at their party's county convention in Hillsborough. To guarantee that enough delegates, many of whom were magistrates, attended the convention, it usually was held the same week as the county court. Approximately sixty to seventy delegates would gather in one of the town's two largest buildings, the courthouse or the Masonic Lodge.[16]

The county convention followed procedures similar to those of the neighborhood caucuses. At the outset a chairman, usually a former standard-bearer of the party who held no further political aspiration, was chosen.[17] Then the convention selected a committee to prepare resolutions that generally avoided issues. For example, the Democratic county convention of 1852 condemned the Whig administration in Washington, endorsed the Compromise of 1850—a dead topic in 1852—and expressed their "devotion to those principles which Jefferson originated and Jackson perpetuated."[18]

The county convention's primary function was to choose candidates for the North Carolina assembly and senate. Nominations were made by a committee of fifteen to twenty men who represented the county's neighborhoods. The committee would leave the meeting and convene in secret. As the convention waited, a prominent party leader would give a speech in which he stressed the need for organization and unity during the upcoming campaign. When the committee returned, it recommended a slate of candidates, who were then formally endorsed by the convention. Although most of these nominations probably had been decided upon even before the convention met, there must have been some spontaneity involved in the nomination process because occasionally a nominee, citing either poor health or business responsibilites, refused the honor.[19]

The men nominated for the state assembly and senate between 1850 and 1860 did not constitute a distinctive social or economic group.[20] North Carolina law required members of the legislature to own real estate, and these nominees had property that averaged $5,938 in value; but holdings were as small as $500 and as large as $25,000. All nominees of both parties owned at least one slave. The average holding was 33.7 slaves; but their holdings ranged from as few as one to as many as 218 slaves.

The largest number of these nominees resided in the towns of Hillsborough or Chapel Hill, which contained only 10 percent of the population but served as a polling place for 40 percent of the voters.[21] Moreover, town residents were likely to be known more widely and to have broader followings throughout the county than those who lived in the rural neighborhoods. The fact that so many nominees resided in the towns did not mean that the interests of agriculture were inadequately represented. All but two of the twelve nominees—lawyers, doctors, merchants, and an architect—who resided in the towns, were also farmers.[22]

But conventions also chose rural candidates. The most desirable nominees were men who resided in the rural neighborhoods where the party had a strong following. For example, the Whigs always tried to include on their ticket a resident—such as William W. Guess—of Flat River, a very strong Whig precinct. Likewise, the Democrats turned to Dr. Bartlett Durham of the Wilkerson precinct in the Durham neighborhood, a banner precinct for them. Because the key to victory in any election hinged not on changing voters' minds but on turning out the party faithful, there was nothing to gain by nominating someone who lived in a neighborhood where the party always was in the minority.

About a month after the nominations were made, the campaign actively began. For many of the affluent nominees who were town dwellers, campaigning among the rural people meant the need to give at least the appearance of being a common man. When William A. Graham started his campaign to represent Orange County in the North Carolina State Senate in 1854, the former governor, United States senator, and secretary of the U.S. Navy was observed to have "put aside his long worn dignity . . . donned a straw hat, the first he has worn in 30 years, flax pants, & spotted calico coat. . . ." He defeated his opponent by only thirty-three votes out of the nearly nine hundred cast.[23]

For most of the electorate the campaign was more a social activity than an enlightening lesson in political doctrine. Candidates emphasized personalities over issues. In their speeches before crowds at tax payment gatherings and general stores in the rural neighborhoods, they often referred to their opponents not as "gentlemen" but as "monkey, goat, &c."[24] As might be expected, such "harsh talking" often would "engender ill feeling & coldness" between the candidates. It seems that once a man accepted his party's nomination he subjected himself to any abuse from his opponent. For example, when campaigning for the state senate in 1858, the Whig nominee, Josiah Turner, Jr., the son of one of Orange County's most affluent men, did not feel it unfair to attack his even more wealthy Demo-

Antebellum political leaders.   *Left:* Paul C. Cameron (1808–91) was the wealthiest man in Orange County both before and after the Civil War. (Photograph courtesy of Manuscript Department, Perkins Library, Duke University.)   *Right:* William A. Graham (1804–75). After serving as governor of North Carolina, United States senator, secretary of the United States Navy, and running unsuccessfully for the vice presidency, in 1854 he campaigned to represent Orange County in the North Carolina state senate. The strongly partisan nature of politics in the county permitted him only a narrow victory. (Photograph courtesy of North Carolina Collection, UNC Library at Chapel Hill.)

cratic opponent, Paul C. Cameron, for wearing gold spectacles.[25] As ludicrous as these speeches often were and as long as they lasted— up to two hours—the crowds generally listened attentively.[26]

The campaigns sometimes included very elaborate activities. For example, in 1852 when the national Whig party nominated William A. Graham of North Carolina to run for vice-president on the ticket with General Winfield Scott, Orange County Whigs organized Scott-Graham clubs and held a barbecue on September 19. At 10 o'clock in the morning on that day, a brass band led a parade of "the aged, the middle aged, the young men . . . and the fair daughters of Orange in all their loveliness and beauty" to a site just south of Hillsborough. After a number of speakers addressed the crowd of about twenty-five hundred, the gathering sat down for an enormous meal. As evening approached, many left the barbecue and marched by candlelight to the courthouse to hear even more speeches. Finally, as a reporter at the event later noted, "The company then dispersed in good order, not a single event having occurred to mar the enjoyment."[27]

As orderly and sober as this gathering may have been, the festive atmosphere of campaigns frequently descended into revels. Usually the crowds could restrain themselves during speeches because they knew rewards would follow the discourses. Once the speeches ended, however, the people quickly found relief in alcohol. After a political gathering in the Flat River neighborhood, Adolphus Mangum, a strong supporter of temperance, observed: "A large number of gentlemen (not gentlemen either but mere dogs) became intoxicated and such a disturbance is rarely witnessed as follows—such were the proceedings that I was ready to wish that every drop of the infernal stuff was *safely landed* in the river Styx or committed to the flames for immediate consumption."[28] Occasionaly the crowds could not restrain themselves until the speeches ended. A spectator at one political meeting recalled "the drunkards, who have procured some stinking whiskey, that a hog would not drink were sporting with it in a brave manner, swallowing glasses full at a time making beast and hogs of themselves. . . ."[29]

As the elections approached, many in the county expressed concern over the role alcohol played. During every campaign the Sons of Temperance chapters waged a "war of extermination against spirits," not only at elections but at all public events.[30] The anxiety over alcohol, however, was not confined to the temperance groups. The county grand jury also was disturbed by the practice of "treating," whereby candidates would provide "meat or drink [more often the latter] as a means of success . . . to the injury of the community, and in opposition to the wishes of the moral portion of the people, who . . . form a majority of the electors."[31]

It was not necessary to "treat" many voters in order to influence an election. Most men would vote for only one party, regardless of its candidate and regardless of rewards promised for switching their allegiance. If unenthusiastic or uninterested, however, they might stay at home and not vote. Because the turnout at every election was so large—nearly 85 percent—and because the county was so evenly divided between the two parties, a candidate needed to treat only a small number of voters—sometimes fewer than twenty—to affect an election.[32]

In 1853 dissatisfaction over treating became quite strong, and the temperance groups met to find a solution to the problem. In late August 1853, the county convention of the Friends of Temperance and Good Order considered a motion to oppose any candidate who treated. Before making a decision on this formula, however, the convention decided, "That the citizens in the different sections of the county be requested to hold meetings in their neighborhoods and make an expression of their opinions upon the subject. . . ."[33] In October and November of 1853 a number of the neighborhood meetings reached a consensus that the best manner to prevent treating was to get two hundred voters from each party to pledge that if a candidate from either was found "to secure his election by treating, directly or indirectly," the two hundred signers of the pledge would vote for the opponent.[34]

Rather than turning to the pledge as the solution to the problem of treating, the county temperance convention could only agree in on 1854 a less severe plan. The convention requested that the nominees for both parties enter into agreement not to treat. Committees were sent by the convention to both of the political party conventions to gain support for this method. The parties had little choice but to endorse this solution strongly.[35]

Although the issue of treating did not arise during the 1854 campaign, apparently the practice did not die. In the 1858 race for the North Carolina State Senate between the Whig, Josiah Turner, Jr., and the Democrat, Paul C. Cameron, the concern over treating was revived. A week before the election Cameron's brother-in-law noted, "It is impossible to tell however what is to be the result of an unlimited use . . . of liquor. . . ."[36]

Although no proof exists that Turner practiced treating, there is a strong possibility that he did. The two Democrats who ran for the state assembly seats were elected by a comfortable margin, while their fellow party member, Cameron, won only 46.4 percent of the vote and lost to Turner.[37] The election was not quickly forgotten.

Two years later, in a letter to his father-in-law, Cameron referred to his "folly" in having "sought to be elected in Orange *without* the use of Whiskey."[38]

Election day tended to be as animated as the campaign. A student at the University of North Carolina described the poll in Chapel Hill as a kind of festival, where there were some "fifty wagons on the ground attended by old men, women, and children who had for sale cakes and beer and cider, and whiskey." He further observed that on election day whites and blacks "mingled together on the most familar terms."[39] Adolphus Mangum found similar conditions at the Flat River poll, where "the negroes had a topsy turvy fandango and finally old & young, and white and black dispersed."[40]

III

Bitter partisan rivalry set the tone for antebellum politics in Orange County. Ideological differences between the two parties, however, were not the basis for this rivalry; rather, the parties were shaped by the county's neighborhood structure and ties of kinship.

During the 1850s a new generation of voters began to dominate politics numerically in Orange. One-third of the voters in 1850 were under thirty years of age. By 1860, nearly 60 percent of the electorate were under age forty.[41] None of these young men had participated in the formation of the Democratic and Whig parties during the 1830s. For these men President Andrew Jackson's veto in 1832 of the bill to recharter the Bank of the United States had little meaning. Further, by 1850 most of the important leaders in forming the parties, such as Andrew Jackson, Martin Van Buren, Henry Clay, and Daniel Webster, were dead or soon would be. Finally, the central issue of the 1830s that had separated the two parties in North Carolina — the role of the state government in the development of internal improvements — was moribund by the mid-nineteenth century. In Orange, members of both parties supported the state's involvement in the completion of the North Carolina Central Railroad through the county in 1855.[42]

Nevertheless, there continued to be an intense interest in party politics. The level of participation was high, with nearly all voters turning out to vote, and the campaigns were warlike. Although few records show how individuals voted, the neighborhoods consistently displayed about the same proportion of Whigs and Democrats in election after election. For example, the residents of Flat River cast 84.5 percent of their vote for the Whig candidate for governor of North Carolina in 1850 and 76.5 percent in 1860. Likewise, the residents of Eno cast 78.7 percent of their vote for the Democratic candidate for governor in 1850 and 88.9 percent in 1860. Moreover, in the county as a whole there was not only a very high correlation between how the electorate cast their votes in 1850 with how they voted in the next five elections, but there was an equally strong relationship between the relative strength of the two parties in 1840 and 1860.[43] Complaining that this continuity in voting was caused by voters following "party spirit" rather than "conscientious political views," Adolphus Mangum, a Whig, concluded, "The Ethiopian's skin & the leopard's spots and a democrat's principles can rarely if ever be changed."[44]

This continuity in voting behavior is hard to explain. Voters may have viewed the two parties as representing different social or economic interests, but, if so, these differences do not show up in a profile of the Whig and Democratic heads of households who actively participated in politics by serving as delegates to the county conventions during the 1850s and in 1860—about one-fourth of the total electorate. In age, occupation, wealth, and slave ownership there were striking similarities between these Democrats and Whigs (see Table 13).

This profile omits the large group of voters who did not head households, mostly young men, and who rarely owned either land or slaves. But it is possible to determine if these very small landowners and nonlandholders were specially attracted to either party. In North Carolina only men who owned at least fifty acres of real estate—about 40 percent of the electorate—could vote for candidates for the state senate, but all could vote for the governor.[45] Virtually identical percentages of the electorate supported the respective Whig and Democratic candidate for both the governorship and the senate.[46]

The Know-Nothing movement between 1854 and 1856 did cause a temporary break in these traditional patterns of party identification. Arising after the Kansas-Nebraska Act split the northern and southern wings of the Whig party, the nativist American, or Know-Nothing party offered the southern Whigs a new political home. In the South and particularly in North Carolina, with its overwhelmingly native-born population, however, there was little basis for a concern over lengthening the naturalization period for aliens and allowing only citizens to vote, issues the national American party stressed. But the new party did provide former Whigs with the means to continue opposing Democrats without alienating a substantial segment of the population. By May 1855, the formerly Whig *Hillsborough Recorder* firmly associated itself with the new party:

> A new party [has come] into existence, known as the American or Know Nothing party, avowing principles in harmony with those held by us for many years. The party itself is new, but the principles are old. ... And when the contest is made to turn upon these principles alone, we shall not hesitate to give them such aid as our ability will enable us to give. ... We shall not strike the Whig flag to do battle, but with the old Star Spangled Banner, ever dear to good Whigs, floating over us ... we presume the American party will not reject an ally under this flag.[47]

The major test of the new party's strength came in the elections of 1856. That year the political process began as usual with the holding of neighborhood caucuses. Unlike in the past, however, the resolutions passed by the American caucuses contained strong ideological statements. For example, the Cane Creek American caucus endorsed a resolution: "That we hold and believe in the doctrine that Americans should rule and govern America; and that those who make our laws and administer the laws, should be native born citizens, and that such should be placed in civil or political stations; and that we are opposed to anything like the union of Church and State."[48] The resolution of the American party caucus of the Flat River neighborhood was more specific: "That native born Americans should rule and govern America; and that the time for the naturalization of foreigners should be extended to twenty years, the same time that our sons have to serve us before we allow them to vote or have any voices in our legislative councils."[49]

The infusion of ideological issues was not the only factor that made the American caucuses differ from the previous Whig and Democratic gatherings. The active participants in the American party—those men who served as delegates to the county convention—were younger than their Whig and Democratic counterparts (see Table 13). Their relative youth probably accounts for their ownership of less land and fewer slaves.[50] Further, although most of the men who had been previously politically active were Whigs, few had any former party affiliation.[51] Again, the relative youth of the American leaders may explain the difference. The greater proportion of blue collar workers in the American leadership indicates that the party may have attracted some "new men" who had been excluded from conventional politics.

Symbolic of the American party's emphasis on youth were their choices as nominees for the state assembly: Frederick Strudwick, aged twenty-three, and William N. Patterson, aged twenty-eight. Because of their youth neither of these men had previously run for office. The American's nominee for the state senate, Josiah Turner, Jr., at thirty-four was also young, but he had been the Whig nominee for the state assembly in the previous three elections. Although he supported the American party and its principles, Turner continually called himself "an old line Whig." [52]

All the American candidates lost in the election of 1856, but they made a respectable showing. Their defeat was not caused by the issues they supported; instead, as the *Hillsborough Recorder* contended, because of their youth they were "not generally known in the county." [53] Even in defeat, the American candidates succeeded in drawing the support of most of the traditional Whig voters.[54] During the next four years the opponents of the Democratic party in Orange dropped the American party title and called themselves, first, the "Opposition" party; by 1860 they had returned to the name "Whig." Through all these combinations and permutations, the strength of the Democratic party in Orange continued to be substantially the same. Their opponents, though experimenting with new leadership in 1856, continued to attract pretty much the same voters who had always supported Whig candidates.

Precinct returns suggest a cause for persistent party affiliation. In the six gubernatorial elections in Orange between 1850 and 1860, the Democrats and their opponents had a nearly equal share of the electorate—an average of 48.8 percent for the Democrats and 51.2 percent for their opponents. Precincts, however, were not usually evenly divided: they were won and lost by landslide proportions.[55]

A list of voters at each precinct in 1850 suggests why these elections were so lopsided. The list indicates that the boundaries of Orange's precincts coincided very closely with those of the neighborhoods. The list also shows that a few families and their relatives dominated each precinct. For instance, the Lloyds, who were faithful and active participants in the Democratic party, along with the various families they had married into comprised 79 of the 122 voters at the White Cross precinct. Therefore, when the voting strength of the Lloyds and their in-laws is combined, it is evident why White Cross was a Democratic stronghold.[56]

Although it is difficult to determine what forces during the 1830s led men to join either of the two parties, once they established their allegiances, they supported their party until the Civil War. Further, in the same manner that men seemed preordained to become members of the neighborhood church and to marry women who resided nearby, the new generation of voters in the 1850s were destined to join the party of their elders and kin in the neighborhood. Politics, like so many other aspects of life in Orange, was shaped by the neighborhood structure.[57]

IV

Unlike other southerners fearful of Abraham Lincoln's election in 1860, the people of Orange were hesitant to see Republican victory as a justifiable cause for secession. The persistence of a two-party system in the county allowed them to put a Republican victory into a different perspective than their neighbors in the lower South who, for a number of years, had lived only under the Democratic party. It permitted them to believe that no party, no matter how threatening it might appear, could dominate for any extended period. Therefore, no political setback justified separation from the Union.[58] A number of weeks before the election this sentiment was expressed by William A. Graham of Orange who asked, " . . . who can prepare for a declaration of independence appealing to a candid world for its approbation and sympathy upon the ground that we have been out-voted in an election in which we took the chance of success . . . ?"[59]

After Lincoln's election in early November the county remained calm. Although, of course, the Republican candidate had won no votes in Orange, there was evidence that most of the voters supported preservation of the Union; the nominee of the Constitutional Union party, John Bell, handily defeated the secessionist-backed candidate, John C. Breckinridge.[60] In the Republican victory, the *Hillsborough Recorder* saw no cause for alarm: "Lincoln, however objectionable he may be, was fairly elected according to the provisions of the Constitution; and we have no right to presume, in the absence of evidence to the contrary, that he will not faithfully perform his duty. . . . "[61]

By late December, after South Carolina's secession from the Union, it became apparent to many in Orange that North Carolina would have to decide whether to hold a convention at least to consider secession. The topic was discussed at a number of neighborhood gatherings. At a meeting in the Cane Creek neighborhood on December 21, participants passed resolutions that pointed to the small plurality of Lincoln's election, recognized the constitutional restrictions on presidential power, and rejected the calls for a state convention to debate secession. Similar thoughts were expressed at a December 28 meeting in the Flat River neighborhood, at which it was resolved: "That we therefore declare ourself opposed to a hasty convention of the people of North Carolina, believing that no good could be accomplished by it. . . ."[62] Finally, that same week a gathering in Hillsborough also acknowledged the restrictions on the new president: "and whilst we vigilantly observe his course of administration . . . we perceive in the fact of his election no sufficient cause for the subversion and abandonment of the Government of our Fathers. . . ."[63]

As the new year began there was little shift in sentiment. Early in January, during the annual celebration of Andrew Jackson's victory at the Battle of New Orleans, when volunteer toasts were presented and the crowd responded with gunshots and cheers, the first two speakers gave pro-Union toasts that were well received by the crowd:

> The whole Union and Major [Robert] Anderson [the commander of U.S. forces in Charleston harbor]—may the former be preserved and the later defend Ft. Sumter.
> (response: 2 guns and 20 cheers.)
> North Carolina, the first to strike a blow for liberty; may she be the last to secede from the union.
> (response: 2 guns and 10 cheers.)

One of the final speakers expressed an entirely different sentiment:

> The immediate secession of North Carolina, a Confederacy of the Southern states—may the flag of a Southern Confederacy wave over a free and independent people, and should we be compelled to give our aggressors a threshing, may we give them a good one.

His toast did not receive as warm a reception—one gun and no cheers.[64]

The question of secession, however, soon was shaped by forces outside the control of Orange. On January 20 the North Carolina legislature passed a bill that called for an election on February 28. In this election the people were to choose delegates and decide whether a secession convention should be convened.[65]

Meetings were held throughout February to select the two delegates to represent Orange if the people approved holding a convention. At the two largest meetings William A. Graham, a Whig, and John Berry, a Democrat, both opponents of secession, were the clear choice of those against holding a convention. This bipartisan coalition demonstrated its strength at the polls on February 28, when Graham and Berry defeated their two pro-secession opponents by a four-to-one margin, the most lopsided antebellum election in Orange. In addition, the voters, by a similar margin, decided against holding a convention. For the first time since its formation in the 1830s, the traditional voting pattern was broken.[66]

Throughout March there was no movement in Orange towards secession. In a letter to the *Hillsborough Recorder* one writer praised the tone of President Lincoln's inaugural address and concluded, "I say the heart of the man is not right who can't see more peace than war in the message."[67] Further, the editor of the *Recorder* went so far as to claim that the seceded states would soon return to the Union. "We think appearances indicate a peaceful termination of existing difficulties," he asserted, "and we have good hope that no long-term will elapse before we shall see returning that 'more perfect union' which the founders of the Republic so earnestly labored to accomplish, and all the stars again shining in one glorious galaxy."[68]

Events outside of the county, however, again forced the people of Orange to face the issue of secession. On April 13 Fort Sumter fell, and two days later President Lincoln called for 75,000 troops. These events undercut the position of those in Orange County who had adopted a "wait and see" attitude, as now the people of North Carolina would be called to aid in putting down what President Lincoln termed an "insurrection." Regretfully the *Recorder* recognized this dramatic change: "We had hoped in a crisis like this, that the conservative spirit of the North would have in a measure checked the ambition of the President; but in this we are disappointed. The

Northern states, all of them, respond with great alacrity to the call of the President, and troops are assembling in large numbers."[69]

Quite rapidly a "marvellous change in public sentiment" was observed in Orange.[70] The county could no longer remain a passive onlooker, as William A. Graham explained, it had to choose "on the one hand to join with him [Lincoln] in a war of conquest, for it is nothing less, against our brethren of the seceding states, or on the other, resistance to throw off the obligations of the Federal Constitution."[71] Reaching a decision was not difficult for most. At a meeting in Hillsborough in support of secession a Confederate flag was raised, and one student noted, "Old gray haired men were ready to fight."[72]

The consensus that quickly formed over the need to separate from the Union did not diminish fears over where that action might lead. "I see no way to escape now from a bloody civil war," Moses Ashley Curtis, the rector of St. Matthew's Episcopal Church in Hillsborough, informed his son. "Both sections are bitterly exasperated. . . . If my fears are realized, we shall see hard times. . . ."[73] When looking to the future, John W. Norwood, an attorney and Curtis's neighbor, reached a similar opinion as he observed that "if the war goes on, it will be one of conquest and extermination." He sadly concluded that there was "not a ray of light yet breaking in the darkness which over hangs us."[74]

In addition to failing to provide comfort about what the future held, the sudden shift in sentiment toward support for separation from the Union did not cause agreement on the grounds justifying such a separation. A division over this topic was reflected in the election on May 13 for delegates in the secession convention. One pair of candidates, Paul C. Cameron and Henry K. Nash, argued for separation on the grounds that secession was a constitutional right. Their opponents, William A. Graham and John Berry ran together, as they had in February; however, they now acknowledged the need for a convention. But they based their support for separation from the Union not on the right of secession which they viewed as an abstract theory of state sovereignty, but on the right of revolution, an argument which they believed linked them to the nation's founding fathers, who had also thrown off what was perceived as a usurping government.[75]

Although the differences between the candidates may appear to be insignificant since all four supported separation from the Union, apparently they had meaning for the electorate. The margin of victory for Graham and Berry in May was much smaller than that in February, when they crushed their two opponents. Some Democrats, who may have believed in the theory of secession but felt its application premature in February, no longer hesitated to support it in May. Most Whigs, particularly after they saw the course being supported by their traditional opponents, easily became supporters of the right of revolution. These shifts resulted in a return to historical patterns, with most Whigs voting for Graham and Berry and Democrats supporting Cameron and Nash.[76]

The decision reached in Orange, as before, was reversed at the state level. When the convention met on May 20 it quickly became apparent that the secessionists outnumbered revolutionists by a comfortable margin. In the vote for president of the convention, the secessionists' candidate, Weldon N. Edwards of Warren County, defeated Orange's William A. Graham by sixty-five to forty-eight. By a similar vote the revolutionists' ordinance of separation was defeated and the secessionists' ordinance of secession was adopted. If it was any consolation for the people of Orange County, the convention also voted to place the date "May 20, 1775" on the state flag to commemorate the "Mecklenburg Declaration of Independence," North Carolina's earliest resolution of independence from Great Britain. In the end, therefore, secession was portrayed not as a radical departure from the past but as an action firmly rooted in honored tradition. The next day Orange County formally became, with North Carolina, a part of the Confederacy.[77]

V

The primary force that shaped administration and politics in Orange County was the neighborhood. If in theory county government was undemocratic, in practice it represented the interests of the neighborhoods. In politics, the neighborhood dominated political machinery and partisan allegiances. Although challenged on numerous occasions, the political strength of the neighborhood persisted up to the county's separation from the Union.

CHAPTER 4

"In A Strange Land And Away From Home"
The War Years

The Civil War was a two-front struggle for the Confederacy. To gain victory entailed not only defeating Union troops in the field but also maintaining the support of the civilians at home. On both fronts the war, which was initiated to preserve a way of life, challenged the traditional structure of Orange County. Some of the changes brought on by the war came slowly, and, relying on ante-bellum precedents, the people adjusted to them. But after a number of years, when war seemed to become a permanent way of life, Orange County residents felt not just challenged but threatened.

I

For the soldiers from Orange County the Civil War was a revolutionary experience. For the first time in their lives a large portion of the adult males were forced to travel far from their neighborhoods.

When the war came, there was already a basis for military organization in Orange County in the state militia. By state law all white males between ages eighteen and forty-five were required to enroll in the regular militia. Each county was divided into captain's districts, each of which provided a company, that is, thirty-six men liable for militia duty. The men from five captain's districts formed a battalion, and two battalions composed a regiment. There were two regiments in Orange County.[1]

In theory the militia appeared formidable; in practice it was weak. Men were only required to report for company musters twice and regimental musters once annually, but by the mid-nineteenth century these attendance laws rarely were enforced. During the 1850s the straggling militia regiments were poorly outfitted and equipped, and leadership was untrained.[2]

The experience of the militia did prove beneficial when the county mobilized in 1861. By having mustered with their neighbors even once a year the men had gained some sense of comradeship. In addition, militia officers, who often later served as officers in the Confederate army, had acquired some knowledge about leading soldiers.[3]

Besides the regular militia companies there were a few volunteer militia companies. Men who joined these companies and served ten years were exempted from militia duty except in case of an invasion or insurrection.[4] The Orange Guards was the most prominent of these volunteer companies. Established in 1855, this company consisted of seven officers and sixty-two privates who resided in the vicinity of Hillsborough. In 1857 another volunteer unit was formed in Chapel Hill. The establishment of the Flat River Guards in 1860 indicates that these volunteer companies were not confined to the county's towns.[5]

The volunteer companies projected a much more martial image than the regular militia. Performing in the 1855 Fourth of July ceremony in Hillsborough, the Orange Guards, which had been in existence for only seven months, was reported to have "made a fine appearance, going through its evolutions with precision creditable to a newly formed company.[6] The Flat River Guards also performed admirably in its appearance. Evidently these new companies drilled more often than the regular militia.[7] The county's volunteer companies took themselves seriously. They mustered with volunteer companies from other counties and sent delegates to Goldsboro, North Carolina, to meet in a volunteer militia company convention. There they composed recommendations calling on the North Carolina legislature to adopt a standardized system of tactics and to furnish improved arms for the militia.[8] The importance of the antebellum militia companies, both regular and volunteer, quickly became evident in the spring of 1861 when, after the fall of Fort Sumter, volunteers from Orange County rushed to the Confederate banner.

The formation of Companies B and C of the Sixth North Carolina Regiment illustrates how mobilization proceeded. Company B was comprised primarily of the members of the Flat River Guards and other men in that neighborhood who enlisted in May 1861. It consisted of eighty-seven men and remained under the command of the same officers who had directed the antebellum volunteer company. Captain Robert F. Webb (later promoted to Colonel) was the unit's commanding officer.[9] Company C, which also was formed by enlistments in May, contained eighty-five men who were residents of the Durham neighborhood. Its commanding officer, Captain William J. Freeland, had been the lieutenant-colonel of the regular militia in the Durham neighborhood. The company, which assumed the name Orange Grays, found a generous benefactor in Orange's wealthiest planter, Paul C. Cameron, who provided the unit with five hundred dollars.[10]

The Sixth North Carolina Regiment, which the Flat River Guards and the Orange Grays joined, was commanded by Colonel Charles F. Fisher, the former president of the North Carolina Central Railroad, who before the war had been instrumental in organizing a number of volunteer militia companies in the counties along the route of the North Carolina Central and the Western North Carolina Railroads. In June the Sixth Regiment, which included eight other companies besides the Flat River Guards and the Orange Grays, assembled at the shops of the North Carolina Central Railroad in Alamance County, Orange's western neighbor. For the next five weeks the regiment drilled, before departing for Richmond, Virginia, on July 11. Ten days later it arrived at Manassas Junction, Virginia, where it encountered Union troops.

In this first battle of Bull Run, sixteen men in the regiment were killed and sixty-four wounded. Among the first to fall on the battlefield was Colonel Fisher.[11] Among the wounded was Lieutenant William Preston Mangum of the Flat River Guards, son of Willie Person Mangum, the former United States senator from North Carolina and a resident of Orange County. Mangum's cousin, Captain Webb, had been instrumental in getting him his commission.[12] Although his prospects of surviving seemed good at first, Mangum died within a week.[13]

Like the Flat River Guards and Orange Grays, most of the other soldiers from Orange County also served in companies recruited from their own neighborhoods. Of the 1558 soldiers who served from Orange County, 1457 (93.5 percent) served in only fourteen different military companies. In these fourteen companies the majority of the soldiers, and in most cases the large majority, were residents of Orange County (see Table 14 and Appendix 2-A). The members of each company were often residents of the same neighborhood. For example, Company G, Twenty-Eighth North Carolina Regiment, was composed of men from White Cross; Company E, Thirty-First North Carolina Regiment, of men from Eno; and Company G, Forty-Fourth North Carolina Regiment, of men from Cane Creek. Each of these companies was commanded by a man from the neighborhood who had been an officer in the antebellum militia.[14]

For many soldiers the war marked their first departure from the borders of their neighborhood and Orange County. To find oneself so quickly "in a strange land and away from home," as one soldier described it, must have been a shocking experience.[15] However, the transition may have been eased for many a volunteer because he was sharing the experience with others from his neighborhood. In addition, the neighborhood orientation may have helped many soldiers to understand the cause for which they were engaged and to define their loyalties; once they faced the enemy, the troops could see that they were literally fighting to defend the lives of their friends, neighbors, and relatives who stood on the battlefield alongside them.

For about a year and a half these military companies consisted primarily of members of the same neighborhood. By 1863 90 percent of the men from Orange who served in the county's fourteen military companies had enlisted. There simply were no longer enough men at home to replace the soldiers from Orange County who were removed from their companies by death, imprisonment, injury, and other causes. The companies, therefore, had to look for new enlistees, and, after 1862, conscripts, from other counties. For example, in 1861 the Flat River Guards consisted almost exclusively of men from that neighborhood. By January 1865, however, more than half the men in the company were residents of other North Carolina counties.[16] As the war wore on, soldiers from Orange County increasingly had to depend on the efforts of men with whom they held no traditional bonds. In turn, these new soldiers from other counties had to accept commands from officers from Orange County with whom they had little or no acquaintance.

Unprepared for war, the government of North Carolina did not have enough arms and clothing to distribute to its troops.[17] Therefore, for the first year and a half of the war, the soldiers from Orange County, even though hundreds of miles from home, depended on their neighborhoods for support. They received it from the women of Orange, who formed ladies' aid societies in both the county's towns and nighborhoods and attempted to meet the basic needs of the county's soldiers.[18]

The women's first goal was to clothe the soldiers. For this purpose they raised funds by a variety of methods. Apparently the patriotic mood that swept the county made it fairly easy to raise money during the first months of the war. Some women went from door to door and solicited donations. The women of Hillsborough gave a concert and charged fifty cents admission.[19] In just a few days the women of Chapel Hill raised $1500 to fit the military company from the village with uniforms and soon were sewing four shirts a day.[20]

The rapid pace set by the women often impaired the quality of their work. Further, it was no easy task to sew for men who were stationed far away and could not try on the clothes. In order to measure the soldiers, Levin Carmichael, Hillsborough's tailor, went to the camps and forts where the men were stationed.[21] Some of the men were nervous about how their uniforms would fit. David Thompson, a private in the Orange Guards, feared that if the ladies of Hillsborough made his uniform that it would be a "botched-up affair." He preferred to have his mother, a resident of Eno, or "anybody in the neighborhood" who knew him, sew it. His fears, however, proved unfounded, for three months later, when the Orange Guards received their uniforms, even Thompson happily declared, "I never saw a set of coats fit as well in my life. . . . " [22]

Few records of the amount of clothes produced by the women have survived, but the results of their efforts must have been significant. The Eno ladies' aid society alone forwarded its soldiers ninety-five shirts and one hundred pairs of stockings.[23] In giving "cordial thanks" to the ladies of Hillsborough for clothing the Orange Cavalry, Lieutenant William A. Graham, Jr., declared that his company would use the money the state government provided for uniforms to purchase comforts for the sick and needy.[24] Colonel Fisher of the Sixth Regiment announced that the women of Orange County who supplied his men uniforms were "rendering to the State a service only second to that of the soldiers in the field and deserve consideration accordingly."[25]

After most of Orange County's soldiers had received their uniforms in 1862, the pace of the ladies' aid societies seems to have slowed considerably. Although they occasionally sent the troops some clothes, blankets, and other comforts, the scale of their labor was never again like that in the first year of the war. As shortages of food and commodities developed at home, women simply could not help the troops. Besides, the soldiers' dependence on the county diminished as the army and the North Carolina government acquired the ability to supply the troops.[26] After nearly a year of military service David Thompson noted that coats, pants, shirts, shoes, stockings, and caps were requisitioned for the Orange Guards.[27]

Even when they no longer depended on their relatives and neighbors at home for their necessities, the soldiers still wanted to receive comforts from their families. Civilians continued to send a flow of supplies to the troops. When home on furlough a soldier was expected to collect goods from the families of the other soldiers in his company and neighborhood and distribute them upon his return. For example, in August 1861 David Thompson requested his sister to give a large box of fruit to a private from the Orange Guards who was on furlough and insisted that the private not return without this treat.[28] A more formal procedure developed late in 1862, when North Carolina commissioned Walter A. Thompson, a retired member of the Orange Guards, as an agent to deliver supplies to the troops. After telling the soldiers' families to bring boxes of goods to the depots along the North Carolina Central Railroad, he traveled from Charlotte to Hillsborough, picked up the boxes, and took them to the troops.[29]

II

Unlike the men of the Sixth Regiment who quickly went to Virginia and met Union forces at Manassas Junction, most of the soldiers from Orange County saw no fighting during the first year of the war. Instead, they were introduced to military life by defending North Carolina's coastal forts.

The experience of the Orange Guards, who were stationed in Fort Macon, located on the Bogue Banks protecting Beaufort harbor, was typical. James A. Graham, a son of William A. Graham and a corporal in this company (later promoted to Captain), told his mother how the troops spent their time in the fort: "We have to get up at a quarter past 5 in the morning and have our beds made up and rolled by 6, at 6 1/2 we have a drill for an hour and then get breakfast. We then have nothing to do till 10, when we have to drill for an hour. Drill again at 5 in the evening. Dress Parade at 6 1/2 and then supper. Answer to roll call again at 9 o'clock and have all lights out by 10."[30] When not drilling, Graham read, studied military tactics, and slept. He felt that the salty ocean air made it difficult to keep awake. Sundays were something of a reprieve from the daily tedium, he explained, because the men did not have to drill and were allowed to listen to preaching.[31] After five months with no action, Graham declared: "I am getting tired of war and wish that it would cease. . . . "[32]

Confined for months in the forts under this monotonous routine, the soldiers, as might be expected, thought about food. Some of the officers, who often were sons of slaveholders, had brought some of their families' slaves to cook their meals.[33] The enlisted men were not so fortunate. Although they had large meals with beef, fish, oysters, potatoes, and cabbage, the men often complained that the food was poorly prepared. Some of the soldiers at Fort Macon, after months of accepting this fare, drew their own rations, purchased a second-hand stove, and began to cook their own meals. "We are getting along with our mess finely," David Thompson proudly announced. "We can cook as good as any woman."[34]

The problem of disease proved less manageable. With three thousand men from all sections of North Carolina cramped into Fort Macon, sickness soon began to spread. Perhaps in part because their neighborhoods were so isolated, many of the soldiers had never been exposed to such childhood diseases as measles and mumps. Many suffered without seeking medical attention. Even doctors devoted to the soldiers' care could do little in the face of epidemics. Others were insensitive to the needs of the men. One physician, requested to attend to a soldier suffering with pneumonia, refused to go and demanded that the sick man come to him; the soldier soon died.[35] By the end of 1861 James Graham reported that six or seven deaths in his company resulted from disease.[36]

In the spring of 1862, after almost a year in the forts, many of the soldiers from Orange County looked forward to encountering the enemy. They got their chance on March 14, 1862, when an expedition of Union forces under the command of General Ambrose E. Burnside moved against the port city of New Bern, North Carolina. In the first hours of the battle the Orange Guards, who had moved to protect the city, stood bravely. When orders were given to retreat, however, all discipline disintegrated. "We then scattered through the woods and every man took care of himself," recalled James A. Graham.[37] After this battle the troops from the county realized that victory might not come as easily as they had previously expected. One soldier wrote the editor of the *Hillsborough Recorder*: "Tell all the seceeders [sic] who could whip twelve Yankees a year ago to come and whip one now and we will give them a furlough after the fight."[38]

The soldiers of Orange County also quickly learned that war was a deadly affair: almost one-third of them died. Many were killed in combat. A large number of the soldiers who were wounded did not die on the battlefield but lingered close to death for days or weeks before finally succumbing (see Appendix 2-B). Major battles at Fredericksburg, Gettysburg, Wilderness, and Chancellorsville accounted for most of the combat-related deaths; Gettysburg alone caused 18 percent of all such deaths.[39] Nevertheless, at least half of the soldiers from Orange who died were victims not of the battlefield but of disease, especially typhoid and pneumonia (see Appendix 2-B).[40]

Perhaps because death was so common, many of the soldiers developed—or at least publicly cultivated—a high degree of indifference to it. After one battle a private coolly described to his sister how in a nearby hospital surgeons were dressing wounds next to a "pile of legs and arms" that stood "half as high" as the soldier's head.[41] Another soldier, while writing to his sister during the shelling of Petersburg, Virginia, broke off his letter abruptly. Resuming, he explained the interruption:

> Mary I came very near being scared out of my senses a moment ago. While sitting here writing with 2 or 3 other fellows I heard a gun fire somewhere on the enemies [sic] lines and after awhile I heard a shell coming whistling over seemingly right towards me. I sat and looked and couldn't help being pleased at the music it made (You know I am a

great lover of music anyway.) until it came down zip in less than ten steps of where I was sitting. Then you ought to have seen me throw paper, ink, and everything else and run and get behind a tree after the danger was all over.[42]

Even the dying often displayed a sense of resignation. "I am lying here severely wounded," one soldier wrote a number of weeks after the battle of Gettysburg. "This is the 22nd day and my wounds do not seem to heal. I feel that my race is about run. . . . My grave, I suppose will be near a barn or house of Mrs. Weible's 2 miles from Gettysburg."[43] He died a few weeks later.

Though the war gave soldiers a chance to see something different from their neighborhood and Orange County, most men nostalgically remembered their home county as being superior to other places where they were garrisoned. Stationed in eastern North Carolina, one Orange County soldier who found the people "ignorant and unrefined," reported that the men of this region "get drunk, curse, steal, and commit every sin in the catalogue," and alleged that the women "chew tobacco, dip snuff, lie, and eat clay." After only one year in the military another soldier boasted, "I have travelled over a great deal of this World, but I have never found no place like old Orange County yet. I have seen a great many girls in my route, but none like those in Orange County."[44]

Many Orange County soldiers were taken prisoner by the enemy. When captured at Gettysburg, Captain Robert Bingham of Company G, Forty-Fourth North Carolina Regiment, was transported west in a box car without windows. In Pittsburgh the inhabitants viewed the prisoners as "caged lions" and began to throw stones at them. Arriving safely at Johnson's Island Prison on Lake Erie, Bingham found his days monotonous and "rippleless." "It really does seem a waste to live so," he lamented, "when life is at best so short & often so sorrowful. . . . "[45] Another prisoner at Johnson's Island, Colonel Robert F. Webb of the Flat River Guards, also reported the boredom of prison life: "The great difficulty with us is to kill time . . . it is terrible hard work doing nothing." After nearly half a year in captivity, Webb could "hardly remember the outside world" and feared that he and his fellow prisoners "would loose [sic] our identity."[46]

Most soldiers from Orange County seem to have had no trouble maintaining their identity because their thoughts continued to center on home. Their constant fear was the possibility that the war zone might reach their county. After seeing how Union troops forced the people of eastern North Carolina from their homes, one soldier declared, "I hope you will never see them in Orange County."[47]

The enthusiasm of soldiers for the Confederate cause varied with the well-being of family and neighbors remaining in the county. As early as August 1861, Adolphus Mangum of Flat River, a chaplain in the Sixth Regiment, warned Henry T. Clark, the governor of North Carolina, that the soldiers of his regiment were disturbed about not being paid because their families depended on their compensation. "If they are neglected thus," Mangum cautioned, "they will become disheartened and will not feel like fighting and suffering for the careless and ungrateful."[48] Apparently Governor Clark was slow to act in this matter because a month later a soldier in the Sixth Regiment, using the pseudonym "Flat River," wrote, "at the request of a respectable majority" of his company to the *Hillsborough Recorder*, that the men still had not been paid and daily were receiving letters from their families who were in need of bread.[49]

As the troops began to realize that the war would last for a long time, they began to inquire, usually around the time of planting and harvesting, about their families' farms. After one harvest a very inquisitive soldier asked, "How much corn did our folks make & how much wheat did they sow & how many hogs have they got & how large are they [?]"[50] An officer complained that the soldiers in his company were constantly petitioning for furloughs to go home and help with the harvest. When informed that he could let those soldiers go home whose families' crops might be "seriously damaged or entirely lost without their help," he reported that every man in his company applied.[51]

The soldiers' concern over the welfare of those at home led them to question the Confederate policy of conscription. Although most soldiers felt that there were a number of men still in the county who were capable of serving in the army, they feared that the conscript acts would merely decrease food production. "I cannot see how farmers will make provisions for us if they all go into service between eighteen and thirty-five," one soldier declared.[52] Another private expressed similar sentiments: "I don't see what the people at home

will do since they are taking everybody that is able to bear arms &
[im]pressing everything. I don't think myself that they can hold up
long at it."[53]

At the same time the soldiers believed that those left behind
should respect the sacrifices being made by the troops. They particularly felt it unfair that civilians, who were far from the front and
ignorant of military matters, should decide whether the war continue. After hearing that some in North Carolina were "down-
hearted and almost ready to give up the contest," James A. Graham
of the Orange Guards announced, "I don't think that the people at
home ought to think about giving up while the soldiers in the field,
who have to bear all the hardships, are so hopeful and in such good
spirits.[54]

Late in the summer of 1863 soldiers became especially discon-
tented over opposition to the war by civilians. At this time William
W. Holden, the editor of the *Raleigh Standard*, was advocating that
North Carolina secede from the Confederacy and reach peace terms
with the Union. One Orange County soldier felt that Holden "ought
to be hung or done something with."[55] Another wished "Holden
and his backers were in Yankeedom where their sentiments are."[56]
Some members of the Sixth Regiment, including many residents of
Orange County, signed a resolution that condemned Holden for
"giving aid and comfort to the enemy."[57]

Soldiers were particularly troubled as it became apparent in 1864
that there were some at home who supported Holden's ideas. Hearing from a member of his company who had just returned from a
furlough that "the folks about home is out for peace and whip[p]ed,"
David Thompson of the Orange Guards wrote angrily: "I think
that they ought to send all of them out to the war for a few
months. . . . "[58] Another soldier, claiming that he wanted peace "as
bad as any one," felt that the "people at home" were "blinded" by
Holden and that the editor's plan would make North Carolinians
"the most degraded people in the world."[59]

Not all of Orange County's soldiers were convinced of the wor-
thiness of the Confederate cause, however, as indicated by the fact
that many deserted. Although it is impossible to be sure exactly how
many fled the army, the records indicate that at least forty-nine
did.[60] From these records some interesting features about desertion
become apparent. Rather than being latecomers or draftees, as one

might expect, deserters were overwhelmingly enlistees, who had signed up during the first two years of the war. In fact, some of them had reenlisted after their initial period of service ended. Further, cowardice does not seem to have been a factor in the Orange County desertions. Although being wounded is not necessarily a sign of courage, it does at least indicate that a soldier was actively involved in the war effort, and one-third of the county's deserters had been wounded, about the same rate as for all Orange County soldiers.[61] Some had been wounded more than once. For example, William S. Watson, who deserted from the Flat River Guards in January of 1864, had been wounded twice in 1862 at the battles of Malvern Hill and Fredericksburg. David C. Paul deserted the Orange Guards in February of 1865 after receiving two hip wounds at the battle of Wilderness and Ream's Station in 1864. That eight deserters actually later joined the U.S. Army is one of the strongest pieces of evidence that they were not simply cowards.

If there was no simple explanation why Orange County soldiers deserted, perhaps it was because individual motives may have been secondary to, or at least reinforced by, collective ones. Just as men had enlisted in military companies along with their relatives and neighbors, many seem to have deserted in the same collective manner. In March of 1865, for example, four of the men who deserted from Company G of the 11th Regiment were George and John Clements and George and Houston Sparrow.[62]

Even for those soldiers who never deserted, the topic seems to have been constantly on their minds. Further, they were reminded of it often when deserters were captured and executed in front of the troops. For example, James A. Graham witnessed the executions of four deserters within one week, most of whom he observed were "caused to desert from letters from home." "It was the saddest sight I have ever witnessed," he noted. "Many a poor soldier has met with the same disgraceful death from the same cause."[63]

Even when they tried not to think about desertion, some of the soldiers dreamed about it. While recovering in a Richmond hospital from wounds he had received at the battle of Bristoe Station, David Thompson wrote his sister of a dream he just had: "I thought I was at home & you & I wanted to go some whare [sic] in a buggy & Pappy to prevent us from going cut every horses [sic] throat on the plantation," he recalled. David's father, as a natural authority figure, may have represented the army for, as David added, "I thought he told me he was going to have me arrested for [being] a deserter."[64]

Desertion, of course, was the strongest sign of discontent among soldiers. When dissatisfied, however, most soldiers complained about the situation but remained in the army. For example, on July 16, 1862, Elijah G. Faucett, a thirty-eight-year-old in the Orange Grays wrote to William A. Graham, who was then representing Orange County in the state senate, and asked why he could not get an exemption because of his age. Faucett wondered why the Confederate Congress seemed "to be governed by military men." He feared that soon "we will have nothing but a military government . . . from which the Lord deliver me from ever seeing. I have seen enough already to satisfy me of the horrors of war." Faucett never received his exemption and a year later was wounded at Gettysburg. Fortunately, he recovered from his wound and survived the war to return to his wife, Martha, and his small farm in the Little River neighborhood.[65]

III

On the home front the Civil War threatened the traditional structure of Orange County. The community no longer could function as a collection of isolated and self-contained neighborhoods; for four years, events and conditions far from the county shaped the lives of county residents. Relatives and neighbors no longer could assist the needy, and the county and state government were forced to assume a far larger role in caring for the welfare of the people.

The loss of men to the military changed the pattern of life in Orange County. Although exact figures on enlistments do not exist, one of the best measures of the number of men who left the county to serve in the army is the record of the poll tax, which all white males between the ages of twenty-one and forty-five were required to pay. In 1861, 1321 paid the tax; one year later, only 774 did so. By 1864, only 341, 25.8 percent of the 1861 number, paid. The military participation rate of all males ages fifteen to thirty-nine was at least 70 percent.[66]

The soldiers included the ablest and most productive workers in the county. Although their ages at the time of enlistment ranged from fourteen to fifty-four, 75 percent of the soldiers were between eighteen and twenty-nine (see Table 15). Like most of the inhabitants of Orange County, the majority of the soldiers were farmers (compare Table 16 and Table 4). The typical soldier was unmarried, and he lived and worked on his parents' farm.[67]

This dramatic withdrawal of men from the county was observed by Mary C. Jones, a young woman who resided in Hillsborough. Writing to her cousin in the army she inquired, "Can't you steal off and come? We are very bad off for gentlemen." Nine months later, when the number of men had become even smaller, she informed her cousin that the shortage of men made weddings "so unusual an occurrence" that it was worthwhile to describe in detail one ceremony which had recently taken place.[68]

The war was a severe burden on the economy of Orange County, where most farmers owned no slaves and worked their land with only their own and their sons' labor. If a volunteer was the eldest son, his father, although perhaps only in his late forties, needed his labor to provide for the younger children. If he was the youngest son, his father may have been in his late fifties or early sixties; although in his absence there were fewer mouths on the farm to feed, his aging parents probably had become increasingly dependent on him.[69]

The war was harshest on the families of those soldiers who were married. Many of these men had been married only a few years, and none of their children was old enough to work their farm in their absence.[70] Their wives could not turn for help to either their husband's or their own relatives, as they might have before the war, because these families also had lost men to the military.

From the beginning of the war the county court recognized that the families of men who volunteered would experience hardship. In May 1861 the court appropriated what was then the enormous sum of fifty thousand dollars to support these families. It also appointed commissioners in each captain's district both to determine who was needy and to administer relief.[71]

Most families seem to have made it through the first year and a half of the war with little difficulty. The crops had been planted in the spring of 1861 before the first wave of soldiers had left the county, and there were enough hands present in the fall for the harvest. Further, although the Union blockade and the effort to supply troops caused shortages of such goods as wool, leather, salt, sugar, and coffee, most residents of the county seem to have had enough food.[72]

In 1862, because most new soldiers did not leave the county until after the planting was completed, the prospects also seemed good for the production of foodstuffs. The absence of these men during the fall, however, apparently hurt the harvest, and by early 1863 acute shortages were being reported to Zebulon Vance, the governor of North Carolina. After telling Governor Vance that she was out of corn, a woman, whose husband had been in the army for more than a year, declared, "It is hard for me and mi [sic] children."[73] A woman whose husband had died in the army informed the governor that she had no meat, corn, or wheat to feed her six children. "We see hard times," she despondently announced. "We have done till we don't know what to do . . . i [sic] am thinking the worst is yet to come."[74] Another mother of six pointed out her desperate need to obtain cotton simply "to clothes [sic] my children."[75] "My family must have something to wear," a woman with four children contended, after describing her difficulty obtaining cotton.[76] Recognizing the inability of Orange County to feed itself, William H. Battle of Chapel Hill underscored the necessity of looking elsewhere for help. "Unless one can get corn from some other county than this," he wrote, "I am afraid there will be great suffering among the poor of this vicinity."[77]

The county court was slow to reach Battle's conclusion. Throughout 1862 the court attempted to meet the needs of the soldiers' families by providing direct grants of money. Realizing that many soldiers' parents were also beginning to suffer, the court extended financial benefits to this group.[78] Because it broadened benefits, the court found it necessary early in 1863 to borrow more money.[79]

The court soon conceded that direct grants of money to the soldiers' families would not solve the problem of the needy. The farmers in the country with a surplus of food were reluctant to sell their farm products because of the rapid rate at which prices were rising. Even though the court quadrupled the amount of benefits between the summer of 1862 and the fall of 1863, the soldiers' families could barely keep up with the increase in prices.[80]

In 1863 the court commissioned an agent to purchase grain both in other counties of North Carolina and elsewhere in the Confederate states. Entering the regional wartime economy was no easy task, however, because goods were in short supply elsewhere and inflation was widespread. The county's agent wrote that it was difficult to purchase food in South Carolina. "It is impossible to get men to stand to a trade when it is made," he explained. "They wont sell corn for Confederate money but will barter for anything they can get in preference to money."[81]

The economic problems in Orange County were complicated by an influx of refugees from the areas of North Carolina under Union occupation. "You would not know old Hillsboro!—so many refugees," Mary Jones informed her cousin.[82] One early refugee, who was fortunate enough to find housing, noted that "more people are anxious to come here than there is now accommodations for."[83] Refugees who did not arrive until 1863 found living space only in offices and schoolhouses.[84]

It was not only the refugees but their slaves who taxed the county's resources. Many refugees fled their homes to keep the approaching enemy from emancipating their slaves. Between 1860 and 1863 the number of slaves in the county rose from 5109 to 6013.[85] Because most refugees neither owned land in Orange County nor felt that their stay would be permanent, few of these slaves were used in farming. As Paul C. Cameron observed, "The poor refugees who have brought their slaves up the country find it impossible to provide a home. . . ."[86]

The presence of these new slaves compounded fears of a slave insurrection. Concerns began to grow in January 1863, with reports that a slave had burned a smokehouse.[87] Panic broke out the next month when, within a ten-day period, two masters in Orange County were murdered by their slaves. "As you might suppose the community is much excited," Paul C. Cameron reported to Governor Vance, "and I am told a strong disposition prevails to take the matter in hand & execute the slaves without waiting the action of the court."[88] The swift holding of a court and rapid convictions and executions of the supposedly guilty slaves, however, calmed the fears of many.[89] Except for a reference to the need of a posse to break up a camp of runaway slaves in 1864, there were no other reports of slave misbehavior during the remainder of the war.[90]

But there were continuing reports about shortages of food. By the end of 1863 the county court took a new direction in the care of the

COUNTY CORN REGULATIONS.

Farmers who have not already delivered their tithe corn to the Confederate Agent are allowed by Capt. Kirkland to deliver it to the Millers appointed to receive it. The farmer will get a receipt from the owner of the mill for the corn in the form below, which receipt he will carry to the Confederate Agent, who will take that receipt up, and give his own receipt in place of it to the farmer.

FORM OF THE MILLER'S RECEIPT.

Received   bushels of Corn from   part of his tithe, which I am to dispose of as directed by the Corn Agents of Orange County, and account to J. W. Norwood, one of the said Agents, for the same.

December   1863.   Signed,

WITNESS.

DIRECTIONS TO THE OWNERS OF THE MILLS.

The Millers will shell and dispose of the tithe corn, and all other County corn delivered to them, as follows:

1st. To soldiers' wives at six dollars a bushel, and take in payment the County orders issued to them by their proper Committee man.

2d. They will sell the corn to such other needy persons as bring orders in writing for it from the Committee man of the Captain's district in which said persons reside, in the quantities and at the prices named in said orders, or without price if so named in the order.

DIRECTIONS TO THE COMMISSIONERS OF THE SOLDIERS' FUND IN EACH TAX DISTRICT.

The orders of the County Court make it the duty of the three Commissioners in each Tax District to decide

First, What soldiers' wives shall have orders for their monthly allowance from the Committee men of their respective Tax Districts

Secondly, What other *needy persons* shall have orders from the Committee men on the keeper of the public corn for said corn, and in what quantities, and at what price, not exceeding six dollars a bushel, (till February Court,) and also what destitute persons shall have such corn without paying anything for it. These orders of theirs to the Committee men must be in writing.

In addition to these duties, the said Commissioners will also, after consulting the Committee men if necessary, select the mills in their respective tax districts at which the tithe corn and other county corn shall be deposited, and in what quantities, according to the number of those around the mills who are entitled to have the corn. And they will make known to the owners of the mills, in writing, how much corn said mill is to receive.

The duty of these Commissioners is a very important one, and unless they exercise a firm discretion in distributing the corn to needy persons, all the corn will soon be gone, and soldiers' families and other really destitute persons, will be left without bread.

The undersigned have published these regulations in pursuance of the duty imposed on them by the County Court.

P. C. CAMERON, } County Corn Agents.
J. W. NORWOOD, }

December 11th, 1863.

NOTE.—The following persons compose the Commissioners:
Hillsborough District—W. F. Strayhorn, Thomas Wilson, Nelson P. Hall.
St. Mary's District—S. D. Umsted, H. Parker, John McCown.
St. Mark's District—C. G. Marcum, R. F. Morris, John Burroughs.
St. Thomas's District—J. W. Carr, Jehiel Atwater, W. J. Hogan.
Caswell District—Alfred Snipes, H. M. C. Strowd, Matthew Atwater.
Orange District—C. E. Smith, F. Walker, Thomas H. Hughes.

Corn regulations of Orange County. Wartime regulations imposed by the Orange County Court to obtain food from the county's farmers in order to provide for the growing number of needy. (Photograph courtesy of the North Carolina Division of Archives and History).

soldiers' families. Rather than continuing to distribute money, it began to provide grain directly to the needy. To obtain food for the needy, the court used the "tax-in-kind" law passed by the Confederate Congress in April 1863, which allowed the government to collect one-tenth of all farm production.[91] In November the court required all farmers to take their tithe to the nearest mill, where it was turned over to agents of the Confederate government; then agents for the county purchased the grain directly from these government officials with Confederate money. The court also had its agents buy the tithe grain grown in other North Carolina counties. Finally, in order to discourage the county's more prosperous farmers from hoarding their grain until prices rose, the court fixed price rates.[92]

The amount of aid given by the court to the needy is striking. Before the war the county had given assistance to fewer than thirty people annually; by the end of 1864, 508 women and 735 children were provided for each month.[93]

But many continued to suffer. Robert F. Morris, the tax commissioner responsible for providing aid to the needy in the Durham neighborhood, noted to John W. Norwood of Hillsborough, the director of aid throughout the county, that soldiers' families in his vicinity were "without a mouthful of bread for themselves or their children." "Our women do not ask for a mouthful of meat," Morris declared, "and I think we ought to not let them suffer for bread."[94] Similar complaints came from other commissioners who felt that their districts were not receiving their share of the grain.[95]

In other parts of the Confederacy the intense civilian suffering such as the people of Orange County experienced frequently was transferred into discontent over the war effort. Often this discontent arose because many believed that planters were not sharing in the cost of the war. This feeling became even more intensified after October 1862, when the Confederate Congress authorized a policy whereby one white man could be exempted from military service for every twenty Negroes under his control.[96] Some small farmers and nonslaveholders saw this law as an attempt by the planter class to protect their sons. In Orange County, however, this issue never caused discontent, probably because the sons of planters participated in the war in nearly an identical proportion to all men countywide.[97] For example, all four of William A. Graham's sons of military age who were residing in Orange County—John, Robert, William, and

James—served. Although none was killed, the latter two were wounded. Alvis K. Norwood, the son of John W. Norwood, the owner of thirty slaves, was killed on June 15, 1864, while serving in the Orange Guards. Few planters themselves served in the army: most men who owned at least twenty slaves were well over military age. Overall, the county board, which gave exemptions, did so on rare occasions. The board "rarely excuses any one from service," one soldier declared, "unless he's almost unable to get about at all." [98] The only evidence that any planter family requested to take advantage of the twenty-slave law was the case of Emily Nunn, whose husband Ilai was an invalid. With the Nunn's two sons, William and Willis, already in the army, there was no white man on the Patterson neighborhood plantation to oversee the family's thirty-three slaves, a number of whom Emily termed "very unmanageable." Her request that William be discharged must have been denied, however, since he served through the entire war. [99]

In addition to contributing their sons, planters probably avoided becoming the object of their less affluent neighbors' ire by bearing a significant share of the financial costs of the war. Whereas, in 1860, county taxes totalled $8548.54, by 1864, to meet the costs of the wartime needs of the county and especially to care for the families of soldiers, they had risen to $35,106.63. The taxes on slaves alone equalled $12,412.20. Further, since taxes alone were not meeting the community's expenses, the county was forced to borrow heavily from the only source of money—planters. For example, at the time of the surrender in 1865 the county still owed Paul C. Cameron $13,040. [100]

If discontent did not arise over the lack of planter participation in the war effort, other issues emerged that did threaten the unity of purpose that had characterized the county during the beginning of the war. The first event that gained the attention of many Orange County residents and raised doubts about the war was the arrest of R.J. Graves in the fall of 1862 by the Confederate government. While on a visit to Virginia, Graves, a minister from the Cane Creek neighborhood, apparently was falsely charged with giving information to Union troops about a gunboat, the defenses around Richmond, and a railroad in North Carolina. Graves's imprisonment in Castle Thunder Prison in Richmond upon his return to the Confederacy became a major civil and states' rights issue in North Carolina and especially in Orange County where, as one resident noted, "Nothing has occured [sic] since the war commenced that has gone so far to make this community feel that the authorities at Richmond are inclined to be despotic." The incident proved to have a short life after Governor Zebulon Vance demanded of President Jefferson Davis that Graves be released and returned to North Carolina. Davis complied, and Graves was never tried.[101]

Evidently the speed with which the Graves affair was settled prevented it from becoming an immediate source of discontent. As evidence of this, when on January 3, 1863, Jefferson Davis passed through Hillsborough, one resident observed that "the whole town turned out to meet him." Although asleep when his train reached the town, President Davis awoke to meet William A. Graham, shake the hands of the assembled crowd, and make a short speech in which he, as Paul Cameron remembered, "said he saw peace ahead — and that we should drive back the hated Yankees." The enthusiasm with which his speech was received indicates that the president and the Confederacy still had the support of the people of Orange County.[102]

President Davis's visit, however, did not prevent the rise of other sources of discontent, especially after the war tide began to turn in mid-1863. By August 15 of that year a meeting was held near the border of the White Cross and Cane Creek neighborhoods, an area of the county which had overwhelmingly opposed secession in 1861, and a series of resolutions was drafted. The sentiment expressed in these resolutions questioned the course of the Confederate government which, they charged, "from the beginning of the war has been somewhat unfair" toward North Carolina. In other resolutions, the meeting's participants opposed the appointment of office holders in North Carolina who were not North Carolinians, advocated that the "people both of the North and South . . . select the ablest and the most unprejudiced statesmen from amongst them" to meet in a peace convention, declared that they would not vote for any Confederate congressmen who opposed negotiations and a peace convention, berated "any man under sixty years" who advocated secession but who avoided military service, and voiced opposition to speculators.[103]

Despite the fact that the wartime consensus had clearly broken down, in the August 1864 gubernatorial election the county overwhelmingly voted for Governor Zebulon Vance against William W.

Holden, the peace-at-nearly-any-cost candidate.[104] Nevertheless, soon after the election, a shift in sentiment against the war began to occur in the county. This shift can best be observed in the actions of Samuel F. Phillips, who was elected Orange County's state senator in 1864.[105] Through the August election Phillips had supported Governor Vance, largely because he, like many of the people of Orange County, had doubts over Holden's character, since the Raleigh newspaper editor initially had been such a strong advocate of secession and the war. By September of 1864, however, Phillips had become a critic of Vance and in December supported North Carolina's independently negotiating a peace. Even after the Hampton Roads Conference on February 3, 1865, when President Lincoln asserted that the southern states would be restored to the Union only under condition of the abolition of slavery, Phillips, rather than criticizing Lincoln, voiced opposition to Jefferson Davis. Further, within a few weeks, at a meeting in Chapel Hill, Phillips advocated peace even under terms which might mean emancipation. When a vote was taken at this meeting on a preamble that stressed the need to continue the war rather than accept peace "upon terms that are both ruinous and dishonorable" — meaning emancipation — Phillips's position lost, although it gained the support of a sizeable minority.[106]

By the last year of the war, even some of the county's wealthiest residents, who had been protected by their savings and their slaves' labor, began to report they were facing difficulties. "I have no confederate money, the taxes on my slaves, stocks and bonds more than absorbed my income, my salary was annihilated, and I was compelled to turn agriculturist or starve," wrote David L. Swain, the president of the University of North Carolina.[107] He told of a formerly "well to do" professor who was "compelled to part with his watch" just to meet his expenses.[108] Even Paul C. Cameron, the county's richest planter, felt that it would be difficult to produce a decent crop unless he was able to obtain new farm equipment.[109]

If a majority of the community's residents did not support Phillips's belief that emancipation was worth peace, by early 1865, hardships, shortages, and military disasters contributed to a growing feeling by many that victory might not be achieved. William H. Battle reported that the inhabitants of Chapel Hill seemed a "good deal depressed at the condition present and prospective of the country." He added, "We have fought bravely, but we seem to be gradually

losing everything but our honor." [110] In the Flat River neighborhood, Martha Mangum observed how "late reverses have disheartened the people." [111]

As the fourth anniversary of the war approached, James Phillips of Chapel Hill, Samuel's father, began, like many others, to assess the results of the struggle. "Secession seems not to have produced the results predicted by its sanguine friends," he declared. "There was to be no war, no taxes worth prating about, but an increase of happiness, boundless prosperity and entire freedom from all Yankee annoyance. . . . " He concluded that all the war had accomplished was to bring the people to "the brink of ruin." [112]

IV

In the closing days of the war, Orange County, which had seen no fighting within its borders, found itself in the direct path of the Union army. Although Robert E. Lee had already surrendered to Ulysses S. Grant on April 9, 1865, at Appomattox Courthouse, Virginia, all Confederate troops had not set down their arms. Under the command of Joseph E. Johnston, Confederate forces were still retreating northwestward across North Carolina from the approaching Union army under William T. Sherman.

On April 13, after one of the last skirmishes of the war, Con-

The Civil War years. *From left to right:* Lieutenant William P. Mangum (1837–61) was a member of the Flat River Guards and one of the first Orange County soldiers to die during the Civil War. Corporal James A. Graham (1841–1908) was the son of William A. Graham and member of the Orange Guards who described the realities of being a soldier. Samuel F. Phillips (1824–1903), Orange County's state senator, came to advocate peace even at the price of emancipation. (Photographs courtesy of North Carolina Division of Archives and History.) John Wall Norwood (1802–85) was a prominent Hillsborough lawyer and planter who, while directing wartime aid to keep the county's needy alive, suffered the loss of his own son Alvis on the battlefield. (From copy in the North Carolina Collection, UNC Library at Chapel Hill.)

federate troops crossed into Orange County. Many of the county's residents, fearing that their own army would pillage them, hid their valuables.[113] But upon reaching Chapel Hill on the afternoon of April 14, the soldiers demonstrated discipline and protected the village from damage for two days. On April 16, Easter Sunday, the Confederates departed, and within hours Union troops entered the village.

The Union soldiers posed no great threat to Chapel Hill. Guards, who were posted to protect the university and homes, were said to have treated the inhabitants with "utmost civility."[114] The only people who seem to have suffered were some of the farmers in the countryside who were forced to provide the occupation troops with supplies until railway transportation could be resumed. Once they began to receive rations by train, the Union soldiers provided food to the needy civilians.[115]

The final moments of the war were played out northeast of the village. General Johnston had requested a meeting with General Sherman at a point equidistant between Hillsborough and Durham. On the morning of April 17, after encountering one another on the road between these two sites, the two generals rode to a small farmhouse owned by James Bennett. Here they quickly reached an agreement on very general terms of peace. A second meeting became necessary when President Andrew Johnson and his cabinet, realizing that Sherman had agreed to terms that might protect the property right of slavery, rejected the agreement. On April 26, therefore, the two generals again met at the farmhouse and agreed to terms similar to those reached at Appomattox Courthouse.[116] Within days a Chapel Hill resident summed up the feeling of many of the county when she exclaimed, "It is all over! . . . Peace is come—but what a peace! How different from what our hopes have so fondly pictured. . . . I cannot think two consecutive thoughts—I can only feel![117]

V

The most severe impact of the war on Orange County came from the removal of a large percentage of the adult, white males. For approximately the first year and a half of the struggle, both the county's soldiers and civilians adjusted to the demands made upon them by the war. The soldiers, hundreds of miles away, maintained their sense of neighborhood through the structure of their military companies and their dependence on those at home. Those remaining in the county were willing to make sustained sacrifices so long as victory seemed imminent. But by 1863 problems began to develop and only worsened as the war continued.

The war had parallel effects on the soldiers and civilians of Orange County. As the war went on, the men in the army came to rely less and less on their families and neighborhoods for support and equipment. At the same time the civilians, no longer able to continue in self-contained neighborhoods, grew increasingly to rely on the county

Bennett Farmhouse surrender. The typical county farmhouse, midway between Durham and Hillsborough, where negotiations were held for the surrender of General Joseph E. Johnston and his Confederate troops to Union general William T. Sherman. (Photograph courtesy of North Carolina Division of Archives and History.)

and state governments. The war thus compelled both the soldiers and civilians of Orange County to become part of a larger world. Whether these changes would be so permanent that they would alter the community's traditional neighborhood structure would be revealed during the immediate postwar years.

CHAPTER 5

One Step Forward, One Step Backward

The Postwar Economic and Social Structure

The instability created by the war continued after the coming of peace in 1865. Although Orange County was spared physical devastation, the death of a large number of white men and the emancipation of over six thousand slaves markedly disrupted its economy and social structure. No longer able to look to the government for help, people turned again to the family and neighborhood to reestablish stability. Although the community experienced many changes during the postwar era, the impact of these changes was lessened by traditional forces.

I

When hostilities ended, most Orange County soldiers returned home. To be sure, because of the large number of soldiers who died in the army, the rate of persistence—the percentage of an age group that remained in the county for a decade—was lower during the 1860s than during the 1850s (see Table 3.A). The most sharp decline in the rate of persistence was among men who had been in their twenties and thirties in 1860; these were the men who served in the war. There were 25 percent fewer white men between the ages of twenty and thirty-nine in 1870 than there had been in 1860, indicative of the many young soldiers from the county who died during the war.[1]

This alteration of the sex ratio in itself caused few changes in the patterns of marriage among whites during the first five years after the war. Although in 1870 there were some war widows with fatherless children, their numbers were much smaller than the loss of so many soldiers might have warranted. Most of the soldiers who died in the war were single, and those who were married had few children. Immediately after the war many couples rushed into marriage. These postwar newlyweds were older than those married before the war.[2] In some cases the conflict had forced them to defer marriage; in others, the brides were war widows who were now owners of their deceased husbands' property and, hence, made attractive wives. For example, when Andrew J. Borland of Company D of the 1st Regiment died in 1862, he was survived by his wife Lydia, aged thirty-two, and five small children. Lydia was left with Andrew's 172 acres of farm land in the Cane Creek neighborhood. In 1866 Lydia married Franklin Lashley, who in 1860 had been a landless farm laborer. By 1870, therefore, Franklin, through his marriage to Lydia, was farming Andrew's land.[3]

Although all the war widows experienced a great personal loss by their husbands' deaths, the economic fortunes of those who chose not to remarry quickly varied widely. While some widows clearly suffered, others adjusted well. For example, before he died in May of 1864 while serving in Company F of the 1st Regiment, James Wilkins had farmed over two hundred acres in the Durham neighborhood. By 1870 his widow, Malinda, however, owned only thirty acres, which she worked with her fifteen-year-old son William. When Sutton Ward died in February of 1865 after serving in Company E of the 31st Regiment, he left his wife Sally with a hundred-acre farm in the Eno neighborhood. Five years later Sally still owned all hundred acres and had converted thirty unimproved acres into farm land. An equally impressive success story was that of Elisha Durham's widow. Before the war Durham was both a blacksmith and farmer. When he died in a Union prison two months after the war ended, his widow, Mary, and sons abandoned Elisha's blacksmith shop and focused strictly on farming. By doing so they added thirty acres to their farm and increased its value by $150.

Apparently after the war some widows, and again there were not many in this category, chose or found it necessary to move in with their kin. When Samuel Blackwood died of disease in 1862 he left his wife Harriett and two small children. At the time of their marriage in 1859 Samuel and Harriett had lived only three households apart in the New Hope neighborhood. Their household in 1860 was located next door to Samuel's mother, a widow, and only six households from Harriett's parents. Not surprisingly, therefore, after Samuel's death Harriett moved in with her parents. Similarly, some-time after John B. Snipes died of disease in 1862 and left his widow Adeline with no land, she decided to move in with her parents, who resided nearby. By 1870 she was still living with her parents, Sauvin and Susan Stanford, on their moderate-sized farm. Her son James, aged thirteen, helped his sixty-four-year-old grandfather, whose seven slaves had been emancipated, work the farm in the White Cross neighborhood.

The deaths of so many soldiers in the war influenced more than just widows. Even for those men who did not participate in or who survived the war there was a significant change in marital patterns during this period. Perhaps in part because the war had given soldiers the opportunity to meet women from different sections of Orange County directly or by word of mouth and because the shortage of eligible grooms forced women to find men who resided further from their homes, brides and grooms came from households more widely separated than in the antebellum years (see Table 1). In addition, from 1865 to 1869 these newlyweds were less likely to establish their own households near their parents and more often lived at a greater distance than before the war (see Table 2).

But these changes in marital patterns, the fundamental bond of the antebellum neighborhood, were only temporary. By 1880, as those boys who had been too young to serve in the army entered their twenties, the sex ratio of the young adults in the county had returned to a more traditional level. As these young men married, even more stayed in the county than in the prewar years (see Tables 3.A and 3.B). Further, they continued to live not merely within the county but in the same neighborhood. Between 1870 and 1880 only 13.5 percent of the men who remained within the county moved from one township—the new civil division created in 1868 that often mirrored neighborhood borders—to another (see Map 5).[4]

By the 1870s, as the county seemed to recover from the tragedy of the war, a return to more traditional marriage patterns occurred. The annual number of marriages and the age at marriage nearly duplicated the antebellum levels. Evidently, for some men, the loss of a brother in the war may have resulted in a more substantial inheritance.[5] This encouraged them not only to persist in Orange

The gravestone of Cabe Lamkin Ray. This Little River neighborhood soldier's death during the last weeks of the Civil War provided his younger brothers, who had been too young to serve in the war, with the incentive to remain in their neighborhood during the 1870s and possibly inherit a larger amount of property. (Photograph by Carol Bleise Kenzer.)

County but, as was just described, to remain in their traditional neighborhoods. For example, Private Cabe Lamkin Ray, the oldest son of Tyre Ray of the Little River neighborhood, died during the last weeks of the war and was survived by his three younger brothers —Herbert, Nazer, and Edwin—all too young to serve in the army. By 1880, perhaps anticipating receiving a larger share of their aging father's estate than if Cabe had survived, Nazer, aged thirty, and Edwin, twenty-three, were still residing in Tyre's household as farm laborers. Continued residence in traditional neighborhoods seems also to have encouraged young men to return to a more local attitude regarding who they married and where they settled. Hence, young men returned to the practice of finding their wives among immediate neighbors and establishing their new households as newlyweds even nearer to their parents than before the war (see Tables 1 and 2).[6]

Social and economic institutions in Orange County also followed traditional neighborhood patterns. For example, in the Cane Creek Baptist Church in 1877, just as before the war, a few families dominated neighborhood church membership. Further, in the postwar

MAP 5   *Township Borders, Post-1868*

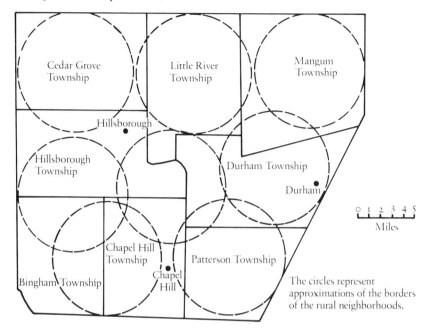

Cedar Grove Township

Little River Township

Mangum Township

Hillsborough

Hillsborough Township

Durham Township

Durham

0 1 2 3 4 5
Miles

Chapel Hill Township

Patterson Township

Bingham Township

Chapel Hill

The circles represent approximations of the borders of the rural neighborhoods.

years the neighborhood general store also continued as the center of credit. Four-fifths of the customers at the Mangum family's general store in the Flat River neighborhood were residents of the Mangum Township. Most of them were farmers unwilling to travel fifteen to twenty miles to make purchases at the larger general stores in Hillsborough.[7]

The only new social institution during the immediate postwar years which might have challenged the traditional neighborhood patterns was the rise of the national Grange movement, or the Patrons of Husbandry, during the mid-1870s. Beginning late in 1873 and continuing through the middle of 1876, ten Grange lodges were established in the county.[8] The Grange, with its emphasis on promoting social and economic solidarity among farmers, might have encouraged a less localized social orientation if it led farmers in the different rural neighborhoods to recognize their common interests. The editor of the *Hillsborough Recorder* described this potential when he observed, "One thing struck us very forcibly as a probable immediate happy effect of . . . the Granges, and that is the bringing of the people of the country together. . . . "[9] However, two factors prevented the Granges from having a long-term impact on the county. First, since the individual Grange lodges were centered within the neighborhoods, the members rarely had contact with those outside their immediate vicinity. Only the leaders of the lodges, all fairly affluent men, met with leaders of the other lodges in a county meeting. Second, although, given more time, the Grange might have overcome the neighborhood unit, its duration—less than three years in Orange County—was far too short to accomplish this. Therefore, although the county was touched by this new national institution, the contact took place through traditional local methods.[10]

II

The degree of continuity of neighborhood social and economic life was matched by that of overall landholding patterns in the county. As in other parts of the South during this period, in Orange County the prewar planters and former slaveholders continued to control most of the land. In part this continuity was maintained because planters and large slaveholders remained in the county during the 1860s to an extent that markedly surpassed that of the nonslaveholders (see Table 3.B).[11]

Although all the capital invested in slaves was lost and the total value of farms in the county fell by over 50 percent between 1860 and 1870, the planters and former slaveholders continued to be wealthy.[12] Of the twenty-three planters who remained in the county from 1860 to 1870, twenty still were among the wealthiest 10 percent of white male household heads.[13] The property of planters who died during the decade was usually retained by their widows and children.[14] For example, in 1860 John Berry, the prominent Hillsborough architect, planter, and politician owned $7000 in real estate and forty-five slaves. By the time the 1870 census was taken John had died, but his wife Elizabeth, despite the county-wide and regional fall in land values, owned $15,000 in real estate. Therefore, the war did not create a large number of new affluent men; the overwhelming majority of the wealthiest landowners in 1870 had either owned or lived in a household where a substantial amount of property and slaves was owned in 1860 (see Table 17).

John Berry (1798–1870) and wife, Elizabeth (1803–88). Despite losing, through emancipation, the capital invested in forty-five slaves, and even after her husband, a prominent architect, planter, and politician, died in 1870, Elizabeth remained one of the wealthiest residents of the county. (Photograph courtesy of North Carolina Collection, UNC at Chapel Hill.)

Even though they were relatively well off, planters still often bemoaned their postwar economic conditions. For example, late in 1869 Paul C. Cameron, the wealthiest planter in the county both in 1860 and 1870, complained, "It filled me with bitter feeling towards those I can't name of impoverishing my wife and dear children when I am too old to rebuild our fortunes and hardly able to take care of myself. . . . "[15] Although Cameron's total estate had drastically fallen during the previous decade, from $267,000 to $100,000, it was difficult for many to believe he could not "take care" of himself. His niece, who noted how during a recent visit to Cameron's house she found "Uncle Paul as blue as he well can be & complaining of dire poverty," jokingly asked, "Ought he not to be 'real poor' just for [a]while to see how it feels?" Cameron would never have that opportunity; rather, within five years his assets in the county would total $298,247.[16]

Such stability among the wealthy meant, of course, that there was little change in the pattern of landholding among the other groups in society. For white farmers the concentration of acreage remained fairly constant (see Table 9). Faced with an unstable black labor force, most planters were forced to take land out of production. Consequently, the average size of farms operated by whites fell from 285.7 acres in 1860 to 198.5 acres in 1870.

Although the most affluent landholders owned a smaller share of the total value of real estate in 1870 than 1860, the decade did not see a revolution in property ownership. One-tenth of the landowners still held about 60 percent of the land (see Table 8). Few of these planters sold or leased their land to whites. More than one-third of all white farmers continued to own no land.[17]

By 1870, freedmen, like the typical white farmers, had made little economic advancement. Only 14.2 percent of black male household heads owned any real estate. The average size of farms operated by black farmers was less than half that of the farms operated by white farmers.[18]

No evidence exists indicating that in Orange County freedmen failed to gain real estate because whites refused to sell it to them on account of race. In fact, it appears that if blacks had money in the depressed immediate postwar economy, whites were very willing to sell them property. For example, Robert Fitzgerald, a black freedmen's schoolteacher who resided near Hillsborough, noted how in the vicinity of his school some Negro families were "very poor, but the general class have bought land and built houses though small."[19] Further, when his father arrived from Delaware with money and expressed a desire to purchase land, Fitzgerald described how he was "invited to a great number of places" by white men to view their property. Eventually after being wooed for ten days by "several gen-

tlemen who offer to sell him land cheap," Fitzgerald's father bought
a 158-acre "plantation," which included "farming utensils, household and kitchen utensils for $1200." [20]

Not all freedmen had the same economic opportunities. Before
the war more than two-thirds of the free blacks were mulattoes, and
they owned considerably more real estate than freedmen of pure
African ancestry. [21] Consequently, mulattoes had a head start over
other freedmen after the war. Mulattoes acquired land with their
earnings as skilled laborers (although they comprised only one-fourth
of the nonwhite population, mulattoes made up nearly half of the
nonwhite skilled labor force in the county [22]), and by 1870 they were
twice as likely to own land as other blacks. [23]

Most Negroes, whether black or mulatto, clearly held an inferior
economic status. In 1870, though free to move from one plantation
to another, most Negro farmers worked under a system of labor not
far removed from slavery. Rather than working a parcel of land on
their own and then paying money or a share of the crop for rent to
the white landlord, they simply labored under the supervision of
another farmer and very likely a white one. [24]

III

The preservation of both the neighborhood's social patterns and
the planters' dominance of property could not hide the fact that the
war had brought about a true social revolution through the emancipation of the county's six thousand slaves. All of the community's
whites, whatever their antebellum economic and social status and
despite any satisfaction they may have found in the continuity of
their family and neighborhood systems, were forced to consider the
implications of this momentous change. Within a few weeks of the
Confederacy's surrender, as one resident of Chapel Hill noted, "The
whole framework of our social system is dissolved. The negroes are
free, leaving their homes with few exceptions, & those exceptions
are only for a time." [25]

A central theme of this social revolution, and one that linked the
whites' and the freedmen's responses to emancipation, was the re-
definition of dependency that took place. Under slavery the master
had always assumed that his slave was dependent on him. Once the
war ended, however, so did that assumption. "Isn't it provoking to
be dependent upon those miserable free negroes [?]" asked a planter's

daughter.[26] Paul Cameron stressed how it had become important for him "to teach the negro that we are *not dependent on him* [his italics]."[27]

This concern about dependency was largely an outgrowth of the diminished financial strength felt by Orange County's planters. Although planters, as has been indicated, continued to own a disproportionate share of the county's land, they seemed less secure of their status than they had before the war. A few months after the war's conclusion William A. Graham declared, "I shall be able to save my crops of this year, but have no assurance for the next. . . . "[28]

For some planters this insecurity was caused partly by the specific concern that they might lose their property as the shortage of money made it difficult to pay their taxes and debts. "Father thinks it would be an everlasting disgrace upon himself and children to be sold out for debt," a planter's daughter lamented. "The thought of being sold out for debt is always on his mind . . . he was constantly referring to it."[29] For many planters, however, the concern was expressed as a more general fear of the future itself. "The people seem to have all of the life crushed out of them and still look forward with fear lest the worst has yet to come to pass," a former resident of the county observed after her return home.[30]

This fear of the future, which is understandable given the insecurity created by four years of war, also resulted from the former master's sense of abandonment by his slaves. No topic was discussed more, and none was more disconcerting. Some whites felt that the freedmen were simply testing their new status. "It is to prove their freedom that they go away," a former slaveholder's daughter declared.[31] William A. Graham observed how the former slaves "leave home in search of freedom, like knights errant in search of adventures."[32]

What often most distressed the planter about the freedmen's apparent abandonment of his former master was their decision simply to establish a separate household. When describing how another planter had just experienced the loss of his freedmen, Paul C. Cameron exclaimed, "What an upturning of all the foundation stones of Domestic life!"[33] "All of our servants seem to be possessed of a desire to go to housekeeping," a Chapel Hill planter announced.[34] "They seem to show no feeling or attachment for their owners—

those who have raised & fed & clothed them," one woman scorn-
fully cried after her neighbor's freedmen left.[35]

The former slaveholders quickly felt the loss of their slaves in a
number of personal ways. The former slave mistress in particular
soon realized how her slaves had shielded her from drudgery. The
wife of one planter told her daughter how the loss of their "servants"
forced "every lady here . . . to learn to cook & most of them
washing." She sadly added, "I dread the ironing worse than anything
else & washing dishes."[36] "Broken-up" without her servant, another
woman reported that she loathed the thought of "cooking & washing & milking."[37]

Even when freedmen decided to remain and work for their former
masters, the new relationship was often strained, especially when the
freedmen insisted on fair treatment. When one mistress scolded her
servant for tardiness, the maid flew "into a rage" and announced
that if she could not please her mistress that perhaps she should "get
a house somewhere else."[38] Upset by the daughter of a planter,
another black servant quickly declared that "her skin was nearly as
white . . . her hair nearly as straight" as her employer's and that "she
was quite as free."[39] When another planter struck one of his servants
for insolence and disobedience, the freedman responded by breaking
his nose, jaw, and teeth.[40]

Irate and insulted, a few Orange County whites hoped that blacks
would leave the South. One resident of Chapel Hill wished that the
freedmen "were all in—shall I say Mass[achusetts] or Conn[ecti-
cut]."[41] But most whites realized that their own economic future
was linked to that of blacks and felt it essential to convince the
freedmen to return to work on the land. Although the freedmen
presently held the "erroneous notion that liberty is the right to do
nothing," one planter's daughter observed, they would soon return
to those masters who had been kind to them, so long as they were
"assured of their liberty."[42]

Despite their belief that if treated fairly the freedmen would return
to work for them, many planters still feared what they perceived
was a shortage of black labor. A former slaveholder told how freedmen had become "very scarce" in the Cane Creek neighborhood.[43] A
resident of Chapel Hill noted, "There has been great difficulty in
getting laborers. Most of our Negroes have quit here for Raleigh

and elsewhere."[44] "Negroes are still leaving this section," a Hillsborough planter informed his son five years after the war had ended.[45]

The planters' concern about the shortage of blacks was only heightened by their realization that there was no alternative source of labor. Planters might have considered attracting white men to work for them by offering favorable terms, but with more than four hundred of the county's white men having died in the war, this was impossible. "There are not many white men to work," Eliza Thompson informed her daughter. "All of the best men we had were either killed or lost their limbs or health in the army."[46]

It is significant that whites came to recognize their dependence on their former slaves just when blacks began to express a sense of their own independence and identity. Unfortunately, since blacks left few personal records, far too often it is only possible to view their expressions of this independence and identity through the critical eyes of whites. Blacks, like whites, continued to follow traditional lines during the postwar years in one important area—familial patterns. The structure of the black family generally paralleled that of the white family. But black males were more mobile than white males (see Table 3.A). Not only were black men less likely to remain in Orange County, many of those who stayed moved from one township to another.[47] Possibly because of their greater mobility, which largely can be attributed to their inferior economic position, blacks were more likely than whites to encounter and later select mates who resided further away (see Table 1). After marriage, blacks also more often established their new household further from their parents (see Table 2). Even so, more than half of the black newlyweds had lived in the same township before marriage, and 80 percent of them settled within the same township as one of their parents.[48]

One area in which blacks asserted a desire to establish their identity as well as gain independence from whites was education. Within five months of the end of the war a notice was placed in the *Hillsborough Recorder* by Job Berry, a freedman, that the "colored citizens of Hillsborough" were to meet within two days to raise money to purchase a building for a school.[49] By the end of 1868 six freedmen's schools had been established throughout the county.[50] Although these schools were subsidized by the Freedmen's Bureau and Quakers, the freedmen themselves made whatever financial contributions they could.[51] Further, the schools' significance as an institution encouraging the freedmen's sense of independence and identity can best be measured by the degree not only to which blacks desired but to which whites opposed them. "All our old negroes have left. . . . It is very difficult to hire them at any price since the 'cussed' . . . Nigger School commenced," a white resident of Hillsborough angrily charged.[52] William A. Graham, noted a bit more sedately, but just as firmly, what he viewed as a link between freedmen attending schools and "equality with whites, & other political topics."[53]

No sign of collective black assertion of independence and identity was stronger than their annual celebration of the Fourth of July. Every year for the first four years after the war the Negroes of Chapel Hill, Hillsborough, and the countryside held large ceremonies and parades on Independence Day. These were not spontaneous celebrations but well-organized events publicized with handbills, arranged by committees, led by chairmen, secretaries, and marshalls, and initiated by a formal reading of the Declaration of Independence.[54] By contrast, it was not until July 4, 1867, a white Chapel Hill resident observed, that the "stars and stripes" were flown over his town's post office and assessor's office, "The first raised by white men in the town in six years."[55]

Despite finding it difficult, therefore, whites grudgingly came to accept the social and economic revolution of emancipation. The frustration they felt over their dependence on blacks, as well as the bitterness with which they viewed blacks' proclaiming their independence, was trying, but they had little choice. Nevertheless, so long as whites retained their superior economic status over and maintained a social distance from blacks, they could tolerate the situation. However, it would not be long before a new challenge arose as blacks gained political rights, and whites, fearing an even greater revolution, reacted. The difference then would be that, whereas whites had generally responded as individuals to the economic and social revolution of emancipation, in politics they could and would act collectively.

IV

Although the experience of every former slaveholder varied, that of Paul C. Cameron, the largest antebellum planter, provides a sense of the complexity of the economic and social relationship between whites and freedmen. Just after the surrender of Johnston to Sherman at the Bennett farmhouse, Cameron proposed a labor contract to his former slaves, detailing what would be expected of the freedmen if they wanted to remain and work for him. In Cameron's view, one shared by many former planters, the proper relationship between the landowner and the freedmen should vary little from that of master and slave on the antebellum plantation.[56] Cameron would provide all the land, mules, horses, carts, wagons, tools, and other farm machinery. As before emancipation, all labor was to be directed by Cameron or his agent. Each worker was expected to work ten hours per day every day but Sunday. All laborers not "perfectly respectful in language and deportment" to Cameron and his agent would be dismissed "without claim for services." The contract further specified that "all the usual work on the farm" was to be "faithfully and cheerfully performed." For 1865 the freedmen would receive one-third of the corn and molasses and one-fourth of the sweet potatoes and peas produced on the plantation. For 1866 they would receive half of the wheat, corn, cotton, tobacco, and various other crops. Any refusal to work was grounds for dismissal without compensation. Finally, there was to be no "large assemblage of negroes" on the plantation except for religious purposes, and no visitors were allowed without Cameron's approval."[57]

Cameron quickly learned that his freedmen were not satisfied with these terms. Within weeks he informed his father-in-law, Judge Thomas Ruffin, that on a recent trip to the plantation Mrs. Cameron found the freedmen "all as idle and indisposed to work or return to their former duties."[58] Further, a five-month supply of food had already been consumed, and worst of all there were reports that the freedmen were excited over talk of gaining ownership of the property.[59]

Throughout the summer of 1865 disorder persisted on Cameron's plantation. A "sort of carnival" atmosphere existed among the freedmen, Cameron reported; during six days in mid-August he failed to see "a single *one* at any sort of work."[60]

After the harvest the freedmen remained dissatisfied. Cameron's overseer observed that some "show a disposition of contrary and make demands about what is due them." Unhappy with the contract, some workers refused to stay for the next year and began leaving.[61] During the last three months of 1865 matters only worsened. The plantation is "going to the devil," declared Cameron. No work was being done, and the freedmen were destroying the stock, buildings, and fences.[62] Unable to command any respect, Cameron's overseer reported that both he and the freedmen had armed themselves. If attacked by the laborers he pledged to leave his "mark." He felt it necessary to call in federal authorities from Raleigh for assistance. Cameron agreed and sought help. Only after some federal troops under the command of a Captain Freeland visited the plantation did the freedmen become less insolent and "more obedient."[63]

The growing season of 1866 proved to be equally troublesome. Cameron briefly considered using foreign laborers. He tried unsuccessfully to sell his land, and finally abandoned his attempt to manage his plantation himself.[64] Instead, he leased his property in large units, under five-year contracts, to white farmers, who in turn hired black laborers. These farmers paid Cameron a cash payment or share of the crop as rent. Once the contracts were signed, Cameron happily announced, "I am no longer a farmer in Orange."[65]

For Cameron, leasing his land to white farmers meant he no longer had to deal directly with the freedmen. He acknowledged that his decision would be a "terrible calamity" for many of the freedmen, "especially the very old and young," but he believed that without this move he would never have "peace or comfort." "It would have been fortunate for me if this step had been taken in May '65," he declared. "If any one want[s] the negro . . . take him!"[66]

Although many planters accepted Cameron's challenge and used black laborers rather than leasing their land to white farmers, the instability found on Cameron's plantation was prevalent throughout Orange County. As a result, five years after the war, corn production stood at 51.7 percent, wheat 81.6 percent, tobacco 54.3 percent, cotton 49.2 percent, and improved acreage 29.2 percent below 1860 levels.[67] These levels of production were also partly the result of the loss of labor of the many white men who died in the war.

V

If there was no change in the pattern of land ownership in Orange County after the war, there was a different, and largely new, form of land tenure: share tenancy. As share tenants, farmers who owned no property were able to work a parcel of land without the direct supervision of the landlord. Most share tenant arrangements specified that the landlord furnish the tenant with land, housing, and farm implements and that the tenant provide for his own board and clothing. After the harvest, all the crops would be divided, with the tenant keeping either one-half or two-thirds. By 1880—the first year the census recorded land tenure—one-fourth of all white farmers and nearly three-fourths of all black farmers were share tenants (see Table 18).[68]

The significance of share tenancy differed for each race. For blacks it represented an escape from the direct supervision of whites. It should be emphasized, however, that even by 1880 most blacks still had not reached the status of share tenant but remained farm laborers.

For whites, share tenancy did not necessarily signify a decline in economic status since most white share tenants had never owned land.[69] For example, Thompson Pendergrass of the Patterson neighborhood owned no land in 1850, 1860, and 1870. By 1880 he was classified as a share tenant. Further, his status was inherited by his sons—Alvis, Munroe, and William—who resided near their father, owned no real estate in 1870, and also were share tenants by 1880.

If share tenancy did not represent a decline in economic status for traditionally landless whites like the Pendergrasses, it may have represented a fall in social status. Before the war, given the kinship ties in Orange County's rural neighborhoods, most of the landless white farmers seem to have been renters or farm laborers on their more affluent relatives' property. During the postwar years, however, perhaps either because poor economic conditions made it impossible for the relatives of these nonlandowning whites to give them renting arrangements as favorable as those that existed before the war or because there simply was little alternative source of employment, now these landless whites had to compete directly against blacks in the labor market. This competition seems to have taken place on fairly equal terms. When making arrangements with white and black farmers, one landlord contended that whites were "not much better than Negroes." Another landlord claimed that the white was "inferior as a laborer to the Negro."[70] A further indication of the declining social status of the landless white can be found in the lower percentage of marriages between his children and those of landowners in the 1870s as compared to those between nonlandowning and landowning whites in the 1850s.[71]

Share tenancy also seems to have permanently altered the kinds of crops produced in Orange County. Share tenants and farm laborers were forced to purchase food from the neighborhood store. In order to obtain credit from the storekeeper, the share tenant needed to take out a lien on his future crop. Because merchants preferred cotton and tobacco as security for this lien, they encouraged the production of these crops. Contributing to this trend was the declining price of cotton throughout the late 1860s and during the 1870s.[72] In addition, the panic of 1873 and the long depression that followed forced more and more farmers to look to the storekeeper, who increasingly took greater risks providing credit during hard times, for credit. In 1870 nearly one-third of the white farmers failed to produce enough corn to meet the needs of their households—more than double the percentage in 1860 (see Table 19). Only half of the black farmers produced enough corn to feed themselves. In the antebellum pattern, farmers rarely purchased grain; by 1869 one-fourth of the customers at a store in the New Hope neighborhood found it necessary to buy grain.[73] By 1880, after accounting for the share tenant's payment of his crop to his landlord, about one-third of all farmers still failed to produce enough corn to meet their households' needs. Among share tenants alone, approximately the same percentage of farmers of both races failed to produce enough corn (see Table 19).

In contrast to the decline in self-sufficiency, by 1880 the county produced as much tobacco as in 1860 and nearly three times more cotton. Although the majority of farmers of both races continued to grow grain, the percentage of farmers producing cotton in 1880 was ten times higher than in 1860 and nearly three times higher than in 1870 (see Table 20). This shift toward cotton production was ominous. The price of the crop was falling. At the same time the number of acres of farmland under cultivation declined between 1860 and 1880.[74] The link between the rise in cotton production and the decline in self-sufficiency was direct; if the acreage used to grow the increase in cotton from 1860 had been farmed in corn, corn production in 1880 would have matched its 1860 level.[75]

Though many farmers found it necessary to purchase grain, there was no major change in the role played by the neighborhood general store. Just as before the war, each rural neighborhood continued to have only one or two stores. In most cases these stores were run by the same affluent families who operated them before the war. For example, the Mangums continued throughout the 1870s to run the store in the Flat River neighborhood that they ran during the 1850s. Likewise, the Halls of Little River, the Webbs of Cane Creek, and the Durhams of White Cross continued to operate their neighborhoods' stores. The few new stores that were established to meet the needs of the growing agricultural population were run mostly by the sons of antebellum planters. For example, in 1875, Samuel F. Patterson, whose father, James N. Patterson, had owned 106 slaves in 1860, established a general store in the Patterson neighborhood.[76]

Despite the significant degree of continuity in the farmer-merchant relationship, it is necessary to recognize that, in addition to the traditional influences of geography, credit, and social function on the farmer's selection of supplier, increasingly, compulsion also played a part. In the mid-1870s the North Carolina legislature passed laws specifying that a merchant who sold tenants and farm laborers goods on credit could assert his claim only after the tenants paid their landlord his share of their crop.[77] This legislation discouraged newcomers who owned no land from opening stores in the rural neighborhoods. Only when the landlord and merchant were the same person or when the two worked closely together could a merchant be sure tenants would repay him.[78] This caused little difficulty in Orange County, as traditionally the rural merchants or their relatives in the neighborhood were substantial landowners.

VI

The most dramatic change in Orange County's economy during the immediate postwar years was the rise of the tobacco industry in Durham. By 1880 Durham had not only surpassed Chapel Hill and Hillsborough in population but also had become a regional trade and industrial center. Despite its tremendous growth, however, Durham successfully blended change with the traditional economic, social, and neighborhood structure of the county.

Durham was built by tobacco. In 1858 Robert F. Morris established a small smoking-tobacco factory in Durham. About four years later, John Ruffin Green of Person County, just north of Orange County, moved to Durham, purchased the Morris factory, and fashioned his product to meet the tastes of the students of the nearby university in Chapel Hill. As many of these students entered the Confederate army and scattered throughout the South, they wrote back to Green for some of his tobacco. Further, when the soldiers of both armies flowed through Durham in 1865, many tried Green's product. After the war ended and the troops returned home to all parts of the country, they served as advertisers of the tobacco produced in Durham.[79]

In 1867 Green took as a partner William T. Blackwell, also a native of Person County. When Green died in 1869 Blackwell purchased the entire company from his partner's estate. He soon added James R. Day and Julian S. Carr as partners in his firm. Carr, the son of an affluent Chapel Hill merchant, was a particularly valuable asset to the firm because of his success at advertising for William T. Blackwell and Company or, as it was generally called by its brand name, "Bull Durham."[80]

A very important turning point in the tobacco industry in Durham occurred in 1871 when the "Bull Durham Company" established a tobacco warehouse in the town. Not only did the warehouse insure a constant supply of tobacco, it made the town the regional center for the tobacco trade. Previously the tobacco grown in North Carolina's northern piedmont had been sent to the tobacco manufacturing centers in Richmond, Danville, and Petersburg, Virginia. Now Durham's immediate proximity to the tobacco fields permitted farmers to take their product directly to the market to receive premium prices. Recognizing the town's favorable economic environment, others with an interest in the tobacco market built warehouses in Durham.[81] Hillsborough, which failed to attract any warehouses, could not prevent its few small tobacco firms from moving to Durham where, according to the editor of the *Recorder*, "superior inducements have been offered them. Our community can ill spare them."[82]

An indication of the strength of the tobacco industry in Durham was its continued rapid growth through the national business panic of 1873 and the subsequent depression, which lasted for approximately five years. In December 1873, the worst of the panic was over in Durham, and the tobacco trade was active. By February 1874, reports of large sales in the tobacco warehouses gave evidence that the tobacco factories were functioning at full capacity.[83]

The flourishing tobacco market soon attracted a number of other tobacco manufacturers to Durham to compete with "Bull Durham." In 1874 Washington Duke and his sons, who quickly emerged as

The "Bull Durham" factory. Its bellowing horn daily called five hundred tobacco employees to work. (Photograph courtesy of North Carolina Collection, UNC Library at Chapel Hill.)

"Bull Durham's" strongest rival, moved into the town. Before the war Duke had owned a small farm just north of Durham. After the war he and his sons began the home manufacture of smoking tobacco. Within ten years of their arrival in Durham they became the town's largest firm, and over the following ten years they created a worldwide tobacco empire, the American Tobacco Company.[84]

Along with the tobacco industry Durham attracted other businesses. In 1874 the town surpassed both Chapel Hill and Hillsborough in its number of firms (see Table 21). Durham's tobacco industry accounted for only one-fourth of these firms. To meet the needs of the town's population, which grew from 256 to 3605 during the 1870s, there were thirty-four general stores, two newspapers, three restaurants, seven bars, and various other enterprises.[85]

Even more striking than the increase in the number of firms was the growth in their estimated worth (see Table 22). By 1880 the "Bull Durham Company" alone was estimated to be worth more than all the firms in Hillsborough combined. The bellowing horn of this firm, which could be heard twelve miles away in Chapel Hill, each morning called 500 employees to work. At the same time the entire population of Hillsborough was only 791.[86]

The tremendous growth of Durham and its tobacco industry did not threaten Orange County's traditional social structure because the leaders in the town's development and its industry were not strangers to the county, were previously affluent, and were either planters or related to planters. Of the fifteen most prominent social, political, and economic leaders of Durham in 1884, nearly all were natives of North Carolina.[87] Six were natives of Orange County, all of whom had been slaveholders or sons of slaveholders in 1860. Another six were born in the counties that bordered Orange County near the town of Durham—Person, Granville, and Wake. By 1870, before the rapid growth of the tobacco industry, two-thirds of these men were already residing in or had previously resided in Orange County. In addition, more than 90 percent of the seventy-eight tobacco manufacturers, tobacco dealers, and tobacco warehouse owners who resided in Durham in 1880 were natives of North Carolina. A large number of them were residents of Orange County before the growth of the tobacco industry. Many had been residents of Durham Township in 1870.[88]

If the men who developed Durham's tobacco industry were not newcomers to the community, neither were they strangers to wealth. Although such prominent leaders of the industry as Washington Duke and Julian S. Carr are often described as men of modest origins, neither was of poor ancestry. Before the war Washington Duke's oldest brother, William, was a justice of the peace in Orange County and the owner of 700 acres worth $5000. Julian S. Carr's father, also a justice of the peace, was one of the largest merchants in Chapel Hill, who in 1860 owned nine slaves and $6000 in real estate.[89]

Many of Durham's tobacco manufacturers were kin to antebellum

Orange County planters. For example, the tobacco manufacturing firm Webb, Roulhac, and Company was composed of three partners: James Webb, William S. Roulhac, and Duncan Cameron. In 1860 Webb's father owned sixteen slaves. Roulhac was both a grandson of Thomas Ruffin, a substantial planter as well as chief justice of the North Carolina Supreme Court, and a nephew of Paul C. Cameron, Orange County's largest planter. In 1871, Cameron contributed $6500 to allow his oldest son, Duncan, to become the firm's third partner. Four years later, William Lipscomb, whose father owned 2500 acres and fifty-two slaves in 1860, joined the firm.[90]

Many of the men who purchased and stored tobacco also were related to antebellum Orange County planters. One of Durham's most prominent warehouse owners, Edward J. Parrish, was the son of Doctor C. Parrish, the master of sixteen slaves in 1860. Likewise, Parrish's brother-in-law, John S. Lockhart, a major tobacco dealer in Durham, was the son of a farmer who had owned eighteen slaves. Both Parrish and Lockhart had other relatives in Orange County who had owned more than twenty slaves.[91]

The leaders of Durham's tobacco industry did not threaten the social position of the planter. Many of these men, especially the younger ones, inherited land during this period and became planters. Others, in fact, were already planters. Further, the tobacco industry, which was necessarily urban, mechanized, and market-oriented, did not challenge the planter's values, since before the war many planters were involved in banking, commerce, transportation, and industry. Finally, the location of Durham only complemented the planter's agricultural interests. If a number of men were profiting by the new industry, a number of planters also were making large sums of money by their vicinity to the growing tobacco market.

Nor did Durham's tobacco industry endanger the traditional role of the family and rural neighborhood. Instead, Durham's growth may have fostered closer family ties because, rather than leaving Orange County and their families to pursue distant economic avenues, a number of young men simply moved into the bustling town. This factor may in part explain why the rate of persistence for the 1870s was even higher than before the war.

Durham attracted restless or ambitious residents of Orange County. One-fourth of the white men and two-fifths of the black men who remained in the county from 1870 to 1880—but changed

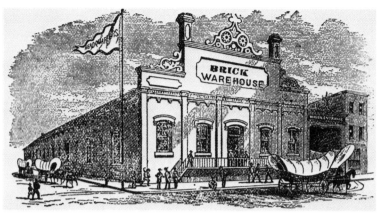

Edward J. Parrish's tobacco Brick Warehouse in Durham. (Photograph courtesy of North Carolina Division of Archives and History.)

townships and therefore probably moved away from their neighborhoods—migrated to Durham Township. Most of this movement took place over very short distances. Few people who lived as far away as Bingham or Cedar Grove (the Cane Creek and Eno neighborhoods) decided to relocate in Durham (see Map 5). Most who chose to move into Durham resided in such nearby townships as Mangum and Patterson. Once these newcomers arrived in Durham, therefore, they continued to live only a short distance from their rural relatives.[92]

The experience of some of the whites who moved to Durham reveals a number of interesting factors that may have shaped their decision to migrate.[93] Many of those who moved already were involved in nonagricultural pursuits. For example, before he moved to Durham to become a tobacconist, Robert F. Webb, a merchant residing in Mangum Township, ran the general store in the Flat River neighborhood. The same was true of John F. Freeland of Chapel Hill. Others who moved had skills which they probably perceived would be in greater demand in the booming community. Before he moved, Thomas A. Cheek was a house carpenter in Chapel Hill, a livelihood he continued in Durham. Thomas Adams, a shoemaker in Hillsborough, apparently found his skill more profitable in the growing tobacco center. Further, his two sons Elmore and Oscar were able to find jobs as factory workers in the city.

Leaders in Durham's postwar economic development. *From left to right:*
Julian S. Carr (1845–1924). The son of a Chapel Hill merchant and a
substantial owner of slaves, his advertising skills made the "Bull Durham"
brand world-famous. Edward J. Parrish (1846–1920). One of Durham's
leading tobacco warehouse owners, his father had been a prominent slaveholder in antebellum Orange County. Washington Duke (1820–1905).
Within a decade after moving from his small farm just north of Durham,
Duke and his sons took advantage of new technology to surpass "Bull

Many of the whites who moved to Durham had nothing to lose
as they were landless farmers or farm laborers with little future in
the countryside. For example, Jacob Crabtree of Hillsborough, Jack
Andrews of Chapel Hill, and Gaston Couch of Little River all were
landless farmers or farm laborers in 1870. After relocating in Durham, Crabtree became a factory worker, Andrews a mason, and
Couch a watchman.

Another factor that may have influenced whites to move to Durham was kin ties. When Robert F. Webb decided to give up his
general store in Mangum to become a tobacconist, he was joined in
North Durham by his in-laws Alvis K. and James N. Umstead and
Robert Harris, all of whom became tobacco dealers.

In their decision to migrate to Durham blacks were influenced by
factors similar to whites. Many black farm laborers also chose to
find new pursuits in Durham. For example, Brown Jefferson and

Durham" in the production of cigarettes. (Photographs courtesy of Manuscript Department, Perkins Library, Duke University.) Colonel Robert F. Webb (1826–91). Upon returning to the Flat River neighborhood to run its general store after the war (in which he spent many months imprisoned at Johnson's Island Prison on Lake Erie), Webb again decided to move into Durham with his inlaws and become a tobacco dealer. (From copy in North Carolina Collection, UNC Library at Chapel Hill.)

Willie Mitchell of Mangum Township and Nelson Mallett of Chapel Hill became teamsters and draymen. All three had sons who became Durham factory workers.

Some of the blacks who already resided in Durham were able to take advantage of the town's development in other ways. Anderson Leathers, a farm laborer in Durham in 1870, became a shoemaker by 1880. His two sons, Jack and Samuel, also farm laborers in 1870, chose to become factory workers. Theophilus Chavis, a particularly enterprising Durham farm laborer, recognizing a growing black clientele in the town, opened a eating saloon.

Finally, as was the case with whites, kinship ties played their part in motivating some blacks to migrate to Durham. Edmund Hall and his two sons, Henry and Lewis, who headed separate households and were all landless farmers in Little River in 1870, moved to Durham by 1880 and lived next door to one another. Unlike the blacks who went to work in the factories, however, the Halls took other routes. Edmund became a woodcutter, perhaps to meet the needs of the townspeople. The fact that Henry and Lewis chose to remain in farming may indicate that they could successfully produce and sell foodstuffs in the town.

The close family relationships of the rural neighborhood were preserved in Durham itself. The town was not a magnet for drifters. In 1880 most white and black males residing in Durham Township who were not farmers lived in a house with their family or a relative. The typical married Durham resident usually headed his own household and lived with his wife and children; the single resident lived with his father and mother.[94]

The rise of Durham's tobacco industry had only a minor impact on the county's traditional occupational structure (see Table 4). Most of the work in the tobacco factories was done by blue collar workers, nearly all of whom were black laborers, mostly under thirty years of age.[95] If the tobacco factories had not existed, these men and boys probably would have been farm laborers. Whether they were tobacco factory workers living in a town or farm laborers living in the country, these black workers labored under the supervision of whites.[96]

The use of black workers may have reduced the possibility of extensive labor-management conflict, as traditional racial attitudes and the surplus of cheap black laborers inhibited blacks from making demands on their employers. When in 1875 some black workers at "Bull Durham" began a strike to raise their salaries, they were immediately fired and quickly replaced.[97] Although, given similar circumstances, "Bull Durham" may have done the same to white workers, it might not have been as easily accepted by the community.

The employment of black workers during the early years of the tobacco factories in Durham also was linked to the low level of technology in the industry.[98] Throughout the 1870s the main product produced in Durham was not cigarettes but smoking tobacco, which would be purchased in bags and then smoked in a pipe or hand-rolled into a cigarette by the individual smoker. The basic task in manufacturing smoking tobacco was granulating the tobacco leaves by passing them through a sieve, a labor-intensive task for which blacks had traditionally been employed. Although on May 29, 1866,

Hiram M. Smith of Richmond, Virginia, patented a cutting machine that threshed tobacco, it was not until the mid-1870s that his steam-powered machine was fully in use in Durham. Further, before the cutting machine could be utilized to its full potential, a packing machine needed to be developed to eliminate the next laborious task in making smoking tobacco. Although this problem was solved in Durham by 1880, it took until 1885 before the process of labeling and stamping the tobacco bags could be mechanized. Even by that year, a large and unskilled labor force still needed to be employed to sew the tobacco bags. As late as 1884 the "Bull Durham Company" employed 250 workers to perform this task, more than one-fourth of its entire labor force. Hence, although the "Bull Durham Company" developed a large-scale business divided into thirteen departments (those for mixing and shipping, handling leaf, cutting leaf, stamping and labeling, flavoring and packing, making cigarettes, cutting, and maintaining machinery, in addition to the wooden box factory, paper box factory, printing office, stables and watchmen, and the outside workers) with each headed by a separate manager, throughout this early stage in the industry it was necessary to rely on low-skilled and inexpensive black labor.[99]

The other emerging product of the Durham factories, manufactured cigarettes, also initially was hampered during this period by technological limits. W. Duke, Sons and Company attempted to gain a share of the tobacco manufacturing business by focusing its efforts in cigarettes, since "Bull Durham" had invested primarily in smoking tobacco. By 1881, after hiring J.M. Siegel, a Russian who had worked for a cigarette-making firm in New York, to head this new line, the Dukes were producing 9.8 million hand-rolled cigarettes annually. "Bull Durham" quickly moved into production of cigarettes and by 1883 produced 14.4 annually. The Dukes ensured their supremacy over cigarette production when, on April 30, 1884, they introduced the Bonsack machine, a recently patented invention that produced cigarettes at a rate equal to forty-eight hand-rollers. Soon the Dukes, through a combination of intense personal efforts and entrepreneurship, gained dominance over not only the Durham but the international cigarette industry.[100]

Even before the phenomenal emergence of the Dukes in the mid-1880s, signs of change were becoming evident in Durham. Since most of those who resided in Durham were simply too busy to notice what changes the town experienced, it took an outside observer to put them into perspective. In 1878, when he looked toward the east, the editor of the *Hillsborough Recorder* noted how the previously "insignificant hamlet" was developing into an "important town" whose population was "even more influential in its effects upon the business of the country than by its numbers." Moreover, summarizing the lessons that already could be learned from the Durham experience, the editor added, "Its growth and its prosperity teach us what manufacturing can do for a country by the stimulus it gives industrial life; and also the wisdom of a diversity of pursuit by departing with discreet adventure from the old and worn highways of commerce and agriculture, the ancient trusted road to wealth and independence." [101]

The people of Durham did not have to be reminded of the changes in their lives, the accelerated pace of which they experienced daily. In 1880 the editor of the town's newspaper, the *Durham Tobacco Plant*, informed his readers that, whereas in 1876 a new house was completed every month, and in 1878 one every week, now one was finished everyday. [102] "You will find many changes on your return, improvements in every direction," one inhabitant of the town informed another who had been away. He added, "We hear the hammer and saw, in every hour of the day." [103]

The town's inhabitants, particularly its leaders, also were aware of their growing collective interest, power, and influence. By 1875 the Durham Board of Trade, consisting of the town's manufacturers, warehousemen, and leaf dealers, was established. The Board's strength became evident in 1877, when it established a committee that successfully worked to have a state tax on tobacco warehouses repealed. Within two years of its establishment, members of the Board of Trade also formed the Durham National Bank to meet the town's financial needs. In addition, members of the Board not only created committees to improve Durham's roads, but they sent representatives to the Orange, Wake, and Granville County Commissions, as well as to state authorities to aid their effort. [104]

For the town's leaders, business and society formed a close network. The best example of this appeared in December of 1880, when a destructive fire consumed more than twenty stores and buildings in the town. Fortunately for the tobacco dealers and manu-

Durham, mid-1880s. Despite their wealth the Dukes, like most of the tobacco factory owners, chose to reside in Durham (family home, Fairview, at left) within a few blocks of their business (at right). Note that after nearly two decades of rapid growth, downtown land was still under cultivation. (Photograph courtesy of Manuscript Department, Perkins Library, Duke University.)

facturers their financial losses were minimal, as they were insured. It was not by chance that James Southgate had issued all of the insurance policies, for he was more than another businessman in the town. When as the chief officer of the new Durham Masonic Lodge, the town's primary fraternal order, Southgate called meetings to order, he literally convened the members of the Durham Board of Trade.[105]

Another factor promoting a sense of tradition was the compactness of the town itself. Throughout the 1880s Durham's city limits extended no more than five or six blocks from the North Carolina Central Railroad. Most of the factories, in fact, were located within a block of the rails. Further, by choosing to reside very close to their establishments, an average distance of only one-fifth of a mile, the factory owners were forced to be involved actively in the town's affairs, particularly its churches, health, and education. From their employees' perspective, as one scholar has pointed out, during its early years of development, Durham's leaders remained both "accessible and visible."[106]

During the decade and a half immediately after the Civil War, therefore, Durham's history was defined by elements of change and continuity. Although the scale of its growth clearly marked it as an emerging city of the New South, the town retained many features of the county's traditional way of life. Perhaps, in part, its short-term economic success can be attributed to this combination. Nevertheless, there were signs by 1881 that Durham would be swept along by more change. In part, these changes were linked to the Dukes' decision to focus their efforts on cigarettes. Equally important, the leaders of the tobacco industry, although sensing their growing collective economic power, were still only part of a largely agriculturally based county. It would not be long before they would choose to transform their economic influence into political power.

VII

The economic and social structure of Orange County after the Civil War was as much the product of an old as the creation of a new era. Just as before the war, a small minority of planters controlled most of the land, most blacks labored upon the land and under the supervision of whites, and the mercantile system continued to be shaped by the neighborhood. Briefly disrupted by the war, this pattern was restored during the Reconstruction years. Again the life of Orange County residents centered on the family and neighborhood. Even the dramatic postwar growth of industry in Durham, which provided some alternatives to agriculture, complemented rather than challenged the traditional economic and social dominance of the planter and the county's family and neighborhood orientation.

CHAPTER 6

No Longer "Among a People of Arcadian Simplicity"

The Postwar Administrative
and Political Structure

In antebellum Orange County, administration and politics were shaped primarily by the neighborhood. During the postwar years, however, decisions made outside of the county bypassed the neighborhood structure and altered Orange's traditional administrative and political organization directly. Whites, who individually had little choice but to accept the economic and social effects of emancipation, acted collectively to check the political power of blacks. With the county's new political structure based upon race, even the goals of politics were altered. Finally, the racial basis of politics may in itself have contributed to the county's division in 1881.

I

The Civil War destroyed Orange County's two-party system. Although Whigs and Democrats disagreed on what grounds justified separation from the Union, both parties supported secession after the fall of Fort Sumter. This unity of purpose showed at the polls. In the two gubernatorial elections during the war, Zebulon B. Vance, the nominee of a coalition of former Whigs and Democrats, twice captured 80 percent of the county vote.[1]

With the end of the war in 1865 there was no attempt to revive the former two-party system. In September, when Orange County had to nominate two delegates to the upcoming state constitutional convention, only enough men could be assembled in Hillsborough to hold what one participant called a "sort of Convention." This meeting nominated John Berry, the former Democrat who had been a strong opponent of secession in 1861, and Samuel F. Phillips, the former Whig who had advocated peace even under terms of emancipation by early 1865. Their only opponent was Jones Watson, a former Whig, who entered the campaign because he had recently had a personal disagreement with Phillips and wanted to embarrass him.[2] Phillips and Berry gained an identical number of votes, and Watson trailed by a wide margin. Only eight hundred voters cast ballots in this election; two thousand had voted in 1860.[3]

Nonpartisanship and apathy characterized North Carolina politics during the first two years after the war.[4] Two factions sought control of state politics: first, a coalition of unionists and reformers led by William W. Holden, the leader of North Carolina's peace movement; second, the former supporters of North Carolina's wartime governor, Zebulon B. Vance, now under the leadership of Jonathan Worth, who attempted to return North Carolina into the Union under the most lenient terms. In the gubernatorial elections of 1865 and 1866, in which only whites could vote, Worth's supporters easily defeated Holden's; in Orange County, Holden won only 21.8 percent of the vote in 1865.[5] In the spring of 1866 at the state constitutional convention, Worth's supporters blocked the passage of democratic reforms proposed by Holden's followers, such as that of abolishing property qualifications for officeholding. By late 1866 Holden saw that the only way to oust Worth was to endorse black suffrage. When Congress passed the Reconstruction Act of March 2, 1867, which enfranchised blacks, Holden endorsed the measure, and his followers launched the Republican party in North Carolina.

The Reconstruction Act reestablished a two-party system, reinvigorated interest in politics, and eventually altered the structure of local government in Orange County. In the fall of 1867 more than twice as many whites registered to vote as had cast ballots in 1866.[6] In the campaign to select delegates to the new state constitutional convention, the supporters of Worth, now termed Conservatives, chose two of the most prominent young men in the county, John W. Graham and Dr. Edwin M. Holt. Graham's father, William A. Graham, and father-in-law, Paul C. Cameron, and Holt's father-in-law, Harrison Parker, were three of Orange County's largest former slaveholders. In contrast, the Republicans nominated Benjamin S. Hedrick and Henry Jones. Hedrick was a former professor at the University of North Carolina who had been dismissed from that position for supporting the Republican nominee for president in 1856, moved to Washington, D.C., and worked in the Patent Office throughout the war. The only thing known about Henry Jones is that he was a black farm laborer.[7] Although registered whites outnumbered blacks by three to two, many whites feared that some members of their race would not go to the polls whereas the blacks would march to them and vote "as one man."[8] In fact whites cast their votes in larger numbers than they had in years. A majority voted against holding another constitutional convention but selected Graham and Holt as delegates if the call for a convention was approved statewide.[9] Since only one county in the state joined Orange in voting against holding a convention, one was convened in January 1868.[10]

With an overwhelming 107 to 13 majority in this convention, the Republicans quickly moved to rewrite the state constitution in a fashion that drastically altered the governmental structure of Orange, as it did of all the counties.[11] The 1868 constitution did away with the antebellum county court, whose members, the justices of the peace, were not elected but received their commission from the governor upon the recommendation of the state legislature, and which exercised nearly exclusive administrative power in the county. The Republicans transferred this power to a board of five county commissioners elected at large in the county. In addition, they divided the counties into new administrative units, townships, whose residents would elect two magistrates and a clerk, who would perform minor administrative and judicial duties in these townships.[12] The constitution also eliminated property qualifications for officeholding and voting, based representation in the state legislature only on population, introduced provisions for stay laws, retroactive homestead protection, penal reform, a limited poll tax, mechanic's and laborer's liens, authorized the formation of a system of public schools with free tuition, and broadened women's rights.

Orange County voters were deeply interested in the spring 1868 election, which decided whether to ratify or reject the new constitution and choose local and state officeholders. The Conservative convention in Hillsborough bluntly declared: "That we are in favor of a White Man's Government in a White Man's Country. That we are in favor of the equality of the negro before the law, but not of his power over the law."[13] In April, 89.1 percent of all registered voters participated in the election. Nearly 60 percent of the electorate voted against the constitution and favored all the local and state Conservative nominees. But in the state as a whole a majority of the voters ratified the constitution and elected William Holden, the Republican candidate, for governor.[14] By 1868, therefore, Orange County had a new structure of county government.

II

When the county commission form of government was established in Orange County it retained some of the fundamental features of the antebellum county court system. The most evident similarity was the personnel. The fifteen men who served as county commissioners during the first eight years of the system were much like the antebellum magistrates appointed by the state government. In fact, nearly all of the commissioners had been antebellum magistrates.[15]

But the structure of the new system of county government made the county commissioners behave differently. Five commissioners now performed the administrative role previously discharged by more than seventy justices of the peace; consequently, the commissioners met more frequently and for longer sessions. The antebellum county court had four sessions annually, and each session rarely lasted for more than six days. The justices of the peace, who were obligated to attend only two sessions and only one day per session, tended to come to court only when it dealt with issues directly affecting their particular neighborhoods. In contrast, during the postwar years the county commissioners convened on the average of sixty days annually, met at least once a month, and generally sat every day for three to four weeks in May and June to revise the county's tax list.[16]

Only a man of substantial wealth could devote as much time as the commissioner's position demanded. Specifically, only a farmer who owned a large amount of property, had his estate managed by an agent, and had his land worked by tenants could leave his farm for extended periods of time. Commissioners who were farmers, therefore, were even wealthier landowners than the very affluent antebellum magistrates.[17] Those who were not farmers—a far higher percentage than was the case for magistrates—were lawyers, doctors, editors, and jewellers. Before the war the residences of the numerous justices were spread proportionately throughout the county's towns and neighborhoods; now three-fourths of the commissioners resided in the towns of Hillsborough, Durham, and Chapel Hill.[18] The antebellum court had been divided equally between Democrats and Whigs. Now, because commissioners were elected at large, the party that dominated the county, the Conservatives, controlled every seat.[19]

In short, the antebellum court had not been a democratic form of government because the magistrates were appointed, not elected, but it proved to be a representative body since the large number of magistrates accurately reflected the diverse interests of the various neighborhoods. By contrast, the newly elected board of commissioners was a democratic form of government, but because its members were men of large wealth, all belonging to the same political party and residing in a narrow geographic area, it failed to be a representative form of government.

The county commission tried to take the interests of the neighborhoods into account. However, it could not meet the general needs of the entire county and also have the expertise necessary to deal with the narrow interests of the individual neighborhoods. When dealing with issues concerning the specific interests of a particular neighborhood, therefore, the commissioners sought advice from the elected township magistrates from that neighborhood. For example, when in September 1873 the commissioners wanted a bridge repaired in the New Hope neighborhood, they appointed Charles W. Johnston, a township magistrate from New Hope to contract for the repairs.[20] Most of the township magistrates would have been used to this practice because a majority of them were justices of the peace before the war.[21]

The fortunes of the new structure of county government were precariously linked to those of the Republican party. The Conservatives continued to wage a vigorous public campaign against the Republicans, and late in 1868 they were aided by the Ku Klux Klan, which declared war on the party. Its attacks, however, were not simply politically motivated; in 1869 five blacks were murdered in Orange County for supposedly burning barns and threatening to commit rape.[22] Nevertheless, the Klan focused its boldest attacks on Republican leaders. For example, in February 1870 klansmen dragged Wyatt Outlaw, the leading black Republican of Alamance

County, Orange's western neighbor, from his house and hanged him in the courthouse square. Three months later they murdered John W. Stephens, the white state senator from Caswell County, Orange's northern neighbor.

After this violence had continued for more than a year, Governor Holden responded by forming a militia of white soldiers and sending it into Alamance and Caswell in July 1870. The militia arrested about one hundred suspects, and, under Holden's order, they denied these suspects release on writs of habeas corpus. To Holden's dismay, a federal district court judge later released the prisoners. The legal setback soon was followed by political defeat. In August the Conservatives, by exploiting both popular reaction against Holden's use of the militia and Klan intimidation of Republicans, captured control of the state legislature. The new Conservative majority quickly moved to impeach Holden for violation of the state constitution in his use of the state militia and, upon his conviction, removed him from office on March 22, 1871.[23] The Conservative victory was far from complete. In August the electorate defeated the Conservatives' call for a new constitutional convention. Further, in 1872 Tod R. Caldwell, who, as the Republican lieutenant-governor, replaced Holden as governor after the conviction, defeated his Conservative opponent Augustus S. Merrimon in the gubernatorial election.

By 1875 the Conservatives succeeded in convening a new constitutional convention, which gave the legislature, also controlled by the Conservatives, the power to alter the structure of county government. In 1877 the Conservative majority in the legislature, for both political and racial reasons, devised a new county government act designed to eliminate black and Republican office holding. The Conservatives reestablished the antebellum procedure of having the state legislature select county magistrates. They retained the board of county commissioners, but this body would no longer be elected but rather chosen by the magistrates appointed by the legislature. The legislature severely limited the board's administrative power, so that significant decisions could only be made with the support of a majority of the magistrates. The new law guaranteed that if the Conservatives continued to control the state government, as they did for the next twenty years, they would also continue to control local government.[24]

The new form of county government had a major impact even in those counties like Orange with white majorities. Before 1877 some Republicans were elected magistrates in those townships with a substantial black population; after 1877 no Republican was chosen by the Conservative members of the legislature.[25] The legislation did not alter the character of the board of commissioners in Orange County, where all commissioners elected since 1868 had been Conservatives.[26] The system that developed after 1877, therefore, was neither representative like the antebellum form nor democratic like the county commission plan of the Republicans.

III

After 1868 a new party system emerged in Orange County. Now the Conservative and Republican banners waved where the traditional Democratic and Whig ones previously had flown. Like the antebellum party system, once formed, the postwar system proved to be quite stable. From one election to the next, the percentage of the vote cast in a precinct for either one of the parties varied little.[27] The cause for this continuity was obvious. Most white voters consistently supported Conservative candidates, and black voters accordingly marched to the polls to cast their votes for Republicans.[28]

Despite the emergence of race as the basic determinant of political allegiance, kinship bonds continued to play a role in party structure. Since nearly all white men were Conservatives during this period, the dominant families continued to control politics in their neighborhoods. In 1876, for example, a number of the men who were selected in Mangum Township to serve as delegates at the Conservative party convention in Hillsborough formed an intricate kinship network. Two of the men chosen as delegates, John W. Umstead and Alvis K. Umstead, were brothers. John's brother-in-law, William W. Mangum, was also selected, as were William's cousin, William K. Parrish, and his brother-in-law, Robert F. Webb. Two other delegates, Duncan Cameron and George Collins, were also brothers-in-law.[29]

The Conservatives needed a more formalized party structure than one based only on neighborhood and kinship bonds in order to bring men together on an equal footing who had previously opposed one another as Whigs and Democrats. Further, they had to make their party not simply a coalition of particular neighborhoods like the antebellum parties but a unified body encompassing all of the white voters throughout the entire county. To meet this objective they based their party's organization on the new townships and the old school districts. During the spring, men who resided in each of the township's five or six school districts held a caucus and selected three men to serve as a school district committee. The caucus then chose delegates to attend the township meeting.[30] At the township meeting, a township executive committee was selected from among various members of the school district committees. The township meeting then selected delegates to attend the party convention in Hillsborough, at which a county executive committee of five was named to plan the forthcoming campaign and keep the party organized between campaigns.

Once the county convention selected the party's nominees, however, the township executive committees took charge of running the campaign. In 1872 Calvin E. Smith, the chairman of the Conservative party's county executive committee, explained to the township executive committees their role in the upcoming campaign: "First you will at your earliest convenience call a meeting of your committee and thoroughly organize the Conservative party in your township for the approaching Summer and Fall elections, put the machinery in good running order, see that all needful and necessary information is obtained and circulated among the people and each man on the committee will consider himself a canvasser for the cause and urge upon the people the necessity of turning out on the day of election."[31] The township committee functioned not only in the countywide campaigns held during the even-numbered years but also in the township campaigns during the odd-numbered years.

The leadership of the Conservative party was not a duplicate of that of either of the prewar parties. To be sure, Conservative leaders continued mostly to be farmers (see Table 23). But the leaders had different political backgrounds. More than half had once been Democrats; slightly fewer had been Whigs. More important, they tended to be wealthier than the antebellum Democrat and Whig leaders.

This change in the composition of leadership was the result of both practical and ideological factors. If the Conservatives had opened the nomination process to everyone and sent as many delegates to the county convention in Hillsborough as the Whigs and Democrats of the 1850s combined had, the delegates would have been so numerous that they would have poured out of the courthouse doors. In addition, because the party stressed the importance of race over other issues, such as economic interests, there was little need to broaden the party's active base by bringing in more men of modest and poor incomes.

In antebellum politics, the election day turnout of the party faithful, as promoted by the neighborhood-orientation of partisanship, was the key to victory. Little effort was wasted on persuading the members of one party, often residents of another neighborhood, to cast their votes for the nominees of another party. Under the new postwar political system, turnout was equally important, as crossover voting now even necessitated crossing socially forbidden racial boundaries. This negative incentive seems to have been a less effective means of encouraging turnout by whites, and although the Conservatives' party organization and the composition of their leadership continued to bring the party victories, voter turnout declined. Where 85.1 percent of the white men had participated in elections prior to the war and 82.2 percent cast their vote in 1868, only 64.3 percent voted by 1880. Perhaps because Conservative victory largely was assured by superior numbers, many whites, especially the poorer one who were no longer encouraged to play a role in party organization and leadership and did not have the rallying point of neighborhood, grew apathetic and did not go to the polls. As a consequence, the Conservatives' margin of victory declined. After winning 58.3 percent of the vote in the gubernatorial election of 1868 in Orange County, they carried only 53.7 percent in 1880.[32]

IV

The Republican party played a much different role in Orange County politics. Because nearly all whites were Conservatives and because whites outnumbered blacks by almost two to one, by 1870 it was apparent to the Republicans that they could never win countywide elections. They sought, therefore, to promote the largest turnout in elections for state and national elections, since these officeholders would be responsible for protecting their local interests by ensuring their right to vote and preserving the gains they had made through the 1868 state constitution. Orange County Republicans also exerted their fullest efforts to win township races.

The Republican political organization also differed from that of the Conservatives. Because there were few school districts in which blacks outnumbered whites, the Republicans bypassed this unit and focused their attention on the townships. In each township they selected an executive committee of three which, along with a number of other township delegates, attended the county convention in Hillsborough. The county convention selected nominees for office and also chose a county executive committee from these township executive committees. Membership on the county executive committee was distributed fairly equally between whites and blacks and among the townships.

White Republicans who participated actively in campaigns were mostly farmers, but, on average, they owned much less land than Conservative activists (see Table 23). Many of the faculty members of the University of North Carolina were Republicans, since they received their appointments with the support of the Republican governors through the mid-1870s. Hence, there was an unusually large number of white Republican professionals. The typical active black Republican was a farmer far more likely to own real estate than was the average black. Because many of the blacks lived in Hillsborough and Chapel Hill, a large number of them were blue collar workers rather than farmers.

For the countywide elections held in August of even-numbered years to elect representatives to the state legislature, the Republicans nominated only whites. Because these nominees had no chance to win, this practice, although discriminatory, was not a large price for blacks to pay in order to provide whites with the incentive for remaining in the party. Although Republicans never won these countywide offices, nominating candidates for these positions gave Republican voters more reason to go to the polls where they could vote for the Republican nominees for the governorship and the other state offices. This also was an excellent way to mobilize voters every fourth year for the national elections held three months after the state contests. The only local elections the Republicans could hope to win were the township contests for magistrates, clerk, constable, and school committee during the even-numbered years. In these campaigns the Republicans nominated both whites and blacks in fairly equal numbers. The party did not make a strong effort in all the townships but focused on those—Chapel Hill, Hillsborough, and Bingham—where they had a chance to win.

In Chapel Hill Township the Republicans' chances for victory were excellent because the percentage of registered voters in the township who were black, 40.6 percent, was fairly high. In addition, the University of North Carolina, with its entire faculty composed of Republicans appointed by the Republican administration in Raleigh, provided a good political base of white Republicans.[33] Finally, other whites became Republicans because they held appointments from the Republican administration in Washington such as postmaster, federal tax collector, and census taker. For example, Hugh B. Guthrie, an antebellum Whig leader, who received income from the federal troops boarding in his Chapel Hill hotel and served as the town's postmaster, was a Republican.[34] The Republican efforts in Chapel Hill were rewarded when they elected a magistrate in 1873.[35]

In Hillsborough Township the Republicans had an even better chance to win office. Here 45.4 percent of the registered voters were black. Patronage was again employed to attract such whites as Isaac Strayhorn who, after becoming a leader in the township's Republican party, saw his mother, Mrs. Harriet Strayhorn, become the county seat's postmistress.[36] The Republican candidates in Hillsborough, both black and white, were exceptionally successful in township elections and won a magistrate's position and a number of seats on the school committee between 1869 and 1875.[37]

In Bingham Township the Republican prospects were also quite good, but for very different reasons. In February 1861, 90.3 percent of the residents in this area (largely the Cane Creek neighborhood) voted against holding a secession convention.[38] During the war, peace meetings were held in this vicinity, and one of its precincts gave Alfred Dockery, Holden's choice for governor, an unusually large share of its votes in 1866.[39] In 1872 this same precinct voted 58.1 percent for the Republicans.[40] Since blacks were only one-fifth of the registered voters in this township—the lowest percentage in the county—its Republicanism cannot be traced to race but to its tradition of dissent.[41] Republicans in Bingham Township were also rewarded by federal patronage. Benjamin S. Hedrick, the former University of North Carolina professor who held the reins of federal patronage for Orange County, obtained positions as federal tax collectors for his in-laws, the Thompsons, residents of Bingham.[42] The largest prize won by the Republicans in Bingham was William E. Thompson's victory in the election for township constable in 1871.[43]

The Republican strategy of focusing on township contests ended in 1877. When the Conservatives gained complete control of the state government that year and abolished the election of magistrates and other township officials, the Republicans lost any chance to gain office in the county. Thereafter, the only way they could challenge the Conservative political organization was to support dissident Conservatives who chose to run as independents.

One of the strangest political marriages of the 1870s was between the Republican party and Josiah Turner, Jr. Turner, an antebellum Whig leader in Orange County, had become one of the most prominent Conservatives in North Carolina during the late 1860s and early 1870s. As editor of the party's state publication, the *Raleigh Sentinel*, Turner defended and so encouraged the Ku Klux Klan that he was arrested by Governor Holden's militia in 1870. In 1876, after he failed to receive his party's nomination for governor, however, Turner announced as an independent candidate for that office.[44] When no support materialized, however, he returned home to Orange County and sought a lesser office. Unfortunately for Turner, the Conservative county convention had already made its nominations. Believing that he was being unfairly blocked from office, Turner ran as an independent for Orange County's seat in the state senate against the Conservative nominee, John W. Graham.

After the Republicans quickly endorsed Turner, the county's Conservative newspapers warned party members not to be deceived by Turner's claim of independence. The *Durham Tobacco Plant* felt that Turner was anything but "independent," because he was "literally . . . dependent" on those whom he had "for years heaped all manner of abuse."[45] The *Hillsborough Recorder* contended that the Republicans were only "fooling" Turner and would drop him "like a hot potato" and run a Republican once they believed they had "drawn off enough Democrats." It urged Turner to withdraw rather than to play the "vain role of the blind Sampson."[46]

When the election was held in November, Graham defeated Turner. Turner was unable to attract many Conservatives to his candidacy (see Table 24).[47] But the Republican organization succeeded in getting a large number of party members to vote for a candidate who recently had been vehemently anti-Republican.

In late 1877 Turner renewed his quest for office. Believing that the Conservative party organization was denying him of the Conservative nomination, he proposed the abolition of the party caucus and convention system and the substitution of a primary election. Both of the county's Conservative publications quickly opposed this suggestion. The *Durham Tobacco Plant* feared that many of the voters would take no interest in a primary and thus would allow a handful of men to practice "wholesale ballot stuffing." Turner, it claimed, had supported the caucus system when it "suited him well enough"; now, when he could not manipulate everything to suit himself," he was trying to "institute some new scheme."[48] The *Hillsborough Recorder* argued that a primary election might work "among a people of Arcadian simplicity," but that too many of the "present generation," trained in "the arts of deception," would take advantage of the system. It felt that "until someone less interested than Mr. Turner" proposed a better plan, the Conservatives should retain the caucus and convention.[49]

In the spring of 1878, after he failed to receive the Conservative nomination, Turner decided to run as an independent for one of the county's two seats in the state assembly. Again he received the Republican endorsement. Basing his campaign exclusively on the need for a primary system, he placed the Conservatives on the defensive. Now they had to explain the virtues of the caucus and convention over the primary. Their only defense was that the caucus and convention instilled discipline among Conservatives and kept the Republicans from office.[50] Otherwise, all they could do was to claim, as they had in 1876, that Turner was a Republican pawn and that a vote for him was cast not for a principle but against "Orange County Democracy."[51]

This time Turner defeated his Conservative opponents by a wide margin. He attracted not only the Republicans, as in 1876, but also gained the support of a large number of Conservatives (see Table 24). The *Hillsborough Recorder* recognized this shift in the electorate: "It would be unfair, nay it would be downright meanness to charge that all who voted for Josiah Turner . . . were Radicals. These very same voters have more than once saved Orange and the district from

Postwar political leaders. *clockwise:*
John W. Graham (1838–1928).
The son of William A. Graham
(a leading Whig) and son-in-law
of Paul Cameron (a leading Democrat), he became a leader of the
postbellum Conservative party
which consolidated the two antebellum parties. (Photograph
courtesy of North Carolina Collec-
tion, UNC Library at Chapel Hill.) Isaac R. Strayhorn (1845–93) was
a prominent white member of the Republican party. (From copy in
the North Carolina Collection, UNC Library at Chapel Hill.) Josiah
Turner, Jr. (1821–1901). Orange County's antebellum Whig leader who
led an independent political movement in the 1870s. (Photograph courtesy
of Manuscript Department, Perkins Library, Duke University.)

Radicalism." Further, it remarked of those who had left the Conservative ranks to join Turner: "They are of us and to us they shall return."[52]

In 1880 the Conservative county executive committee devised a plan to defeat Turner's exploitation of the primary election issue. It decided to preserve the convention but also to introduce a modified primary system. In August a primary election was held in each township at which, as the *Chapel Hill Ledger* explained, "those who belong or expect to act with the Democratic party" were to vote for delegates to represent the townships at the county convention.[53] Each township was entitled to send one delegate for every twenty-five votes it had cast for Zebulon B. Vance, the Conservative nominee for governor in 1876. In each township voters were to indicate the candidates they wanted to receive their party's nominations for the various county and state offices; in this way, the delegates could know their township's preference.[54]

Since the preference primary failed to bind delegates to support their township's selections, Turner could attack the plan and again run for the state assembly as an independent with Republican support.[55] Although he lost the election, his showing was better than in his 1876 defeat.[56] This time Turner seemed to have won the votes of some, but not all, of the Conservatives who had supported him in 1878 (see Table 24).

Although it never won them any office, the Republican strategy of supporting independents was effective. By using Turner, the Republicans encouraged a number of white voters to challenge their party's authority. Their strategy forced the Conservatives to alter their nomination process. Even after this change, however, a number of Conservatives still refused to support their party.

V

The emergence of Durham as an industrial center during the 1870s had significant political implications. As its population leaped from 256 to 3605, the town demanded more political power. Once it obtained this power, Durham used it to sever ties with Orange County and establish a new county.

Before 1874 no resident of Durham had ever represented Orange County in the state legislature, and only one of the fifteen county commissioners had ever been from the town.[57] In contrast, nine residents of Hillsborough and Chapel Hill townships had been county commissioners since 1868. Aware of these developments, a resident of Durham wrote to the editor of the *Hillsborough Recorder* in April, 1874: "Durham claims, and justly so, the right to a representative in our next legislature."[58] The Conservative convention, recognizing Durham's increasingly large share of the county vote, nominated a resident of Durham for the county commission and the state assembly.[59]

Four years later, although Durham had grown, it no longer was represented on either the county commission or in the state legislature. Speaking for a number of Durham's citizens who demanded power commensurate with their numbers, one resident declared, "I think . . . it is the feeling of the good people of the county that Durham, the metropolis of the county, shall furnish at least one of our Representatives."[60] Because Josiah Turner was campaigning as an independent and it was feared that Durham might defect to his banner, the Conservatives nominated M.A. Angier of Durham, along with John R. Huchins of Chapel Hill, for Orange County's two seats in the state assembly. Angier, with strong support from Durham's voters, easily won one of these seats. Hutchins, who trailed Angier in Durham, lost the other seat to Turner.[61]

In 1880 the Conservatives gave Durham not one but both of the county's state assembly seats. The party nominated Caleb B. Green, the editor of the *Durham Tobacco Plant*, and William K. Parrish, a substantial landholder and a relative of some of Durham's tobacco manufacturers. Despite a strong challenge from Josiah Turner, Green and Parrish, largely because of their ability to win an equally large share of Durham's vote, carried the election.[62]

Durham rapidly took advantage of this new political power. When the state legislature assembled in 1881, Green, with the active support of Durham's tobacco manufacturers, introduced a bill for the division of Orange County and the creation of Durham County from parts of eastern Orange County and a number of townships from neighboring Chatham, Granville, and Wake counties. The state assembly passed a modified version of his bill on February 10. In the state senate the bill encountered stiff opposition from Senator Calvin E. Parrish of Hillsborough, who spoke for the residents of western Orange County who expressed their opposition to the "dismemberment of 'Old Orange.' " Nearly one hundred of the more prominent white residents of the western part of the county signed a petition to influence the state senate. Although it initially appeared as if their efforts might persuade the senate to kill the bill, as one observer noted, "Blackwell & Carr" ["Bull Durham"] began to get "hard at work . . . to change the votes." When the Republicans in the senate threw their support in favor of the bill, it was passed on February 28.[63]

As for how the bill actually passed the senate, the records are unclear. Although it is obvious that the Durham tobacco interests played a major role, that fact alone does not explain the entire motivation for its introduction and passage. No one doubted, noted Walter Clark, an opponent of the bill, that "Blackwell & Co." wanted "to have a little county in which they will virtually appoint the members of the state legislature & all the county officers."[64]

Racial politics, the basis of the postwar party structure, may have been an equally powerful force behind the bill. The role race might have played was described in a letter published in the *Orange County Observer* a month after the senate passed the bill. "Cates Baby," as the letter's author termed himself (probably a reference to the numerous members of the Cates clan who lived near Orange's western border), suggested two interesting reasons why the Durham bill had been passed. First, he explained, the bill was passed because "old Orange" had supported the independent candidacy of Joe [Josiah] Turner. Second, he stressed, "Because if this county is not dismembered, the Radicals generally known as the 'thieves and niggers' will carry old Orange, and that it is far better to divide Orange than to submit to negro rule and Radical Supremacy—as much as they love old Orange and Hillsboro, 'The City of the Dead.' " In this rather cryptic way "Cates Baby" was referring to the fact that by 1880 western Orange County ("Old Orange") had become the foundation of both Josiah Turner's and the Republican's strength. In 1880 both of the major towns of western Orange, Hillsborough and Chapel Hill, had cast a majority of their votes for the Republican nominee for governor and for Josiah Turner. Further, the center of white rural Republicanism was the "Cates" precinct just southwest of Hillsborough in the Cane Creek neighborhood. Finally, Josiah Turner, as a resident of Hillsborough, would be eliminated entirely from having any influence over Durham politics if he was isolated in his own county.[65]

MAP 6 *The Division of Orange County and Creation of Durham County, 1881*

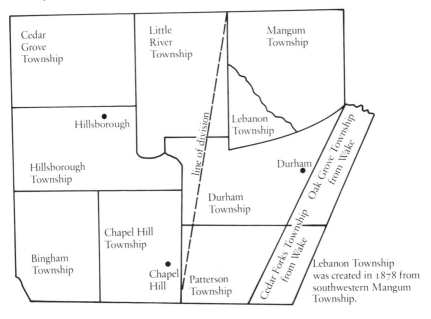

SOURCE: "Map of Durham County, North Carolina," originally drawn by D.G. Mc-Duffie, 1881, North Carolina Division of Archives and History, Raleigh, N.C.

What makes the role of race even more interesting is that Washington Duke, the tobacco manufacturer and leading white Republican, supported the creation of Durham County, and, as was previously noted, the bill passed the senate after the Republican members threw their support behind it. Although Duke may have seen the economic advantages of a tobacco manufacturing county, perhaps he and the Republicans also realized that their chances would be much better of gaining control of a half of Orange than all of it.[66] Hence, in the division of Orange County, both the Democrat tobacco interests of Durham and the Republicans found one issue on which they could unite, to the displeasure of the Democrats of western Orange County. Postbellum politics, based on the tradition of racism, was indeed a novel creation.

The bill called for a referendum on April 14 by people residing within the boundaries of the proposed new county: Patterson, Durham, Lebanon, and Mangum townships of Orange County; and Oak Grove and Cedar Forks townships from Wake County (see Map 6). During the campaign for the referendum, Durham's tobacco manufacturers argued that the creation of the new county not only benefitted their interests but also those of the farmers. They contended that the town's industry and commerce were so dependent on agricultural products that the new county government would be obliged to pay careful attention to the rural interests. They also claimed that Durham was more centrally located in the new county than was Hillsborough in Orange County.[67]

There was little doubt that the referendum would be approved. To defeat its passage the majority of voters throughout the new county would have to reject it; Durham Township, which was sure to support the referendum overwhelmingly, alone represented more than half the voters.[68] Even townships opposed to the referendum would still have to become part of Durham County. Aware of these odds, a planter from Mangum Township who was against forming the new county, predicted that the turnout on the referendum would be light in the countryside because no farmer would "consume so much valuable time to ride four or five miles to a precinct & back home again, first to register & then to vote on a question on which the town of Durham has a majority sufficient to carry it."[69] Although some rural precincts did oppose the referendum, it passed county-wide by a vote of 1464 to 250.[70] Two days later Governor Thomas J. Jarvis signed the bill creating Durham County, and for the sixth time in 129 years Orange County was divided.

VI

The central theme of the postwar administration and politics in Orange County was the willingness of whites to sacrifice many traditions in order to preserve what they viewed as their society's single most important tradition—racism. When it became apparent that the antebellum role of neighborhood in administration and politics might jeopardize white supremacy, it was cast aside. In order to reach that goal, whites without hesitation abandoned traditional local autonomy and the representative nature of their old system of administration as well as the new democratic features introduced in 1868. In addition, by basing partisanship along strict racial lines, they created a new political system that diminished the historical importance both of neighborhoods and of the less affluent white voters.

Epilogue

The continuity of the traditional neighborhood and kinship structure of Orange County extended beyond the immediate postwar years. Despite the tremendous changes during the century after the division of the county in 1881, much of the county's traditional structure remained intact.

Although the Civil War clearly had a significant impact on Orange County's demographic and family structure, as was previously shown, the extent of that impact was limited. Despite the obvious personal sense of grief experienced by the families who lost sons, husbands, or fathers, the tragedy of the war was somewhat mitigated by its enhancement of economic opportunity. Since most of the men who served in the war were too young to be married, the potential number of widows and fatherless children was restricted. Furthermore, war widows left with estates made attractive choices for marriage, a fact that ensured that their children would not remain fatherless. Further, it should not be surprising that the rate of persistence for white men was highest during the 1870s, a period when many of them inherited larger estates than they would have if their brothers had survived the war. Finally, it must be remembered that at any particular point in time marriage affects only a relatively small share of the adult population. If in the first few years after the war traditional marriage patterns were disrupted, particularly given the severely unbalanced sex ratio, during the 1870s the county's wounds were healed. A substantial share of those men who married during this decade were too young to have served in the army.

With the rapid return to traditional patterns, the continuation of close family ties among the residents of the county was ensured. For example, in 1912 a student of the University of North Carolina, venturing out of Chapel Hill, noted the predominance of "certain family names" among the people living in the countryside northwest of the university. He discovered that three-fourths of the residents of the area around White Cross shared the surnames "Lloyd" or "Cates."[1]

The neighborhoods went on to survive both world wars and the Depression. In 1948 another student at the University of North Carolina found that after two hundred years the New Hope church continued to be the "strongest integrating factor in the life of the New Hope neighborhood." Although improvements in transportation allowed the residents to shop in Hillsborough, Chapel Hill, or Durham, the student found that the "social and religious life" of the New Hope people continued to center in their neighborhood.[2]

Even those people who moved out of the countryside and into the towns preserved their sense of kinship and neighborhood. In his 1970 comparative study of Hillsborough, North Carolina, and Lincoln, Nebraska, Alfred M. Mirande discovered that the residents of Hillsborough were approximately seven times more likely to make regular visits to a large number of relatives (eight or more) than those of Lincoln. Hillsborough's "stable pattern of residence" caused its inhabitants to share a "comparable life history" which, according to Mirande, precluded the necessity for people to search out those friends who were not relatives. Because of their "closer fidelity to kin," Hillsborough's residents were half as likely to have a large number of close friends (six or more) as Lincoln's.[3]

If any area of the South today should have broken its ties with the past, it would have to be the Orange and Durham County area, which has experienced unprecedented changes since the 1960s. Its population, which had grown from 23,698 in 1880 to 156,965 in 1960, reached 229,830 by 1980. Further, by the latter year, the counties had become part of a metropolitan area of over half a million people.[4] Much of this growth was due to the continued development of the tobacco industry in Durham as well as of the textile factories that began to be built before the turn of the century. In addition, the expansion of the two major universities within its borders, the University of North Carolina and Duke University—

both of which have become institutions of national prestige—has also significantly contributed to the population growth. Equally important, since 1960 when it was partially located in eastern Durham County, the Research Triangle Park has attracted major national corporate, scientific, and high technology firms and their thousands of employees. As a result of these combined factors, the area probably has one of the highest percentages of non-southern-born people within the entire region. Nevertheless, as recently as 1985 the Orange County Tax Supervisor was Kermit Lloyd whose great-great-great-great-great-great grandfather, Major General Thomas Lloyd, had served as sheriff, justice of the peace, and member of the general assembly for Orange County under King George III. As sheriff, two centuries before, Thomas Lloyd was also responsible for assessing and collecting taxes.[5]

The question whether the rural neighborhoods were unique to either Orange County or the South must remain largely unanswered.[6] Since, to date, studies of other regions have shown no similar pattern, it is impossible to draw any generalization. It needs to be kept in mind that the South was relatively unaffected by the system of land surveying that dominated the public domain states of the Midwest and Far West. Many parts of these regions were surveyed and divided into thirty-six-square-mile, rectangular townships, slightly less than half the size of Orange County's rural neighborhoods. These distinctly artificial boundaries were created well before most settlers arrived. As a result, the county histories of the states of these regions are generally divided into the histories of the individual townships. These histories reveal that these townships did not have the self-contained character of rural neighborhoods. For example, a person who lived in one township might buy goods from a general store in a neighboring township but attend church in still another. It is interesting that when North Carolina created townships in 1868, when the new system of local government was instituted, the borders of these townships in Orange County often mirrored traditional neighborhood borders.

The parochialism or localism so evident in Orange County, however, does seem to fit into a larger and enduring regional pattern. Although no other historical study of the South has focused on the role of rural neighborhoods, in his 1972 study of regional characteristics, John Shelton Reed found that southerners were nearly twice as likely as non-southerners to claim that the most admirable men and women they knew were either relatives or neighbors. Southerners, Reed concludes, "to a greater degree than other Americans" have maintained a "localistic orientation—an attachment to their place and people."[7]

An investigation of a single county over a thirty-two-year period cannot serve as a definitive study of southern culture, nor is it likely to end the debate about whether the Civil War had a significant impact on the South. Much research during the last decade has, by stressing elements of continuity, found that the Civil War had a relatively minor influence on the South. For example, Jonathan M. Wiener traces the importance of planter persistence throughout the era. In her description of the relationship between woman and the evangelical community in the South during the mid to late nineteenth century, Jean E. Friedman also argues that the role of the Civil War was minor. Randolph B. Campbell not only explains how continuity "matched change" in his description of the impact of the Civil War on Harrison County in northeastern Texas, he also claims that "the majority of the community's white population had supported the Confederate revolution primarily to keep things the same and failure on the battlefield did not destroy their purpose." In his examination of the social and economic elites of North Carolina from 1850 to 1900, which has applicability far beyond that single state's borders, Paul Escott contends that continuity was a primary theme of both "power relationships" and "undemocratic attitudes." Nevertheless, an equally impressive collection of studies of the same period by Roger Ransom and Richard Sutch, Steven Hahn, and Michael Wayne have emphasized the war's impact on the South. As C. Vann Woodward, whose *Origins of the New South* stimulated much of the controversy over the importance of continuity or discontinuity during this era, has recently noted, "No end to the debate seems yet in sight, though it threatens the exhaustion of patience."[8]

Clearly Orange County was influenced by the Civil War, the single most important event in the lives of the community's residents during the nineteenth century. However, when the change and continuity these people experienced is compared, it is important to consider that any attempt to determine of which force was greater must recognize that tradition often defines the direction of change.

At the very least this study has identified the broadest elements of the impact of the Civil War and tried to place them in the historical perspective of Orange County. At the very most it has permitted that community's social, economic, administrative, and political structure to be viewed in a single portrait—a portrait revealing the continuing importance of family, kinship, and neighborhood.

Using the Federal Manuscript Census to Determine Distance

A. Previous Use of the Methodology

I am not the first historian to use the federal manuscript census to measure where southerners lived in relation to one another. For instance, Frank L. Owsley, in *Plain Folk of the Old South* (Baton Rouge: Louisiana State Univ. Press, 1949), 76, contended that the order of households in the census demonstrated that both nonslaveholders and small slaveholders lived in close proximity to large slaveholders and therefore farmed lands of fairly equal quality. This methodology was challenged by Fabian Linden, in "Economic Democracy in the Slave South: An Appraisal of Some Recent Views," *Journal of Negro History* 31 (Apr. 1946), 140–89. Linden noted that farmers listed in the 1850 census as neighbors "were quite often recorded apart in the schedule the following census year." He felt that this was caused by the census taker's canvass being "not sufficiently systematic." He concluded, therefore, that the order in which a person appeared in the census should not be a factor to "allow major historical generalizations."

Both Owsley and Linden were correct about the manuscript census. Owsley's assertion that the manuscript census was a valuable tool in determining residence patterns was valid. Linden's claim that people listed as neighbors in one census rarely were found to live next door to one another in the following census also was correct. It is unfortunate that Owsley and Linden's major differences on other points prevented other scholars from employing Owsley's methodology.

MAP 7 *Approximate Route of Census Taker in 1850*

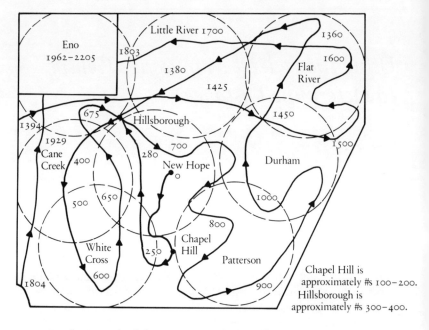

Owsley's methodology is particularly difficult to apply in the case of Orange County. It was not until North Carolina's new constitution in 1868 that Orange was divided into townships that indicated in what area of the county a person resided. Nevertheless, by knowing where a few of the more prominent residents of the county lived, it becomes possible to provide some idea of the route followed by the census taker.

In 1850 the census taker followed a rather complex route over a number of weeks (see Map 7). He started out in the New Hope neighborhood, crossed through the edge of the White Cross neighborhood, went to Chapel Hill, and worked his way north to Hillsborough. During the rest of his route, however, the census taker stopped twice (at #1393 and #1803) and then started up again somewhere else in the county. He finished by enumerating 243 households in the northwest corner of the county.

By 1860, with the completion of the North Carolina Central Railroad through the county in 1855, the census takers had a slightly

MAP 8 *Approximate Route of Census Taker in 1860*

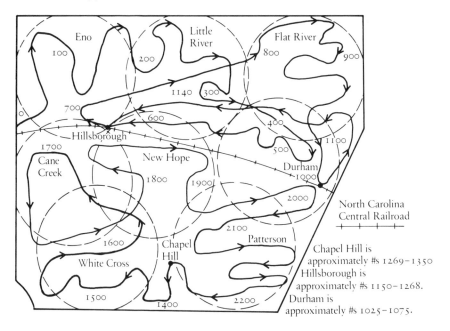

more systematic route (see Map 8). One of the census takers enu-merated the households north of the railroad and the other those south of the railroad. Even with a plan more systematic than that used in 1850, the census takers traveled some rather circuitous routes. This was caused, as in 1850, by their attempt to follow the country roads and paths as much as possible but also to work their way along the rivers and creeks where most of the people lived. On the whole the census of 1860 is more valuable than that of 1850 because it indicates at least whether the household was north or south of the railroad. However, the railroad often divided families sharing the same surname and thus made them appear to reside quite far from one another. It is only when the two censuses are compared that it becomes evident how close families and their relatives resided.

B. Average Distance between Households
The average distance between households in 1860 was calculated by dividing the average area of the county by the total number of house-

holds. Since my primary concern was the distance between households in the rural neighborhoods, I excluded the area of and households in Hillsborough, Chapel Hill, and Durham. I have assumed, for the purpose of this calculation, that all of the neighborhoods were of approximately equal size and population.

area of county   = 652 square miles
number of households   = 2253 households

area of towns approximately 2 square miles
number of households in towns approximately 253

652 square miles − 2 square miles   = 650 square miles
2253 households − 253 households   = 2000 households

650 square miles ÷ 8 neighborhoods   = 81.2 square miles per
                                                                          neighborhood
2000 households ÷ 8 neighborhoods   = 250 households per neighborhood
250 households ÷ 81.2 square miles   = 3.1 households per square mile
1 square mile   = 640 acres
640 acres / 3.1 households   = 206 acres per household

One important point not yet made concerning the neighborhoods was the impact of divisions of the county. With successive divisions of the county, neighborhoods were divided by the new borders. For example, the Barbee family of Orange by 1850 had kin in Chatham County to the south and Wake County to the east of their residence in the Patterson neighborhood. The new borders did not prevent contact between these relatives. For a genealogy of the Barbees, see Ruth Herndon Shields et al., compilers, *A Study of the Barbee Families of Chatham, Orange, and Wake Counties in North Carolina* (Boulder, Colorado: privately published, 1971), copy in North Carolina Collection, Univ. of North Carolina Library, Chapel Hill, N.C.

*C. Measuring the Distance between Households
of the Bride and Groom, 1850–59*
There were 906 marriages among whites between 1850 and 1859. Unfortunately, the marriage records did not note the names of the newlywed's parents. In order to calculate the distance between the bride and groom's households in 1850 I began with only those marriages where the newlyweds headed their own household in the 1860 census. Knowing what their ages were in 1860, I then searched the

1850 census in order to find the bride and groom in their parents' households. Because people often shared the exact same name, I only accepted those cases where the bride and groom in 1860 were nine to eleven years older than they appeared in the 1850 census. Further, only those cases were used when both the bride and groom would have been at least fifteen years old at the time of marriage. Once I identified both the bride and groom's parents' households in 1850, I calculated the difference between their household numbers. For example, William H. Atkins married Demarius Leigh (both of Patterson neighborhood) in 1855. His parents' household was #880, and her parents' was #895 in the 1850 census. The distance between their households was $895 - 880 = 15$ households. Even with this more strict requirement, it was only possible to calculate the distance for 58 marriages (6.4 percent of all marriages).

It is evident from the two maps in Appendix 1-A that this methodology underestimates how close people resided. Households located within a short distance, such as #500 and #1804, appear numerically to be quite far from one another. Therefore, in fact probably more than half of the newlyweds would have resided less than 100 households apart before marriage. When these distances are compared to those of another era, such as in the case of marriages after the Civil War, the numbers will prove to be more meaningful. Finally it should be noted that the methodology necessarily biases my conclusion since all those who married outside of the county are excluded and the sample is only based on persistent newlyweds.

D. Measuring the Distance of the Newlyweds' Household from Their Parents' Households, 1860

In measuring this distance the same process was used as in Appendix 1-C, except it was not necessary to find both of the newlyweds' parents' households in 1850. Once I found the newlyweds' and one, the other, or both of their parents' households in 1860, I calculated the number of households between them. For example, the household of William H. Atkins and his wife Demarius was #1938 in the 1860 census. William's parents that same year resided in household #1941. Demarius's parents resided in household #1936. Therefore, the distance of William and Demarius from his parents was $#1941 - 1938 = 3$ households. The distance from her parents was $#1938 - 1936 = 2$ households. The distance from the closest parent, therefore, was 2 households. This was calculated first for the husband's parents (88 cases), then for the wife's parents (53 cases), and finally for the closest of the two sets of parents (113 cases). This methodology has the same biases as described in Appendix 1-C.

E. Measuring the Age at Marriage, 1850–59

Since a few people married more than once, this age at marriage should not be interpreted as the age at which men and women first married. To calculate the age at marriage it was necessary to find the bride's and groom's ages in the 1850 census. I added the number of years their marriage took place after the 1850 census to their age in 1850 to determine their age at marriage. I used only those cases when the person was at least fifteen years old when the marriage occurred. If, because of the commonality of names, there were two or more possibilities, I did not use those cases. For example, William Henry Lloyd, aged 23 in 1850, was married in 1854. Therefore, his age at marriage was 27 years. This age should only be thought of as an approximation, plus or minus one year, since the date of marriage cannot be compared to the actual date of birth. It was possible to conduct this measurement for 379 cases (41.8 percent of all marriages).

The Records of Orange County's Soldiers in the Civil War

A. The Number of Soldiers from Orange County
The extent of Orange County's participation in the Civil War can be found in two published sources. First, there is John W. Moore's four-volume work, *Roster of North Carolina Troops in the War Between The States* (Raleigh: North Carolina State, 1882) [hereinafter cited as Moore's *Roster*]. Moore's *Roster* covers all of the North Carolina troops. Second, there is an on-going project by the North Carolina Department of Archives and History, Weymouth T. Jordan, Jr., and Louis H. Manarin, eds., 10 vols. *North Carolina Troops, 1861–1865: A Roster* (Raleigh: North Carolina Department of Archives and History, 1961–) [hereinafter cited as Jordan and Manarin Study]. Because only nine of a projected thirteen volumes were completed when I did my analysis, I was only able to use the material covering the first thirty-seven infantry regiments and the cavalry and artillery units from North Carolina.

The major flaw of these sources is their failure to specify in all cases whether a man who enlisted in Orange County was a resident of the community. Moore's *Roster* only notes the place of enlistment. The Jordan and Manarin Study attempts, when the material was available, to list place of residence. It indicates that most of the men who enlisted in Orange County were residents of the community.

Number of Soldiers from Orange County
Listed in Jordan and Manarin Study (1st–37th
infantry regiments and cavalry and artillery units):   1061
Listed in Moore's *Roster* (28th–74th regiments):   <u>497</u>

Total: 1558

B. *Casualty Rate of Orange County Soldiers*

The Jordan and Manarin Study provides a more complete picture of the total number of casualties than Moore's *Roster*. This can be demonstrated by comparing how these works record the total number of deaths in the same companies. For example, according to Moore's *Roster* only 55 men died while serving in Companies B and C, the Flat River Guards and Orange Grays, of the Sixth North Carolina Regiment. The Jordan and Manarin Study indicates that 73 men died in these units. Because the Jordan and Manarin Study drew on more records than Moore's *Roster*, I believe that the casualty rate indicated by the former is more accurate.

Jordan and Manarin Study:

Total Number of Soldiers:	1061	
Total Number of Deaths:	339	(32.0%)
Total Number of Wounded:	253	(23.8%)
Total Number of Casualties:	592	(55.8%)

Moore's Roster:

Total Number of Soldiers:	497	
Total Number of Deaths:	70	(14.1%)
Total Number of Wounded:	21	(4.2%)
Total Number of Casualties:	91	(18.3%)

APPENDIX 3

Tables

TABLE 1 *Distance between Household of Bride and Groom, 1850–80*

		Distance in Households[a]			
		1–99	*100–499*	*500+ or Different Township*[b]	*No. of Marriages*
For Whites:	in 1850s	50.0%	36.2%	13.8%	58
	1865–1869	37.0	37.0	26.0	81
	in 1870s	64.0	34.4	1.6	64
For Blacks:	in 1870s	25.0	75.0	0	12

SOURCES: U.S. Census MS., Orange County, 1850, 1860, 1870, 1880, Schedule 1; *Orange County Marriage Bonds to 1868* (Salt Lake City: Genealogical Society of Utah, n.d.), North Carolina Division of Archives and History, Raleigh, N.C. [hereinafter cited as NCDAH]; Orange County Marriage Register, 1868–81, Office of the Register of Deeds, Orange County Courthouse, Hillsborough, N.C.
[a]For the methodology used to calculate distances using the federal manuscript census, see Appendix 1-A to C.
[b]The designation of different townships is only applicable during the 1870s.

TABLE 2 *Distance of Newlyweds' Household from Parents' Household, 1860–80*

	Distance in Households from Closer of Spouses' Parents[a]				
	5 or less	under 100	100–499	500+ or Different Township[b]	No. of Marriages
For Whites:					
in 1860	31.0%	58.4%	28.3%	13.3%	113
in 1870	22.5	57.5	12.5	30.0	40
in 1880	43.1	74.1	15.5	10.4	58
For Blacks:					
in 1880	19.4	51.6	29.0	19.4	31

SOURCES: Same as Table 1.
[a]For methodology, see Appendix 1-D.
[b]The different township designation is applicable for 1870 and 1880.

TABLE 3 *Rates of Persistence in Orange County, 1850–80*

A. All Men Age 20+[a]

Ages	White Men 1850–60	White Men 1860–70	White Men 1870–80	Black Men 1870–80
20–29	46.6%	31.6%	54.0%	31.8%
(Ages 20–39)	(51.2%)	(36.8%)	(56.8%)	(35.5%)
30–39	57.6	45.3	62.2	40.6
40–49	64.3	56.0	67.0	51.0
50–59	56.5	56.5	59.6	43.9
60+	35.7	34.2	34.2	23.2
Total Average:	52.2%	42.3%	56.3%	37.5%

TABLE 3 *Continued*

B. *Rate of Persistence by Household Status and Slaveholding, 1850–80*

	1850–60	1860–70	1870–80
White Men Age 20+ Who Are:			
Not Head of Household	43.2%	28.3%	50.2%
Head of Household	55.9	48.3	58.7
Nonslaveholding Head of Household	54.7	45.4	
Slaveholding Head of Household	58.4	56.7	
Planters (own 20+ slaves)	53.5	54.8	

C. *Rate of Persistence by Surname, 1850-60* [a]

White Men Sharing Surname with 7 or More Male Household Heads:	60.9% persisted
White Men Sharing Surname with 4–6 Male Household Heads:	51.3% persisted
White Men Sharing Surname with Fewer Than 4 Male Household Heads:	46.0% persisted
Total:	52.9% persisted [b]

SOURCE: U.S. Census MS., Orange County, 1850, 1860, 1870, 1880, Schedules 1 and 2.

[a] The surnames of all students age 20 and over—clearly students attending the University of North Carolina at Chapel Hill and of course not persistent for ten years—were omitted.

[b] The rate of persistence during the 1850s in Table 3.A and 3.C vary slightly because in Table 3.C it was necessary to omit eight surnames. Two were excluded because these surnames were spelled differently each time the census taker enumerated them. The other six surnames (Brown, Davis, Jones, Smith, Williams, Wilson) were omitted because, while there might have been some kin connections between men sharing these surnames, they are very common surnames. If included in Table 3.C, these surnames would not have markedly changed the rate.

TABLE 4 *Occupational Structure of Orange County 1850–80*

Classification of Primary Occupations[a] for All Males Age 20+	White Males				Black Males	
	1850	1860	1870	1880	1870	1880
Professional	2.8%	2.4%	3.3%	2.4%	.1%	.4%
White Collar	3.0	2.8	3.6	6.3	0	.9
Blue Collar	12.9	16.2	11.2	14.0	14.0	27.6
Merchant	1.1	1.1	1.2	2.1	0	.3
Manufacturer	0	.6	.6	1.1	0	0
Farmer, Farm Laborer, and Overseer	79.3	74.8 [b]	80.1	72.2	85.9	70.8
Other	.9	2.1	0	1.9[c]	0	0

SOURCE: U.S. Census MS., Orange County, 1850, 1860, 1870, 1880, Schedule 1.
[a]These are the occupations as listed in Schedule 1 of the federal manuscript census. Many men who were listed with a non-farming occupation often also were involved in agriculture.
[b]The difference between 1850 and 1860 in the percentage of men who were farmers is the result of the increase in the number of men listed with no occupation. Since most of these men lived in the rural sections of the county, where there were no other possible occupations, they probably were farmers or farm laborers.
[c]This includes tobacco dealers and warehouse owners.

TABLE 5 *Distribution of Slaveholding for White Male Household Heads, 1850–60*

Level of Slaveholding	Percent of White Male Household Heads	
	1850	*1860*
0	67.4%	71.5%
1–9	24.4	21.6
10–19	5.7	4.6
20–29	1.5	1.3
30–39	.2	.4
40–49	.5	.3
50+	.3	.3
	100.0%	100.0%

SOURCE: U.S. Census MS., Orange County, 1850, 1860, Schedules 1 and 2.

TABLE 6 *Concentration of Slaveholding among White Male Household Heads, 1850–60*

	1[a]	2	3	4	5	6	7	8	9	10
1850	0	0	0	0	0	0	1.0	6.6	19.6	72.8%
1860	0	0	0	0	0	0	0	5.1	17.4	77.5%

SOURCE: Same as Table 5.
[a]The household heads were ranked in the order of the number of slaves they owned. After this ranking was completed, they were divided into ten equal divisions (deciles), and the total share of all slaves owned by each division was calculated.

TABLE 7 *Distribution of Real Estate Ownership for*
White Male Household Heads, 1850–70

Value of Real Estate (in dollars)	Percent of White Male Household Heads		
	1850	1860 [a]	1870
0	40.0%	41.1%	37.2%
1–99	2.1	1.1	.9
100–249	10.8	3.9	8.2
250–499	13.5	9.1	15.5
500–999	16.0	16.1	18.6
1000–2499	11.8	15.8	14.0
2500–4999	3.6	7.3	3.7
5000–9999	1.6	4.4	1.1
10,000–24,999	.4	.8	.7
25,000+	.2	.4	.1
	100.0%	100.0%	100.0%

SOURCE: U.S. Census MS., Orange County, 1850, 1860, 1870, Schedule 1.

[a] In 1860, for no apparent reason, the census taker for the area north of the railroad listed real estate for only 9 out of 929 consecutive households and therefore clearly underestimated property ownership. Therefore, for 1860 I have used only the 1012 households located south of the railroad.

TABLE 8   *Concentration of Value of Real Estate among White Male Household Heads, 1850–70*

	1 [a]	2	3	4	5	6	7	8	9	10	Gini Index [b]
1850	0	0	0	0	1.9	3.9	6.5	9.9	16.0	61.8%	.7392
1860	0	0	0	0	1.7	3.5	5.7	8.7	16.8	63.6%	.7524
1870	0	0	0	.3	2.9	5.0	7.2	10.6	16.3	57.7%	.7092

SOURCE: U.S. Census MS., Orange County, 1850, 1860, 1870, Schedule 1.
[a]For methodology, see Table 6.
[b]The Gini Index measures the overall degree of equality of wealth. It ranges from 0, signifying that wealth was equally distributed among all household heads, to 1, signifying that one household head owned everything. For a description of the methodology for calculating the Gini Index, see Charles M. Dollar and Richard Jensen, *A Historian's Guide to Statistics: Quantitative Analysis and Historical Research* (New York: Holt, Rinehart, and Winston, 1971), 121–24.

TABLE 9   *Concentration of Total Acreage among White Male Household Heads, 1850–70*

	1 [a]	2	3	4	5	6	7	8	9	10	Gini Index [b]
1850	1.7	2.9	3.5	4.6	5.7	6.9	8.5	11.0	12.7	42.4%	.4857
1860	1.3	2.4	3.5	4.6	5.4	6.8	8.2	10.8	16.1	40.9%	.5010
1870	1.2	2.3	3.9	5.2	6.8	8.4	10.3	12.9	16.7	32.3%	.4426

SOURCE: U.S. Census MS., Orange County, 1850, 1860, 1870, Schedules 1 and 4.
[a]For methodology, see Table 6.
[b]For methodology, see Table 8.

TABLE 10 *Change in Total Acreage for Persistent White Male Household Heads, 1850–60*

Level of Total Acreage in 1850[a]	Level of Total Acreage in 1860:[a]					Cumulative Change:			
	None	Small	Medium	Large	Very Large	Down	Stable	Up	#
None	58.9%	17.6%	15.5%	5.9%	2.1%	0%	58.9%	41.1%	336
Small	24.7	25.8	43.8	5.7	0	24.7	25.8	49.5	89
Medium	15.5	9.0	53.6	21.5	.4	24.5	53.6	21.9	278
Large	10.6	2.4	16.3	49.6	21.1	29.3	49.6	21.1	123
Very Large	6.2	2.5	2.5	11.3	77.5	22.5	77.5	0	88
Total:						15.9%	54.4%	29.7%	914
						(144)	(493)	(269)	
Total at Risk:[b]						29.4%	56.5%	14.1%	
						(144)	(277)	(69)	

SOURCE: U.S. Census MS., Orange County, 1850, 1860, Schedules 1 and 4.

[a]The number of total acres in each designation include: None=0 total acres, Small=1–99 total acres, Medium=100–249 total acres, Large=250–499 total acres, Very Large=500+ total acres.

[b]Since those in the None designation are not at risk to move downward and those in the Very Large designation are not at risk to move upward, both designations are subtracted from the total to determine those at risk to experience change in either direction.

TABLE 11 Marriage between Slaveholding and Nonslaveholding Households, 1850–59

		0	1	2–4	5–9	10–14	15–19	20–24	25–29	Total
					Number of Slaves in Groom's Household in 1850					
Number of Slaves in Bride's Household in 1850:	0	46	8	5	3	0	0	0	0	62
	1	7	1	1	0	0	0	1	0	10
	2–4	2	1	3	3	1	0	2	0	12
	5–9	6	0	1	1	3	0	0	1	12
	10–14	1	0	2	3	2	1	0	0	9
	15–19	0	0	0	0	0	0	0	0	0
	20–24	0	0	0	0	0	0	0	0	0
	25–29	0	0	0	0	1	0	0	0	1
	Total:	62	10	12	10	7	1	3	1	106[a]

SOURCES: U.S. Census MS., Orange County, 1850, 1860, Schedules 1 and 2; *Orange County Marriage Bonds to 1868*, NCDAH.
[a] These are only the cases where the bride and groom each lived in a household in 1850 that was headed by a male. Because of this requirement and the problem of making perfect matches with the 1850 federal manuscript census, these 106 cases represent only 11.7 percent of all the marriages during the 1850s.

TABLE 12 *Marriage between Landholding and Nonlandholding Households, 1850–59*

Value of Real Estate in Bride's Household in 1850 (in dollars)	Value of Real Estate in Groom's Household in 1850 (in dollars)								
	0	1–99	100–249	250–499	500–999	1000–2499	2500–4999	5000–9999	Total
0	19	0	3	4	3	2	0	0	31
1–99	1	0	0	0	1	0	0	0	2
100–249	4	0	2	2	2	1	0	0	11
250–499	4	0	1	5	0	0	0	0	10
500–999	5	0	4	2	8	2	2	0	23
1000–2499	3	0	0	7	8	2	1	1	22
2500–4999	1	0	1	0	1	1	0	0	4
5000–9999	1	0	0	0	0	0	1	1	3
Total:	38	0	11	20	23	8	4	2	106[a]

SOURCE: U.S. Census MS, Orange County, 1850, Schedule 1; *Orange County Marriage Bonds to 1868*, NCDAH.
[a]For an explanation of number of cases, see Table 11.

TABLE 13 *Profile of Antebellum Magistrates and Active Party Participants*

A. *Age in 1850*

	21–29	30–39	40–49	50–59	60–69	70+	Average
Magistrates[a]	0	22.8%	40.0%	24.3%	11.4%	1.4%	46.4
Whigs[b]	9.9	30.2	32.1	21.0	5.6	1.2	43.5
Democrats[b]	17.4	24.8	31.7	18.0	5.6	2.5	42.0
Americans[c]	31.4	40.0	17.2	5.7	5.7	0	35.9

B. *Primary Occupation in 1850*

	Farmer	Professional	White Collar	Blue Collar	Merchant	None
Magistrates	77.1%	4.3%	7.2%	4.3%	7.1%	0%
Whigs	71.6	7.4	4.3	13.6	3.1	0
Democrats	75.2	5.0	5.0	8.7	5.0	1.1
Americans	62.9	2.8	11.4	22.9	0	0

C. *Level of Slaveholding in 1850*

	0	1–4	5–9	10–19	20–49	50+	Average
Magistrates	12.9%	24.3%	25.7%	20.0%	14.3%	2.8%	10.7
Whigs	29.6	25.9	19.8	14.8	8.6	1.2	6.4
Democrats	32.3	27.9	16.8	14.9	6.2	1.9	6.5
Americans	45.7	20.0	25.7	8.6	0	0	3.2

D. *Amount of Real Estate Owned (in dollars) in 1850*

	$0	1–249	250–499	500–999	1000–2499	2500–4999	5000–9999	25,000+	Average
Magistrates	7.1%	1.4%	8.6%	14.3%	27.1%	24.1%	12.9%	4.3%	$2771.08
Whigs	11.7	7.3	10.4	20.3	28.3	12.9	6.7	2.4	1740.14
Democrats	10.6	6.8	16.2	26.7	22.4	8.1	7.4	1.9	1657.70
Americans	28.6	5.7	25.7	14.3	20.0	0	5.7	0	960.11

TABLE 13 *Continued*

E. *Party Affiliation*

	Whigs	Democrats	Switched Party in 1850s	Party Unknown
Magistrates	35.7%	40.0%	2.9%	21.4%
Americans	86.4	14.0	(former affiliations when known)	

SOURCES: Orange County Court Minutes, 1850, NCDAH; U.S. Census MS., Orange County, 1850, Schedules 1 and 2. The names of the active party participants were obtained from the *Hillsborough Recorder*, Mar. 24, 29, Apr. 7, 21, May 12, 15, 19, June 25, 1852; Mar. 29, May 17, 24, 31, 1854; Mar. 21, 1855; Apr. 19, 30, May 14, 21, Sept. 17, 1856; Mar. 18, 1857; Mar. 3, 1858; Mar. 23, 1859; Mar. 7, 21, May 16, 23, July 18, 1860.

[a] Although there were 77 magistrates in 1850, 7 could not be used in constructing the profile because either they could not be found in the manuscript census or they shared their surname with another man.

[b] There was a total of 526 active Whig and Democrat party participants. However, it was only possible to provide a profile for the 323 (162 Whigs and 161 Democrats) who headed households in 1850 and did not have the same name as another man. Although the age, real estate ownership, and slaveholdings all would have changed by the late 1850s, there is no reason to believe that the extent of this change would have varied for the two parties.

Because Paul C. Cameron, with 218 slaves, had four times more slaves than anyone else in the county, his slaves were excluded from the Democrats' average. If his slaves were included, the Democrats would have averaged 7.8 slaves.

[c] Although there was a total of 147 active American Party participants, it was possible to provide a profile for only the 35 of them who headed households in 1850 and did not have an identical name with another man. Because it was not necessary to use only heads of households, the sample for former party affiliations was larger.

TABLE 14   *The Fourteen Primary Military Companies in Which Orange County Soldiers Served, 1861–65*

North Carolina Regiment Number and Company (and company name if any)	Number of Orange County Soldiers in Company, 1861–65	Percent of Orange County Soldiers in Company, 1861–62[a]
"Bethel" — D (6 Month Troops)	79	96.3%
1st — D ("Orange Light Infantry")	81	48.8
6th — B ("Flat River Guards")	122	83.7
6th — C ("Orange Grays")	117	85.9
11th — G	104	77.0
19th — K ("Orange Cavalry")	85	76.2
27th — G ("Orange Guards")	121	84.6
28th — G ("Guards of Independence")	147	96.4
31st — E	94	88.8
33rd — F	59	36.7
40th — G ("Orange Artillery")	123	76.1
44th — G	72	53.7
56th — D	139	99.2
66th — A ("Durham Grays")	114	88.5
	1457/1558 = 93.5%	76.1%

SOURCES: John W. Moore, ed., *Register of North Carolina Troops in The War Between The States* (Raleigh: North Carolina State Publisher, 1882), 1–4; Weymouth T. Jordan and Louis H. Manarin, eds., *North Carolina Troops, 1861–1865: A Roster*, (Raleigh: North Carolina Department of Archives and History, 1961–), 1–10.
[a]This percentage is calculated by dividing the total number of men from Orange County who served in each company by the total number of men in each company. Only the years 1861–62 are used because, as noted in chapter 3, as the war advanced, these percentages declined rapidly.

TABLE 15 *Age of Orange County Soldiers at Time of Enlistment, 1861–65*

Age at Time of Enlistment	Number of Soldiers	Percent of Soldiers
14–17	30	3.7%
18–19	152 ⎤	19.2 ⎤
20–24	299 (598)	37.8 (75.5%)
25–29	147 ⎦	18.5 ⎦
30–34	73	9.2
35–39	48	6.1
40–44	22	2.8
45–49	15	1.9
50–54	6	.8
	792	100.0%

SOURCE: Jordan and Manarin, eds., *North Carolina Troops*, 1–9.

TABLE 16 *Occupations of Orange County Soldiers at Time of Enlistment, 1861–65*

Occupation Classification[a]	Number of Soldiers	Percent of Soldiers
Professional	4	1.4%
White Collar	14	4.8
Blue Collar	49	17.0
Merchant	7	2.4
Manufacturer	1	.3
Farmer	212	73.4
Other	2	.7
	289	100.0%

SOURCE: Same as Table 15.
[a]Occupations were only listed, as was the case with ages, for seven regiments. However, they were listed less often.

TABLE 17   *Prior Economic Status of the Wealthiest White Landowners, 1870*

Value of Real Estate Owned in 1860 (in dollars)	Number[a]	Percent	Number of Slaves Owned in 1860	Number	Percent
0	2	3.8 %	0	26	17.9 %
250–999	2	3.8	1–4	30	20.7
1000–2499	8	15.1	5–9	34	23.4
2500–4999	21	39.6	10–19	28	19.3
5000–9999	15	28.3	20+	27	18.6
10,000–24,999	4	7.5		145	100.0 %
25,000+	1	1.9			
	53	100.0 %			

SOURCE: U.S. Census MS., Orange County, 1860, 1870, Schedules 1 and 2.
[a]Of the 1647 white male household heads in 1870, 194 (11.8%) owned at least $1500 worth of real estate. I have been able to find 145 of these 194 household heads in the 1860 federal manuscript census. Because the census taker in 1860 failed to record the real estate holdings for many of the households in the northern half of the county, I have only used real estate values for those households in 1860 that were located in the southern half of the county.

TABLE 18 *Tenure of Farmers, 1880*

Form of Tenure	White Farmers		Black Farmers	
	Number	*Percent*	*Number*	*Percent*
Owner-Operator [a]	1104	70.1	110	25.8
Non-Owners [a]				
Cash Tenant	65	4.1	18	4.2
Share Tenant	405	25.8	298	70.0
	1574	100.0	426	100.0
Total cash and share tenants	470		316	
Farm laborers [b]	316		559	
Total who owned no land	786	41.6	875	88.8
Owner-Operator [a]	1104		110	
Total	1890		985	

SOURCE: U.S. Census MS., Orange County, 1880, Schedules 1 and 4.
[a] As listed in the agricultural schedule. Only those male farmers who were household heads were selected.
[b] Agricultural workers (also all household heads) listed in the population schedule but not in the agricultural schedule.

TABLE 19   *Percentage of Farmers Not Producing Enough Corn to Meet the Needs of Their Households, 1860–80*

| | Percent of Farmers not Producing Enough Corn[a] | | |
	White	Black	Total
Farmers			
1860	13.7%	——	13.7%
1870	29.9	53.3	32.0
1880[b]	24.2–28.5%	46.0–55.6%	28.8–34.2%
Share Tenants			
1880[b]	41.0–57.5%	45.6–59.4%	43.1–58.3%

SOURCE: U.S. Census MS., Orange County, 1860, 1870, 1880, Schedules 1 and 4.
[a]"Farmers" are defined as male household heads who were recorded in the agriculture schedule.
[b]Since it is impossible to determine what percent of the share tenants in 1880 were sharecroppers, it is necessary to give a range of percent of farmers and share tenants who did not produce enough corn. The lower percentage is based on the assumption that all of the share tenants were giving only one-third of their corn to the landlord. The higher percent is based on the assumption that all of the share tenants were sharecroppers and therefore were giving one-half of their corn to the landlord.

TABLE 20   *Percentage of Farmers Involved in the Production of Crops, 1860–80*

Percent of Farmers Producing[a]	White Farmers 1860	White Farmers 1870	Black Farmers 1870	Total Farmers 1870	White Farmers 1880	Black Farmers 1880	Total Farmers 1880
Corn	96.7%	97.6%	95.6%	97.4%	94.0%	91.7%	93.5%
Wheat	94.2	93.2	78.9	92.0	87.6	75.7	83.6
Cotton	3.7	13.3	3.3	12.4	34.1	25.2	33.1

SOURCE: U.S. Census MS., Orange County, 1860, 1870, 1880, Schedules 1 and 4.
[a]"Farmers" are defined as male household heads who were recorded in the agriculture schedule.

TABLE 21   *Business Firms in Orange County's Towns, 1866–80*

	Number of Firms in		
	Chapel Hill	Hillsborough	Durham
1866	12	34	5
1867	17	31	8
1868	14	32	11
1869	14	26	10
1870	14	28	13
1871	16	33	15
1872	15	35	25
1873	11	31	35
1874	19	30	40
1875	12	31	43
1876	15	36	66
1877	16	28	67
1878	16	26	72
1879	20	30	83
1880	18	31	100

SOURCE: R.G. Dun & Co., *The Mercantile Agency Reference Book*, 1866–80, 15 vols., July issue, Library of Congress.

TABLE 22 Estimated Worth of Business Firms in Orange County's Towns: 1870, 1875, 1880

Estimated Worth	1870			1875			1880		
	Chapel Hill	Hillsborough	Durham	Chapel Hill	Hillsborough	Durham	Chapel Hill	Hillsborough	Durham
$250,000+	0	0	0	0	0	0	0	0	2
$100,000–249,999	0	0	0	0	0	0	0	0	1
$50,000–99,999	0	1	0	0	0	2	0	0	1
$25,000–49,999	1	0	0	2	0	1	0	1	7
$10,000–24,999	0	0	1	2	4	8	3	5	7
$5000–9999	1	3	1	3	3	7	3	1	8
$2000–4999	1	4	3	0	5	9	1	4	12
Under $2000	11	20	8	5	19	16	11	20	62
	14	28	13	12	31	43	18	31	100

SOURCE: Same as Table 21.

TABLE 23 *Profile of Postbellum Active Party Participants, 1868–78*

A. *Primary Occupation in 1870*

	Farmer	Profes-sional	White Collar	Blue Collar	Merchant	Manu-facturer	None
Conservative[a]	74.4%	6.6%	5.4%	3.6%	4.2%	.6%	1.2%
White Republican[b]	71.0	19.4	3.2	6.4	0	0	0
Black Republican[b]	64.7	0	0	35.3	0	0	0

B. *Value of Real Estate in 1870*

	$0	Less than $250	Less than $500	Less than $1000	More than $1000
Antebellum Whigs and Democrats[c]	11.1%	18.3%	31.9%	55.4%	44.6%
Conservative[c]	6.6	7.2	16.2	38.9	61.1
White Republican	29.0	32.2	45.1	70.9	29.1
Black Republican	64.7	70.3	88.2	94.1	5.9

C. *Former Party Affiliation of Conservatives in 1870*

Whig	46.7%	(The antebellum party affiliations could only be
Democrat	53.3%	identified for 60 of the 167 Conservatives.)

SOURCES: U.S. Census MS., Orange County, Schedules 1 and 2. For the names of the Conservative active party participants, see *Hillsborough Recorder*, Mar. 3, Aug. 5, 19, 1868; Apr. 27, May 4, June 1, 1870; Apr. 18, 29, May 6, 13, 1874; Sept. 9, 1875; Mar. 29, Apr. 26, May 24, 31, Aug. 2, 30, 1876; Apr. 24, May 16, 22, 29, Oct. 9, 1878; *Durham Tobacco Plant*, May 9, 1876; *Chapel Hill Ledger*, May 18, Oct. 10, 1878. For the names of the Republican active party participants, see *Hillsborough Recorder*, July 28, 1869; July 13, 1870; June 3, 1874; July 5, 1876; Mary Hastings et al. to William W. Holden, May 23, 1868, William N. Craige to William W. Holden, June 21, 1868, William W. Holden Papers, North Carolina Division of Archives and History, Raleigh, N.C.; "National Republican Ticket," Dec. 1870, in William A. Graham Papers, Southern Historical Collection, University of North Carolina Library, Chapel Hill, N.C.; Robert G. Fitzgerald Diary, Jan. 2, 1869, Fitzgerald Family Papers, microfilm copy, Southern Historical Collection.

TABLE 23 *Continued*

^aAlthough 293 active participants could be identified for the Conservative party, it was possible to provide a profile only for those 167 who headed a household and did not share their name with another man.

^bAlthough 81 active participants could be identified for the Republican party, it was possible to provide a profile for only 48 (31 white and 17 black) who headed a household and did not share their name with another man. More white Republican active participants could be found because the rate of persistence for whites on the whole was considerably higher. This also meant that the real estate holdings of those blacks who could be found— who persisted from the 1870 federal manuscript census until the time they were noted as belonging to the party—tended to be unusually high for blacks.

^cBecause the distribution and concentration of real estate was nearly identical in 1850 and 1870 for all white male household heads (see Table 7 and Table 8), the variation between the periods was not caused by a change in land values.

TABLE 24 *Correlations for Elections in which Josiah Turner Ran as an Independent, 1876–80*

	Republican Vote for Governor, 1876	Vote for Turner, 1876	Vote for Turner, 1878	Republican Vote for Governor, 1880
Vote for Turner, 1876	.80			
Vote for Turner, 1878	.41	.57		
Republican Vote for Governor, 1880	.92	.64	.48	
Vote for Turner, 1880	.66	.66	.67	.79

SOURCES: *Hillsborough Recorder*, Nov. 15, 1876; Aug. 14, 1878; Records of Elections By Precincts, Orange County Miscellaneous Papers, Nov. 1880, North Carolina Division of Archives and History, Raleigh, N.C.

Notes

*Abbreviations of Manuscript Collections
Used in Notes*

DU   Manuscript Department, William R. Perkins Library, Duke
University, Durham, N.C.

NCC   North Carolina Collection, University of North Carolina
Library, Chapel Hill, N.C.

SHC   Southern Historical Collection, University of North Carolina
Library, Chapel Hill, N.C.

NCDAH   North Carolina Division of Archives and History,
Raleigh, N.C.

BL-HBS   Baker Library, Harvard University Graduate School of Business
Administration, Boston, Mass.

Chapter 1

1. Ruth Blackwelder, *The Age of Orange: Political and Intellectual Leadership in North Carolina, 1752–1861* (Charlotte, N.C.: William Loftin, 1961), 9.

2. For the reasons for their migration to North Carolina, see Robert W. Ramsey, *Carolina Cradle: Settlement of the Northwest Carolina Frontier, 1747–1762* (Chapel Hill: Univ. of North Carolina Press, 1964), 3–50; Harry Roy Merrens, *Colonial North Carolina in the Eighteenth Century: A Study in Historical Geography* (Chapel Hill: Univ. of North Carolina Press, 1964), 3–31. Merrens provides the best description of the demographic factors in migration.

3. For evidence of their Old World bond, see David I. Craig, *A Historical Sketch of the New Hope Church, in Orange County, North Carolina* (Reidsville, N.C.: S.W. Paisley, 1886), 5–10; Luther M. Sharpe Genealogy, Luther M. Sharpe Papers, DU. The Luther M. Sharpe Genealogy indicates that John Freeland was born in County Londonderry, the probable residence of the other families in northern Ireland.

4. Craig, *Historical Sketch of New Hope*, 16–17; Henry Poellnitz Johnston, *The Gentle Johnstons and Their Kin* (Birmingham: Featon Press, 1966), 86.

5. Craig, *Historical Sketch of New Hope*, 7–10; Herbert Snipes Turner, *Church in the Old Fields: Hawfields Presbyterian Church and Community in North Carolina* (Chapel Hill: Univ. of North Carolina Press, 1962), 34–36. Turner believes that both Gilbert Strayhorn and William Craig first went to the Hawfields and marked the area.

6. Craig, *Historical Sketch of New Hope*, 9–11; Turner, *Church in the Old Fields*, 22.

7. Blackwelder, *Age of Orange*, 11–12.

8. "Autobiography of Col. William Few of Georgia," *Magazine of American History* 7 (Nov. 1881): 344.

9. Francis Nash, "The History of Orange County—Part I," *North Carolina Booklet* 11 (Oct. 1916): 63–68. For a discussion of the development of settlement systems in another southern county during the late seventeenth and early eighteenth centuries, see Darrett B. and Anita H. Rutman, *A Place in Time: Middlesex County, Virginia, 1650–1750* (New York: Norton, 1984), ch. 4.

10. For a description of the Virginian migration to North Carolina, see Merrens, *Colonial North Carolina*, 61–69. For a similar discussion of the relationship between southern migration and church settlement, see Jean E. Friedman, *The Enclosed Garden: Women and the Evangelical South, 1830–1900* (Chapel Hill: Univ. of North Carolina Press, 1984), 7–8.

11. Ruth Herndon Shields et al., comps., *A Study of the Barbee Families of Chatham, Orange, and Wake Counties in North Carolina* (Boulder, Col.: privately published, 1971), 10, copy in NCC.

12. Nash, "The History of Orange," 69–70; L.J. Phipps, "The Churches of Orange County," in Hugh Lefler and Paul Wager, eds., *Orange County, 1752–1952* (Chapel Hill, N.C.: Orange Printshop, 1953), 290–92. In an interview conducted on June 21, 1980, with Mrs. Alfred Engstrom, an expert on the Quakers in Orange County, I was informed of the movement of Quakers into the Presbyterian churches.

13. Phipps, "The Churches in Orange County," 300. Most of the Germans from Pennsylvania settled west of the Haw River.

14. For a list tracing all of the most common surnames in Orange

County from 1775 to 1850, see Robert C. Kenzer, "Portrait of a Southern Community, 1849–1881: Family, Kinship, and Neighborhood in Orange County, North Carolina" (Ph.D. diss., Harvard Univ., 1982), 11–13.

15. For a description of methodology, see Appendix 1-A.

16. Ibid. For another study of an antebellum southern community which uses the term "neighborhood" to designate a unit of a county, see Orville Vernon Burton, *In My Father's House Are Many Mansions: Family and Community in Edgefield, South Carolina* (Chapel Hill: Univ. of North Carolina Press, 1985), 21.

17. I selected the Lloyds because the genealogical papers for this family were more complete than for any other family in the county. Robert Bruce Cooke, "The Thomas Lloyds of North Carolina" (1926), mimeographed copy, NCC.

18. For genealogical charts identifying all of the Lloyd households in 1850 and 1860, see Kenzer, "Orange County," 18–19.

For other studies of the South which examine family ties, see Bertram Wyatt-Brown, "The Ideal Typology and Ante-Bellum Southern History: A Testing of a New Approach," *Societas* 5 (Winter 1975): 1–30; Steven Hahn, *The Roots of Southern Populism: Yeoman Farmers and the Transformation of the Georgia Upcountry, 1850–1880* (New York: Oxford Univ. Press, 1983), 52–54.

19. William L. Saunders, ed., *Colonial Records of North Carolina*, vol. 9 (Raleigh, N.C.: M.P. Hale, 1866–90), 311.

20. *Hillsborough Recorder*, Jan. 6, 1855. The completion of the railroad in 1855 seems to have had a minor impact on the county and especially its rural neighborhoods. The best indication of this, as described in ch. 2, is that the population of the town with the primary depot, Hillsborough, experienced little population change during the 1850s. Because only two depots were built, in Hillsborough and Durham, neighborhood residents probably still had to travel to one of these towns to take advantage of this new form of transportation.

21. Adolphus Williamson Mangum Diary, June 24, 1852 and Feb. 8, 1857, Mangum Family Papers, SHC.

22. Minutes of the Orange County Board of Commissioners, Dec. 17, 1868, NCDAH. Although this concern was not expressed in writing until after the Civil War, it was demonstrated prior to 1860 by how the school borders were drawn.

23. Of the 42 different surnames of white male members of the Little River Presbyterian Church from 1823 to 1860, the 16 most common ones (38.1% of all surnames) composed 89 out of 115 members (77.4% of members). An examination of the rural churches throughout the county demonstrates the same pattern. For example, in the Eno Presbyterian

Church from 1822 to 1860, 34.8% of the most common surnames composed 70.9% of the membership; in the Cane Creek Baptist Church in 1856, 33.3% composed 66.3%; in the New Hope Presbyterian Church from 1820 to 1851, 34.6% composed 60.6%; and in the Mount Moriah Baptist from 1840 to 1867, 33.3% composed 60.5% (Little River Presbyterian Church Session Books, 1-2, Little River Presbyterian Church, microfilm copy in NCDAH; Eno Presbyterian Church Session Minutes, 1822–74, microfilm copy, ibid.; Cane Creek Baptist Church Roll, 1829–56, microfilm copy, ibid.; New Hope Presbyterian Church Register and Session Minutes, 1816–1950, microfilm copy, ibid.; Charles Edward Maddry, "History of Mount Moriah Church," SHC).

For two additional studies which note the role of the church within the context of the rural neighborhood, see Burton, *In My Father's House Are Many Mansions*, 31–32; Friedman, *The Enclosed Garden*, 7.

24. Little River Presbyterian Session Books, July 18, Sept. 17, 1847.

25. Donald G. Mathews, *Religion in the Old South* (Chicago: Univ. of Chicago Press, 1977), ch. 2.

26. This low rate of excommunication for the Little River Presbyterian Church was similar to that of other denominations in North Carolina. See Cortland Victor Smith, "Church Organization as an Agency of Social Control: Church Discipline in North Carolina, 1800–1860" (Ph.D. diss., Univ. of North Carolina at Chapel Hill, 1966).

27. Mathews, *Religion in the Old South*, 40–46. Mathews points out how discipline was used to preserve the bonds of the community rather than to drive out members and how "sincere repentence" usually prevented permanent excommunication. For another excellent discussion of the role of church discipline, see Friedman, *The Enclosed Garden*, 11–15.

28. Lambert W. Hall to Frances N. Bennett, Sept. 14, 1857, Frances N. Bennett Papers, DU. Few letters of this type exist from this period because, as will be discussed shortly, fiancés rarely lived far enough from one another to make corresponding necessary. In this case this woman lived just across the county border in Caswell County and apparently did not often see her fiancé.

29. Ibid., Nov. 18, 1857.

30. Dr. Benjamin F. Mebane to Frances L. Kerr, Aug. 22, 1857, Mebane Family Papers, SHC. For another example of these visits, see Bettie Stanford to Ellen Hedrick, Sept. 9, 1859, Benjamin Sherwood Hedrick Papers, DU.

31. This does not mean that marriage did not occur between people who lived in two different neighborhoods. In fact, there seems to have been a number of marriages between residents of White Cross and neighboring Cane Creek. This was probably the case because the Lloyds and

many of the other residents of White Cross were, like most of the families of Cane Creek, Baptists. Therefore, many of the people who lived on the northern border of the White Cross neighborhood resided as close to the Cane Creek Baptist Church as to the Bethel Baptist Church in White Cross. Further, since preachers would hold services in one rural church one week and another church the next week, those members who resided within traveling distance of the two churches could attend services at both.

32. Sharpe Genealogy. As an example, Mary Jane Strayhorn had both an aunt and uncle who were Freelands.

33. The close parent-child residence was not the result of early marriages, as newlyweds in Orange, particularly grooms, were married at a rather late age for American society. During the 1850s in Orange the mean age at marriage for grooms was 27.1 years and for brides 22.8 years. Unfortunately, the records do not indicate whether it was the first marriage. For a distribution of the age at marriage and the methodology used to calculate the age, see Kenzer, "Orange County," 26, 190.

Although there has been little research done on the age at marriage for whites in mid-nineteenth-century America, the age at marriage for men in Orange seems to be higher than for other communities. For Orange and Greene counties, Virginia, John T. Schlotterbeck has found the age at first marriage from 1856–60 to be 25.5 years for men and 22.8 years for women, in "Plantation and Farm: Social and Economic Change in Orange and Greene Counties, Virginia, 1716 to 1860" (Ph.D. diss., Johns Hopkins Univ., 1980), 100. For New Jersey in this period Thomas P. Monahan has calculated that the age at first marriage for native-born white men was 25.3 years, in *Pattern of Age at Marriage in the United States*, vol. 2 (Philadelphia: privately published, 1951), 253. For the various regions of Alabama, William L. Barney has found age at marriage for white men to range from 21.5 to 26.2 years, in "Patterns of Crisis: Alabama White Families and Social Change, 1850–1870," *Sociology and Social Research* 63 (Apr. 1979): 540n.

34. Only a small amount of correspondence exists from this period because little was written. The neighborhood structure made it unnecessary for someone to correspond with a relative or close friend who resided within a few miles. By the time a letter was written, mailed, and received, the sender and recipient would have seen one another.

35. Mangum Diary, July 9, 1852.

36. One scholar who has observed this relationship between people and place, though for an earlier era, is Rhys Isaac, "Dramatizing the Revolution: Popular Mobilization in Virginia, 1774 to 1776," *William and Mary Quarterly* 33 (July 1976): 357–85, esp. 364–65.

37. Mangum Diary, July 2, 1852; Oct. 19, 1854.

38. Ibid., Aug. 3, 1852.

39. *Hillsborough Recorder*, May 19, 1852; Nov. 2, 1853; May 16, 1860.

40. Mangum Diary, June 24, 27, July 9, 20, 26; Aug. 8, 9, 11, 1852. For a description of close kin residential and visiting patterns in another Southern location during this era, see Schlotterbeck, "Plantation and Farm," 150, 242–44.

41. Ibid., July 9, Aug. 15, 1852.

42. U.S. Census MS., Orange County, 1860, Schedule 1. Of the 2125 white household heads in 1860, 357 (16.8%) were women. Of the 1768 white male household heads in 1860, 106 (6.0%) were men aged 70 or older.

43. Ibid. Of the 106 men aged seventy or over who headed households, 25 (23.6%) resided next door to some one with the same surname. This was true for 60 of the 357 women (16.8%) who headed households.

44. Patterson H. McDade to John A. McDade, Dec. 5, 1853, John A. McDade Letters and Papers, DU.

45. Orange County Court Minutes, 1850–54. In 23 out of 52 cases (44.2%), the guardian had the same name as the orphan.

46. It is difficult to compare rates of persistence because various writers have used different groups to calculate this measurement. Two writers, however, have selected a similar group to the one provided here in their studies of southern counties. For Clarke County, Georgia, Frank J. Huffman, Jr., found that 41.2% of the men aged 20 and over were persistent during the 1850s. William L. Barney has found rates of persistence for this group ranging from 24.5% to 36.6%, depending on the region investigated in Alabama. For their findings, see Frank J. Huffman, Jr., "Old South, New South: Continuity and Change in a Georgia County, 1850–1880," (Ph.D. diss., Yale Univ., 1974), 35; Barney, "Patterns of Crisis," 532. In his work, *In My Father's House Are Many Mansions*, 31–32, Orville Vernon Burton notes that the rate of persistence for white household heads in Edgefield, South Carolina, during the 1850s was "slightly more than 40 percent," but he includes women household heads.

The rate of persistence in Orange was much higher than in Midwest communities, which averaged around 30 percent for this period. For two of the better community studies that measure the rate of persistence for this period, see Mildred Throne, "A Population Study of an Iowa County in 1850," *Iowa Journal of History* 27 (Oct. 1959): 305–30; Don Harrison Doyle, *The Social Order of a Frontier Community: Jacksonville, Illinois, 1825–1870* (Urbana: Univ. of Illinois Press, 1978), 261.

47. Death as a factor in rate of persistence can be removed by calculating survival rates for the age cohorts for this period. For one study that

TABLE A *Rate of Persistence and Survival Rate, 1850–60*

Age	White Male Household Heads	All White Males Age 20 and Older
20–29	52.6%	50.7%
30–39	69.0	65.0
40–49	79.8	77.7
50–59	80.7	80.0
60–69	100.0	98.8
70+	93.8	85.0
Total:	71.8%	64.7%

TABLE B *Rate of Persistence by Name, 1850–60*

	Percent Persistent, 1850–60	Percent with No Real Estate in 1850	Percent with No Slaves in 1850
All White Male Household Heads in 1850	55.9%	40.0%	67.4%
White Male Household Heads in 1850 Who Shared Their Surname with 7 or More Others	64.1%	37.1%	70.4%

provides these survival rates, see Michael B. Katz et al., "Migration and the Social Order in Erie County, New York: 1855," *Journal of Interdisciplinary History* 8 (Spring 1978): 678. With death removed as a factor, the rates of persistence in Orange, using the survival rate suggested by Katz et al., are listed in table A.

48. U.S. Census MS., Orange County, 1850, 1860, Schedules 1, 2, and 4. The rate of persistence for male household heads who owned slaves was 58.4%, compared to 54.7% for nonslaveholders.

Another indication that there was no significant link between the rate of persistence and ownership of real estate and slaves is found by comparing the wealth of the most persistent men, white male household heads in 1850 who shared their surname with seven or more other household heads, with the wealth of all white male household heads in 1850. As table B indicates, however, there was little difference between these two groups.

49. In 1860, less than 10% of the total number of whites in Orange County lived in the towns of Hillsborough, Chapel Hill, and Durham. Many of these town residents were in fact farmers and planters and therefore should not be considered as true urban dwellers. Of the 11,311 whites in 1860, 567 lived in Hillsborough, about 250 lived in Chapel Hill, and fewer than 100 in Durham. For population figures for Hillsborough and Durham, see *Hillsborough Recorder*, Oct. 24, 1860; William Kenneth Boyd, *The Story of Durham: City of the New South* (Durham, N.C.: Duke Univ. Press, 1925), 97.

50. In 1860, the distribution of heads of household in Orange by place of birth was 97.1% born in North Carolina, 2.5% born in United States but not North Carolina, and .4% foreign born.

The impact of the foreign-born population in lowering the rate of persistence has been documented in Merle Curti, *The Making of an American Community: A Case Study of Democracy in a Frontier Community* (Stanford, Calif.: Stanford Univ. Press, 1959), 72–73; Michael B. Katz et al., "Migration and the Social Order," 682–93; Peter R. Knights, *The Plain People of Boston, 1830–1860* (New York: Oxford Univ. Press, 1971), 63.

Orange County's predominantly native-born population was the norm for southern states. Further, it appears that the older states of the South were not only inhabited by a native-born population but by a population born within the borders of those states. Given more time to develop, the states on the southern frontier would have probably evolved more like the states to the east. For a comparison of the regional structure of the native-born population, see U.S. Census Office, Eighth Census (1860), *Population of the United States in 1860 Compiled from the Original Returns of the Eighth Census* (Washington, D.C.: Government Printing Office, 1864), 622–23.

51. Hugh Talmadge Lefler and Albert Ray Newsome, *The History of a Southern State: North Carolina*, 3rd ed. (Chapel Hill: Univ. of North Carolina Press, 1973), 321.

52. The sex ratio for 20- and 30-year-olds was 89.6 men per 100 women in 1850 and 88.9 men per 100 women in 1860.

53. In his study of Chelsea Township, *Those Who Stayed Behind: Rural Society in Nineteenth-Century New England* (Cambridge: Cambridge Univ. Press, 1984), Hal Barron indicates that Chelsea's rate of persistence for white male household heads between 1860 and 1880 was 34.3%. For the same two decades in Orange County, North Carolina, the rate was

28.0%. The difference between the rates can be accounted for by the fact that in 1860 only 32.8% of Chelsea's male household heads were ages 20 to 39, the ages when men were most likely to migrate or, during the 1860s, die in the Civil War. By comparison, in 1860, 43.7% of Orange County's male household heads were in this age range. Even more striking is the difference between the percent of all white men in 1860 between ages 20 and 39. In Chelsea only 43.4% of its men were in this age range compared to Orange County where 59.9% were.

There also is reason to believe that the Civil War had a much more severe impact on Orange County's white male population, and therefore lowered its rate of persistence, than it did on Chelsea's. Between 1860 and 1870 the sex ratio between the number of white men and women ages 20 to 39 in Chelsea declined, but from only 90.8 to 88.0 men per 100 women. In Orange County it fell from 88.9 to 61.6. See U.S. Census MS., Orange County, N.C., and Chelsea Township (Orange County), Vt., 1860 and 1870, Schedule 1.

54. By "traditional" it is meant the interpretation of Frederick Jackson Turner, who attempted to draw a distinction between the liberating quality of the frontier where, he believed, every family was a "self-sufficing" unit and the tradition-bound structure of society to the east. For this interpretation, see Frederick Jackson Turner, *The Frontier in American History* (New York: Holt, 1920), 153-54. For a much different interpretation, one which is similar to my findings for Orange, see Doyle, *The Social Order of a Frontier Community*, 92-118.

55. Johnston, *The Gentle Johnstons*, 138-42, 152, 172-75, 216-22, 235-46. Within one generation cousins in Greene were marrying one another, as were their relatives in Orange.

56. For examples of relatives moving to the same types of communities in the border states and in the Midwest, see Florence (Ray) Lewis and William A. Ray, "The Rays (Raes) Down through the Years," 1-10, copy in Hillsborough Public Library, Hillsborough, N.C.; Johnston, *The Gentle Johnstons*, 107-19.

57. Blackwelder, *The Age of Orange*, 9-10. In 1860 blacks composed 33.2% of the total population. Of the 5636 blacks, 5108 (90.6%) were slaves.

58. George P. Rawick, ed., *The American Slave: A Composite Autobiography*, vol. 15 (Westport, Conn.: Greenwood, 1972), 313.

59. Ibid., vol. 14, 303.

60. U.S. Census MS., Orange County, 1860, Schedules 1 and 2.

61. Rawick, *The American Slave*, vol. 15, 35. For a similar account by another of the Cameron slaves, see ibid., vol. 14, 296.

62. Guion Griffis Johnson, *Ante-bellum North Carolina: A Social His-*

tory (Chapel Hill: Univ. of North Carolina Press, 1937), 538–39. Johnson presents an excellent discussion of the legal question of slave marriages.

63. Rawick, *The American Slave*, vol. 14, 329.

64. Ibid., 360.

65. Orange County Negro Cohabitation Certificates, 1866–68, NCDAH. Of 897 certificates noting the year of marriage, 588 (65.5%) were before 1860.

66. Herbert G. Gutman, *The Black Family in Slavery and Freedom, 1750–1925* (New York: Pantheon, 1976), 169–90. Gutman focuses specifically on the Cameron plantation of Orange County.

67. An example of how these slaves chose spouses who lived nearby is shown in the testimony of ex-slave Robert Glenn, who noted that his mother belonged to Robert Hall and his father to the Glenns (probably the family of James S. Glenn, who resided in household #1640 in the 1860 census). In 1860 Robert Hall resided in the Little River neighborhood, and his household in the census was #1636. For Robert Glenn's testimony, see Rawick, *The American Slave*, vol. 14, 329. For a detailed analysis of slave inheritance patterns, see ch. 2.

Chapter 2

1. U.S. Census MS., Orange County, 1850, 1860, Schedules 1 and 4. There was a substantial difference between the percentages of household heads, normally middle-aged and older men, and nonhousehold heads, primarily younger men, whose primary occupation was not farming but who were listed in the agriculture schedule as farm operators. In 1850, 17.2% of the men who were household heads but were not classified as farmers by occupation were listed in the agriculture schedule as farm operators. In comparison, only .5% of the nonhousehold heads were listed. In 1860, the figures for household heads was 15.1% and for nonhousehold heads, 5.0%. This pattern was most pronounced for those men who were classified as professionals and white collar workers. In 1850, 38.7% of household heads and none of nonhousehold heads who were professionals and white collar workers were listed in the agriculture schedule as farm operators. In 1860 the comparable measurement was 23.2% for household heads and 5.1% for nonhousehold heads.

2. U.S. Census MS., Orange County, 1860, Schedule 5. In 1860, 26 of the 53 manufacturing firms were mills.

3. U.S. Census MS., Orange County, 1860, Schedules 4 and 5. The tanners, blacksmiths, wool carders, wagon makers, and carriage builders accounted for 19 of the 53 manufacturing firms. The capital invested in

these firms, with but one exception, was less than $2300 and averaged $692. This compares to $2165 for the average value of a farm, including implements and machinery.

4. U.S. Census MS., Orange County, 1860, Schedules 1 and 5. Of the 50 workers for Orange Factory, 30 were women. Of the 20 women who worked for the factory that I have been able to find in the population schedule, 7 were under 20 and 8 were in their 20s.

5. Ibid. The value of the finished cotton yarn and plug tobacco was less than twice the amount of the raw materials, cotton and tobacco. This increase in value was similar to that for such skilled crafts as blacksmithing and tanning. If the final products had been cloth or cigarettes, the increase in value would have been much greater.

For the reliance of the cotton firms on the locally grown cotton, see D.C. Parrish to John H. Webb and John C. Douglass, Apr. 10, 1854; M. Harris to John H. Webb and John C. Douglass, May 9, 1854; Thomas Ferrill to John H. Webb and John C. Douglass, Sept. 9, 1854, James Webb Papers, SHC.

6. Boyd, *The Story of Durham*, 25–32, 58–59.

7. U.S. Census MS., Orange County, 1860, Schedule 1. For a business directory of Chapel Hill, see *Chapel Hill Literary Gazette*, Dec. 25, 1857.

8. Lucy Battle to a brother, Mar. 7, 1851, Battle Family Papers, SHC.

9. Kemp P. Battle, *History of the University of North Carolina*, vol. 1 (Raleigh, N.C.: Edwards and Broughton, 1907), 607–91.

10. Jesse H. Persons to a sister, July 28, 1860, Southgate-Jones Papers, DU; Battle, *History of the University*, vol. 1 690–91, 832–33.

11. U.S. Census MS., Orange County, 1860, Schedule 1.

12. For Hillsborough's population, see *Hillsborough Recorder*, Nov. 13, 1850; Oct. 24, 1860.

13. William S. Powell, "Dictionary of Orange County Biography," in Lefler and Wager, eds., *Orange County*, 328.

14. Allen Alexander Lloyd and Pauline O. Lloyd, *History of the Town of Hillsborough, 1754–1966* (n.p.: privately published, n.d.), 117–19, 149–54.

15. Eva Ingersoll Gatling, "John Berry of Hillsboro, North Carolina," *Journal of Architecture Historians* 10 (1951): 18–22. For Berry's work on Hillsborough homes, see Lucile Noell Dula, *Hillsborough: Historic Orange County, North Carolina* (Gretna, La.: Pelican, 1979); U.S. Census MS., Orange County, 1860, Schedule 1.

16. Since there are no soil survey maps for Orange County from the mid-nineteenth century, I have relied on maps from the 1920s. There is no reason to believe that the soil had changed considerably by this later period. In addition, because of their complex shapes, I have only portrayed the

TABLE C *Crop Population by Location, 1860*

Percent of Farmers Producing	North of Railroad	South of Railroad	Total
Cotton	2.5%	5.0%	3.7%
Tobacco	74.9	6.8	45.7
Corn	94.4	99.2	96.7
Wheat	93.0	95.6	94.2

approximate borders of the soil types in order to fit them to the scale of Map 3.

17. U.S. Census MS., Orange County, 1860, Schedules 1 and 4. Table C shows crop production by location in 1860. Note that all agricultural statistics are actually for the production years 1849, 1859, 1869, 1879, but for the simplicity of expression they will be termed 1850, 1860, 1870, 1880.

18. In his excellent study of antebellum tobacco production John Clarke Robert shows that the southern border of the tobacco area of Virginia and North Carolina in 1860 coincided almost perfectly with the North Carolina Central Railroad. See Joseph Clarke Robert, *The Tobacco Kingdom* (Durham, N.C.: Duke Univ. Press, 1938), esp. map facing p. 18.

19. Nannie May Tilley, *The Bright-Tobacco Industry, 1860–1929* (Chapel Hill: Univ. of North Carolina Press, 1948), 14.

20. For information on the yield for tobacco, see Robert, *The Tobacco Kingdom*, 18, 249–51. I believe Robert's estimate of 650 to 700 pounds per acre may be a bit too high for Orange County, where I think the average was about 500 pounds per acre.

21. For the following account of the various stages of tobacco production, see Tilley, *The Bright-Tobacco Industry*, 37–82; Robert, *The Tobacco Kingdom*, 32–50.

22. U.S. Census MS., Orange County, 1860, Schedules 1, 2, and 4. The 37 slaveholders—8.2% of the tobacco growers—who produced more than 5000 pounds of tobacco, grew a total of 307,122 pounds, or 30.3% of the county's entire crop.

23. U.S. Census MS., Orange County, 1860, Schedules 1 and 4. Sam Bowers Hilliard, *Hog Meat and Hoecake: Food Supply in the Old South, 1840–1860* (Carbondale: Southern Illinois Univ. Press, 1972), esp. 150–71.

Although I have used Hilliard's formula for annual human corn consumption (13 bushels), I have omitted his figures for consumption by livestock. It seems to me that if farmers were not producing enough corn for themselves, they would have slaughtered their swine rather than feed them corn. In addition, since most farmers in Orange grew sufficient amounts of oats to provide for their horses and mules, corn consumption by these animals would have been insignificant. I have not converted all grains into corn-equivalents based on nutritional content, as others have who have studied this question, because in 1850 so few farmers fell below the human consumption average and because production of most grains followed the patterns of corn. It should be stressed that it is only possible to measure self-sufficiency for those farmers who headed households and were listed in the agriculture schedule of the census as farm operators. Only 144 of the 1051 farmers (13.7%) were not producing enough corn for the needs of the free and slave populations of their household. For a number of reasons, however, all 144 of these farmers should not be thought of as having consumed less than the necessary amount of food. Since 33 of them had occupations in addition to farming, they could have purchased food from the income they made from these other pursuits. Equally important, 95 of the remaining 111 farmers (85.6%) produced amounts of wheat above the national average for per capita consumption. Therefore, they could have supplemented their diets with this grain. Finally, tobacco production does not seem to have prevented food production. Of the 144 farmers who did not produce enough corn, only 53 of them (36.5%) grew tobacco. Of these 53, only 7 (13.2%) did not produce enough wheat to make up for the shortage of corn. For two other studies of southern communities during this era which measure self-sufficiency, see Schlotterbeck, "Farm and Plantation," 166–67, 228–29; J. William Harris, *Plain Folk and Gentry in a Slave Society: White Liberty and Black Slavery in Augusta's Hinterlands* (Middletown, Conn.: Wesleyan Univ. Press, 1985), 30–32.

24. Records of the Wardens of the Orange County Poorhouse, 1850–60, NCDAH; U.S. Census MS., Orange County, 1850, 1860, Schedule 1.

Of the 47 people in the poorhouse in 1850 and 1860, 61.7%, were either under 9 years of age or over 60. In 1850, of the 25 people in the poorhouse, 4 were orphans and 6 were classified as being either "insane" or "idiots." For an analysis of the treatment of these mentally disturbed individuals, see *Hillsborough Recorder*, Sept. 7, 1853. For Adolphus Mangum's assistance to his aunt Dicey, see ch. 1.

25. Long, Webb and Co. Account Book, 1847–48, Richard D. White Collection, NCDAH; Leathers, Latta and Co. Day Book, 1854–56, DU.

26. Long, Webb and Co. Account Book, June 17 to Nov. 17, 1848; U.S. Census MS., Orange County, 1850, Schedule 1. Only those customers are listed who were male household heads and could be found in the manuscript census.

27. Ibid.; Parker and Nelson Account Book, 1847–53, SHC. Nearly

half of the 77 male household heads who made at least 10 purchases at this store in 1850 and could be found in the census resided directly in the town or to its immediate north or northwest. This fact is confirmed by tracing the 42 of these men who remained in Orange until 1860. Only 7 of these 42 men lived south of the North Carolina Central Railroad which ran directly south of the town.

28. For evidence that nearly all purchases in general stores, whether in the rural neighborhoods or in the towns, were made on credit, see Long, Webb and Co. Account Book, Dec. 1847 to Oct. 1848; Leathers, Latta and Co. Day Book, 1854 to 1856, North Carolina Mercantile Books, SHC; Leathers, Latta and Co. Day Book, Sept. to Dec. 1854, DU; Parker and Nelson Account Book, 1850, SHC; Stephen Moore Ledger, 1850, Stephen Moore Papers, SHC. For a comparable discussion of the role of credit in rural general stores, see Schlotterbeck, "Farm and Plantation," 220.

29. U.S. Census MS., Orange County, 1850, 1860, Schedules 1 and 2. In 1850, of these white male household heads who were either classified as farmers or were listed in the agriculture schedule of the manuscript census as farm operators, 33.6% owned slaves. By 1860, this figure had fallen to 30.5%.

30. Ibid. For farmers alone, the top 10% owned 70.7% of all slaves in 1850 and 76.9% in 1860.

31. Ibid. For farmers alone, 36.4% owned no real estate in 1850.

32. Ibid., Schedule 1 and 4. It should be stressed that total acreage was even more concentrated than is indicated by Table 9 because I omitted farmers who were not listed in the agriculture schedule. In addition, many who were listed in the agriculture schedule did not own the land they farmed but were farm laborers or renters.

33. Michael B. Katz, *The People of Hamilton Canada West: Family and Class in a Mid-Nineteenth Century City* (Cambridge: Harvard Univ. Press, 1975), 112. For some of the studies which have investigated the distribution of wealth in the United States in this era, see Lee Soltow, *Men and Wealth in the United States, 1850–1870* (New Haven: Yale Univ. Press, 1975); Edward Pessen, *Riches, Classes, and Power before the Civil Power* (Lexington, Mass.: Heath, 1973), Richard B. Campbell and Richard G. Lowe, *Wealth and Power in Antebellum Texas* (College Station: Texas A&M Univ. Press, 1977); Frank L. Owsley, *Plain Folk of the Old South* (Baton Rouge: Louisiana State Univ. Press, 1949); Gavin Wright, *The Political Economy of the Cotton South: Household, Markets, and Wealth in the Nineteenth Century* (New York: Norton, 1978).

34. For the relationship between wealth and rate of persistence, see ch. 1, n. 48 and Table 3.B.

35. Ibid. Between 1850 and 1860, 50 out of 581 nonslaveholders

TABLE D   *Individuals Inheriting Slaves in Twenty-four Wills, 1850–61*

Relationship to Testator	Different Surname Than Testator	Same Surname As Testator
wife	0	2
son(s)	0	8
daughter(s)	9 (all married)	2
grandchildren	1	4
sister	1	0
niece or nephew	2	0
wife's children by previous marriage	1	0
relationship not specified	1	0

NOTE: that more than one person could inherit a slave in each will.

(8.6%) gained the following numbers of slaves: 1 slave, 22 nonslaveholders; 2–4 slaves, 18; 5–9 slaves, 8; 10–14 slaves, 1; 15–19 slaves, 1.

Between 1850 and 1860, 59 out of 325 persistent slaveholders (18.2%) lost all of their slaves after beginning the decade with the following numbers of slaves: 1 slave, 28 slaveholders; 2–4 slaves, 22; 5–9 slaves, 6; 10–14 slaves, 1; 15–19 slaves, 2. For a comparative examination, see Harris, *Plain Folk and Gentry*, 87, 205.

36. Some historical accounts describing the ownership of real estate and slaves include Wright, *The Political Economy of the Cotton South*; Campbell and Lowe, *Wealth and Power in Antebellum Texas*.

37. Orange County Wills, vols. F and G, Office of the Clerk of the Civil Court, Orange County Courthouse, Hillsborough, N.C. Only those wills that were written by male testators between 1850 and 1861 (prior to the outbreak of the Civil War) and probated within five years were analyzed. Only 24 of these 50 wills involved the transfer of property, as many parents gave their adult children property previous to their death.

In 15 out of 24 wills (62.5%) the heir who inherited slaves had a different surname from the testator (see table D).

38. Hahn, *The Roots of Southern Populism*, 69.

39. Orange County Wills, vols. F and G. For documentation of the transfer of personal estate, see Inventories, Sales, and Accounts of Estates for Orange County, 1849–60, NCDAH. See "The Property of Delia Lloyd Sold by Thomas M. Lloyd," Inventories, February Term, 1852.

40. U.S. Census MS., Orange County, 1850, 1860, Schedules 1 and 2. There were 43 male household heads in 1850 and 42 in 1860 who owned at least 20 slaves. The problem with the contention that those who owned 20 slaves formed a distinct group becomes evident from the outset because a number of these men had sons who were household heads but owned fewer than 20 slaves.

Although it would be helpful to describe how large each of these two groups of planters were, it is impossible because of the intermarriage which began to take place between them to make a firm distinction between them (see note 45 below). Nevertheless, if they are defined strictly in terms of having or not having an ancestor who was an original settler of the county, the two groups would be fairly equal in size by 1860.

An excellent analysis of the diversity of slaveholders and planters can be found in James Oakes, *The Ruling Race: A History of American Slave-holders* (New York: Knopf, 1982), ch. 2.

41. Fletcher M. Green, "Slavery in Orange County," in Lefler and Wager, eds., *Orange County*, 95-96.

42. U.S. Census MS., Orange County, 1850, 1860, Schedules 1, 2, 4; Shields et al., comps., *A Study of the Barbee Families.*

43. For their membership in this church, see Maddry, "History of Mount Moriah Church," SHC.

44. For a few examples of their involvement in banking and transportation, see *Hillsborough Recorder*, Mar. 21, 1849, Dec. 5, 1849; Sept. 20, 1854; Mar. 5, 1859.

45. For example, in 1819, Willie P. Mangum married Charity Cain, William Cain's sister. The Mangums resided in the Flat River neighborhood and the Cains in the neighboring Little River neighborhood.

46. Charles Richard Sanders, *The Cameron Plantation in Central North Carolina, 1776-1973* (Durham, N.C.: Seeman, 1974); U.S. Census MS., Orange County, 1860, Schedules 1 and 2.

47. See note 13 above.

48. See note 44 above.

49. St. Matthew's Episcopal Church Records, 1824-60, microfilm copy in NCDAH. St. Matthew's was the Episcopal Church in Hillsborough.

50. Of the 42 men in 1860 with 20 or more slaves, 5 lived in Chapel Hill and 10 in Hillsborough. Of these 15 men, 12 fit into the description of this second group of planters.

51. For Orville Vernon Burton's description of the diversity of the planter elite in Edgefield, South Carolina, see *In My Father's House Are Many Mansions*, 69.

52. For community studies of the Midwest and East which describe the role of voluntary associations during this era, see Doyle, *The Social*

Order of a Frontier Community, 178–93; Stuart M. Blumin, *The Urban Threshold: Growth and Change in a Nineteenth Century American Community* (Chicago: Univ. of Chicago Press, 1976), 150–89; Mary P. Ryan, *Cradle of the Middle Class: The Family in Oneida County, New York, 1790–1865* (Cambridge: Cambridge Univ. Press, 1981), 105–44.

53. Wallace E. Caldwell, "Fraternal Orders in Orange County," in Lefler and Wager, eds., *Orange County*, 318–20.

54. Proceedings of the Grand Royal Arch Chapter [a listing of the Masonic lodges and their members for North Carolina in 1860], 67–68, 103, copy in NCC; U.S. Census MS., Orange County, 1860, Schedules 1 and 2.

55. James Gill to Thomas Gill, Nov. 11, 1852, Gill Family Papers, DU; "Circular on Masonic Festival for the Anniversary of St. John the Baptist," June 24, 1858, Heartt and Wilson Family Papers, SHC.

56. Only 43 of the 76 members of the Eagle Lodge in 1860 could be identified as household heads. Of the 43, 24 (55.8%) owned slaves. This was nearly twice the countywide average for slaveholding (28.4%). Equally significant, of the 25 Masons who resided on the north side of the North Carolina Central Railroad but not directly within Hillsborough's borders, 17 (68.0%) owned slaves.

In the Caldwell Lodge, 18 of the 28 members in 1860 could be identified as household heads. Of the 18, 10 (55.6%) owned slaves. Of the 12 Masons who resided outside of Chapel Hill's borders, 8 (66.7%) owned slaves.

57. Paul C. Cameron, "An Address before the Orange County Society for the Promotion of Agriculture, the Mechanical Arts, and Manufactures," 16, in NCC. Only the 1853 membership list for the Agricultural Society exists. This list can be found in "Agricultural Society and Exposition," 1853, Miscellaneous Papers of Orange County, NCDAH. Of the 89 members, 71 could be identified as household heads in 1860. Of these 71, 64 (90.1%) owned slaves.

Of the 21 members of the Agricultural Society's Executive Committee in 1857, 20 (95.2%) owned slaves in 1860. In fact, 11 of the 21 were planters. For a list of the names of the members of the Executive Committee, see *Hillsborough Recorder*, Nov. 4, 1857.

58. See note 52 above, esp. Doyle, *The Social Order of a Frontier Community*, 178–93, for the role played by voluntary associations in communities outside of the South. The other two important voluntary associations in Orange County were the Sons of Temperance and the militia units. These are described in detail in chs. 3 and 4. What is significant about these two associations is that they were centered strictly within the traditional rural neighborhoods. The Sons of Temperance worked directly

through the rural churches. When county conventions of the society met, the neighborhoods were usually represented only by the neighborhood minister or an affluent neighborhood spokesman. The militia units were confined to the the rural neighborhoods in terms of both leadership and membership. For the structure of the Sons of Temperance, see *Hillsborough Recorder*, Aug. 31, Sept. 14, Oct. 12, Nov. 2, 1853; Apr. 19, May 24, 1854.

Chapter 3

1. For the duties of the county court, see Johnson, *Ante-Bellum North Carolina*, 620–22; Thomas Edward Jeffrey, "The Second Party System in North Carolina, 1836–1860" (Ph.D. diss., Catholic Univ. of America, 1976), 85–93; Paul W. Wager, "History of County Government," in Lefler and Wager, eds., *Orange County*, 172–90.

2. Jeffrey, "The Second Party System in North Carolina," 86–87.

3. Orange County Court Minutes, 1850–59, NCDAH. For a discussion of the rapid turnover of the justices of the peace, see Jeffrey, "The Second Party System in North Carolina," 88–89.

4. Ralph A. Wooster, *Politicians, Planters and Plain Folk: Courthouse and Statehouse in the Upper South, 1850–1860* (Knoxville: Univ. of Tennessee Press, 1975), 105–7. Wooster demonstrates how North Carolina experienced the least amount of democratic reforms of any southern state after the 1830s.

5. Ibid., 114–15. The justices of the peace in Orange tended to own about the same amount of real estate as the justices Wooster chose for his North Carolina sample. However, the justices in Orange were more likely to own slaves than those in the Wooster sample. For a description of the wealth of magistrates in other North Carolina counties in 1860, see Paul D. Escott, *Many Excellent People: Power and Privilege in North Carolina, 1850–1900* (Chapel Hill: Univ. of North Carolina Press, 1985), 20.

6. Jeffrey, "The Second Party System in North Carolina," 88–89. Jeffrey provides one of the best discussions of the magistrate's office.

7. Ibid., 89. Since so many justices were often absent, it was necessary before 1855 to establish a Special Court of five magistrates to guarantee that a court session could be held. This Special Court held the potential of promoting stability because the five justices tended to hold their positions on the Special Court for a number of years. In February 1855, however, the Special Court was abolished in favor of a system of rotation which insured that five different justices would be present at each session. For the abolition of the Special Court, see Orange County Court Minutes, Feb. 26, 1855, NCDAH.

TABLE E   *Distribution of Expenditures for County Contingencies*

Year	Total Expenditures	Salaries	Common Schools	Aid For Poor
1856	$ 9432.53	65.2%	18.0%	16.8%
1857	9800.37	66.3	17.4	16.3
1858	9421.03	55.4	15.8	28.8
1859	9837.02	57.7	15.4	26.9

8. *Report of the North Carolina Comptroller of Public Accounts*, 1856–59. The amount of tax per capita was calculated by dividing the average total white and black population in 1850 and 1860 (16,776) by the total expenditures in 1856 ($9432.53). The result was $1.78 per capita. Beginning in 1856, the county's expenditures were distributed as shown in table E.

9. Orange County Court Minutes, 1850–59, NCDAH; U.S. Census MS., Orange County, 1850, Schedule 1. A total of 123 magistrates attended court during the 1850s. Of this total, it was possible to find 106 who headed households in the 1850 census.

10. Orange County Court Minutes, May 27, 1850, NCDAH.

11. For examples of the contractors chosen by the bridge commissioners, see ibid., Feb. 26, 1850; Feb. 26, 1856.

12. Although the following description of the political process is similar to that provided by Jeffrey, "The Second Party System in North Carolina," 119–53, I reached my conclusions by a different method. My description is based strictly on reading the *Hillsborough Recorder* and noting the common patterns from one election year to the next. In contrast, Jeffrey's excellent analysis is based primarily on his use of various newspapers from throughout the state, complemented by correspondences from the 1840s.

My description is of biennial elections in which North Carolina state officials were elected. For off-year elections, when members of the United States House of Representatives were elected, the political process was quite similar.

13. *Hillsborough Recorder*, May 8, 1850.

14. Ibid., May 12, 1852.

15. Ibid., May 19, 1852; May 23, 1860.

16. Although there was no stated reason for it, the Whigs usually met in the courthouse and the Democrats in the Masonic Lodge. Possibly this was a result, as Lee Benson has argued, of the Whigs being in a general sense the successors of the Anti-Masonic movement, in *The Concept of*

Jacksonian Democracy: New York as a Test Case (Princeton: Princeton Univ. Press, 1961), 3–46.

17. For example, in 1854 Willie P. Mangum, the retired United States Senator, served as chairman of the Whig County convention. For his service, see *Hillsborough Recorder*, May 31, 1854.

18. Ibid., Mar. 24, 1852.

19. For example, in 1852 Abner Parker, citing poor health, refused the Whig nomination for the North Carolina State Assembly. For his refusal, see *Hillsborough Recorder*, June 30, 1852.

20. This profile was based on the 20 men who ran for these offices in the 1850s. The level of slaveholding, occupation, and value of real estate owned was calculated only for those who headed a household in 1850. The age was determined at the time the nominees ran for office. For this information, see U.S. Census MS., Orange County, 1850, Schedules 1 and 2.

21. This was calculated by dividing the total number of men voting for governor in Hillsborough and Chapel Hill by the total vote cast for governor in the county. The result was 1850 = 41.2%, 1852 = 40.2%, 1854 = 42.5%, 1856 = 42.9%, 1858 = 39.8%, and 1860 = 40.2%.

22. See note 20 above.

23. Thomas R. Cain to Minerva Cain Caldwell, July 10, 1854, John Caldwell Papers, SHC; *Hillsborough Recorder*, Aug. 9, 1854.

24. Thomas Miles Garrett Diary, Aug. 1, 1849, SHC.

25. Thomas R. Cain to Minerva Cain Caldwell, July 10, 1854, John Caldwell Papers; Moses Ashley Curtis, Jr., to Mary J. Curtis, July 20, 1858, Moses Ashley Curtis Papers, SHC.

26. For the length of political speeches, see *Hillsborough Recorder*, Sept. 15, 1852; June 26, 1855.

27. Hillsborough Recorder, Sept. 22, 1852.

28. Mangum Diary, July 3, 1852.

29. Garrett Diary, July 10, 1849.

30. *Hillsborough Recorder*, July 4, 1849. The Sons of Temperance were particularly active on the 4th of July, when they would have an annual parade.

31. *Hillsborough Recorder*, Mar. 22, 1854. Charles S. Sydnor notes how the practice of treating was an old one in Southern politics in *Gentlemen Freeholders: Political Parties in Washington's Virginia* (Chapel Hill: Univ. of North Carolina Press, 1952), 51–59, 73.

32. The turnout at elections was calculated by dividing the total number of votes cast for governor by the number of men over age 20 in the nearest census (1850 for the 1850-52-54 elections and 1860 for the 1856-58-60 elections). Because it was necessary to use this age, the following estimates of turnout are probably slightly underestimated: 1850 = 84.4%

turnout; 1852 = 86.1%; 1854 = 86.5%; 1856 = 83.7%; 1858 = 79.3%; and 1860 = 90.8%.

For a discussion of turnout in North Carolina elections which points to rates similar to those in Orange, see J.R. Pole, "Election Statistics in North Carolina to 1861," *Journal of Southern History* 24 (May 1958): 225–28.

33. *Hillsborough Recorder*, Aug. 31, 1853.

34. Ibid., Oct. 12, Nov. 2, 1853.

35. Ibid., Mar. 29, May 24, May 31, 1854.

36. James H. Ruffin to Thomas Ruffin, Jr., July 26, 1858, Thomas Ruffin Papers, SHC.

37. For an interpretation of this election which contends that Turner won because of his support of the ad valorem tax, see Donald C. Butts, "A Challenge to Planter Rule: The Controversy over the Ad Valorem Taxation of Slaves in North Carolina, 1858–1862" (Ph.D. diss., Duke Univ., 1978), 23. I differ from Butts for two reasons. First, if the ad valorem issue was central to the election results, as he contends, then it is unclear why the two Democrats who ran for the assembly and who opposed ad valorem were victorious. Second, Butts's claim that the "poorer voters, newly enfranchised by the free suffrage amendment" were attracted to Turner's advocacy of the ad valorem tax is never proved. In fact, the most striking feature of voting patterns from 1856 to 1858 was not change but continuity. For evidence of this continuity, see note 46 below.

38. Paul C. Cameron to Thomas Ruffin, Jan. 28, 1860, in Joseph G. de Roulhac Hamilton, ed., *The Papers of Thomas Ruffin*, vol. 3 (Raleigh: The North Carolina Historical Commission, 1918–1920), 68.

39. Garrett Diary, Aug. 1, 1849.

40. Mangum Diary, Aug. 5, 1852.

41. U.S. Census MS., Orange County, 1850, 1860, Schedule 1. In 1850, of the 2362 men over age 20, 810 (34.3%) were aged 20 to 29. By 1860, this group, now in their 30s, and the new group of voters in their 20s (a total of 1493) formed 57.8% of all men (2585) over age 20.

42. For two monographs on the two political parties which point to the internal improvements issue as the basis for party differences, see Clarence Clifford Norton, *The Democratic Party in Ante-Bellum North Carolina, 1835–1861* (Chapel Hill: Univ. of North Carolina Press, 1930); Herbert Dale Pegg, *The Whig Party in North Carolina* (Chapel Hill: Colonial Press, n.d.).

For a revisionist interpretation that contends that the internal improvements issue merely symbolized the two parties' differing views of progress, see Harry Legare Watson II, *Jacksonian Politics and Community Conflict: The Emergence of the Second American Party System in Cumberland County, North Carolina* (Baton Rouge: Louisiana State Univ. Press, 1981). For one study which argues that by the mid 1850s the differences over internal improvements had diminished, see Marc W. Kruman, *Parties and Politics in North Carolina, 1836-1865* (Baton Rouge: Louisiana State Univ. Press, 1983), 55-85, esp. 68-85.

For support of the North Carolina Central Railroad and other internal improvements in Orange County, see *Hillsborough Recorder*, Nov. 21, 1849; Feb. 1, May 17, 1854.

43. Election Returns by Precincts, Orange County Miscellaneous Papers, NCDAH. The continuity of party identification by voters can actually be measured and expressed as a coefficient of correlation. This measurement determines the stability of party strength in the election precincts over time. The coefficient of correlation can range from −1.00, indicating a complete shift in party strength, to +1.00, indicating absolute stability. Unless a coefficient of correlation is ±.50 or greater, no significant relationship is expressed. This study utilizes the Pearson Product Moment formula.

The coefficient of correlation for the years between 1850 and 1860 is based on the county's twelve precincts. Although some of these precincts changed their names during the decade, their borders remained fairly stable. The coefficient for 1840 and 1860 is based on the nine precincts whose borders I was sure remained stable over the two decades. The coefficient of correlation is calculated in this case by comparing the percentage of the vote cast for one party at all the precincts in one election with the percentage of the vote cast for that same party at the same precincts in another election.

The vote for governor was selected because it was the only election in which all men were qualified to vote and in which there were only two candidates. The coefficient of correlation of the precinct-by-precinct vote for governor in 1850 with the precinct-by-precinct vote for governor in the following elections was: 1852 = +.93, 1854 = .89, 1856 = .91, 1858 = .86, 1860 = .95. The coefficient of correlation of the precinct-by-precinct vote for governor in 1840 and 1860 was +.88.

44. Mangum Diary, Aug. 6, 1852.

45. The percent of men eligible to vote for the North Carolina State Senate was calculated by dividing the number of men who voted for the senate by the number of men who voted for the governor. The results were: 1850 = 44.6%,; 1852 = 43.2%, 1854 = 44.0%, 1856 = 41.4%.

46. The Pearson Product Moment Formula (see note 43 above) coefficient of correlation of the precinct-by-precinct vote for governor and state senate was: 1850 = +.96, 1852 = .98, 1854 = .97, 1856 = .97, 1858 = .97, 1860 = .99.

This similarity is underscored by a comparison of the vote for the state senate in 1856 and that in 1858, the first election in which there was no restriction on who could vote for the senate. The coefficient of correlation between the vote in 1856 and 1858 was +.95. For a similar conclusion that dual suffrage indicates the lack of class parties, see Richard P. McCormick, "Suffrage, Classes and Party Alignments," *Mississippi Valley Historical Review* 46 (Dec. 1959): 397–410, 402–3.

47. *Hillsborough Recorder*, May 30, 1855.

48. Ibid., May 14, 1856.

49. Ibid.

50. For another analysis of the American party leaders that points to their relative youth and argues that this factor accounts for their ownership of less wealth, see Jean H. Baker, *Ambivalent Americans: The Know-Nothing Party in Maryland* (Baltimore: Johns Hopkins Univ. Press, 1977), 63–79, esp. 67.

Younger men might have been particularly attracted to the changes that the Know-Nothings introduced into politics. By 1850, an increasingly large share of the electorate consisted of young men who could not be motivated by the traditional appeals of the parties. Therefore, the American's infusion of new ideological issues may have been particularly appealing to these young men.

51. The former party affiliations of the 147 active American party participants were: no party = 61.2%, Whig = 33.3%, Democrat = 5.5%.

52. To calculate the ages of these three men, I first found them in the 1850 manuscript census and then added six years to their age. For Turner's continuing attachment to the Whig name, see *Hillsborough Recorder*, Aug. 27, 1856.

53. Ibid.

54. The coefficient of correlation between the vote for the senate in 1854 and 1856 was +.95.

55. There were 12 precincts for each of the 6 elections or a total of 72 precinct returns for the decade. The Democrats received 0–39.9% of the vote in 54.1% of the precinct returns; 40–59.9% in 14.0% of the precinct returns, and 60–100% in 31.9% of the precinct returns.

56. For the lists of voters at each precinct, see Election Returns By Precincts, 1850, Orange County Miscellaneous Papers, NCDAH. All 3 of the Lloyds who were listed as active party participants were Democrats. Further, of the 22 men with the surname "Lloyd" who voted in 1850, 17 cast their vote at the White Cross precinct. The other 5 evidently resided on the borders of the White Cross precinct and therefore voted at the Chapel Hill and Brewer's precinct. All of the Lloyds' in-laws who could be found among the active participants of either party, a total of 7, were Democrats.

57. Jeffrey points to the role of traditional affiliations on partisanship in

North Carolina when he contends that party alignments during "The Age of Jackson were, to a large extent, continuations of the local rivalries of early generations." For his discussion of this topic, see "The Second Party System in North Carolina, 1836–1860," 6.

58. For two scholars who have formulated this thesis for the upper South and North Carolina, see Michael F. Holt, *The Political Crisis of the 1850s* (New York: 1978), 219–59, esp. 254–57; Kruman, *Parties and Politics in North Carolina*, 180–221.

59. Speech given on Oct. 12, 1860, in Joseph G. de Roulhac Hamilton and Max R. Williams, eds., *The Papers of William Alexander Graham*, vol. 5 (Raleigh: North Carolina Division of Archives and History, 1961–), 178–79.

60. Election Returns By Precinct, 1860, Orange County Miscellaneous Papers, NCDAH. The county vote for president in 1860 was John Bell 52.7%, John C. Beckinridge 43.3%, Stephen A. Douglas 4.0%.

61. *Hillsborough Recorder*, Nov. 1860.

62. Ibid., Jan. 1, 1861.

63. Ibid., Jan. 16, 1861.

64. Ibid., Dec. 26, 1860.

65. Joseph Carlyle Sitterson, *The Secession Movement in North Carolina* (Chapel Hill: Univ. of North Carolina Press, 1939), 208.

66. The coefficient of correlation between the Whig vote for governor in 1860 and the vote against holding a convention in February of 1861 was only +.35.

67. *Hillsborough Recorder*, Mar. 13, 1861.

68. Ibid., Mar. 20, 1861.

69. Ibid., Apr. 24, 1861.

70. Charles Phillips to John W. Ellis, Apr. 23, 1861, in Noble J. Tolbert, ed., *The Papers of John Willis Ellis*, vol. 2 (Raleigh: North Carolina Division of Archives and History, 1964), 672–73.

71. Speech given on Apr. 27, 1861, in Hamilton and Williams, eds., *Graham Papers*, vol. 5, 243–48.

72. William C. Calder Diary, Apr. 18, 1861, William C. Calder Papers, SHC.

73. Moses Ashley Curtis to Moses Ashley Curtis, Jr., Apr. 23, 1861, Curtis Papers.

74. John W. Norwood to Joseph Norwood, May 8, 1861, Lenoir Family Papers, SHC.

75. Sitterson, *The Secession Movement in North Carolina*, 245. For William A. Graham's discussion of this, see his speech cited in note 70 above.

For an interesting discussion of Lincoln and the right of revolution topic, see Thomas J. Pressly, "Bullets and Ballots: Lincoln and the 'Right of Revolution,'" *American Historical Review* 47 (Apr. 1962): 647–62.

76. As previously shown, the coefficient of correlation between the Whig vote for governor in 1860 and the vote in February of 1861 was only +.35. However, for the Whig vote for governor in 1860 and the vote for Graham and Berry in May of 1861 the coefficient of correlation was +.72.

77. For the use of the terms "revolutionists" and "secessionists" see Sitterson, *The Secession Movement in North Carolina*, 245–49. For the placing of the date May 20, 1775, on the state flag, see Lefler and Newsome, *The History of a Southern State*, 205. Sitterson neither notes the significance of the date of the convention meeting nor the placing of this date on the flag.

Chapter 4

1. *Revised Code of North Carolina*, 1855, ch. 70, sections 1, 7–8.

2. Raymond Heath, Jr., "The North Carolina Militia on the Eve of the Civil War" (M.A. thesis, Univ. of North Carolina at Chapel Hill, 1974), 9–82; *Revised Code*, 1855, ch. 70, sections 16, 21.

3. For a list of some of the officers in the regular militia, see *Hillsborough Recorder*, Apr. 13, 1861.

4. *Revised Code*, 1855, ch. 70, section 91.

5. *Hillsborough Recorder*, Nov. 7, 1855; Nov. 23, 1857; Feb. 15, 1860.

6. Ibid., July 9, 1855.

7. Ibid., July 11, 1860.

8. Ibid., Feb. 18, 1857; July 21, 1858; July 13, 1859; July 18, Oct. 3, 1860.

9. Richard W. Iobst, *The Bloody Sixth: The Sixth North Carolina Regiment, Confederate States of America* (Raleigh: North Carolina Confederate Centennial Commission, 1965), 304–20. For the unit's antebellum officers, see *Hillsborough Recorder*, Feb. 15, 1860.

10. Iobst, *Bloody Sixth*, 320–35; *Hillsborough Recorder*, Apr. 24, 1861.

11. Iobst, *Bloody Sixth*, 3–27.

12. Robert F. Webb to Martha P. Mangum, June 30, 1861, in Henry T. Shanks, ed., *The Papers of Willie Person Mangum*, vol. 5 (Raleigh: North Carolina Department of Archives and History, 1950-56), 391.

13. For reports on Mangum's condition, see Robert F. Webb to Willie P. Mangum, July 22, 1861; Addison Mangum to Martha P. Mangum, July 24, 1861; J.P. Moore to Willie P. Mangum, July 26, 1861; A.W.

Mangum to Martha P. Mangum, July 27, 1861; Josiah Turner, Jr., to Willie P. Mangum, July 28, 1861, in Shanks, ed., *Mangum Papers*, vol. 5, 396–98, 402–4.

14. See note 3 above.

15. James W. Bacon to Ellen Lockhart, Jan. 1, 1863, Hugh Conway Browning Papers, DU; for another southern community study which also points to the role that family, kin, and neighborhood may have played in motivating soldiers, see Burton, *In My Father's Home Are Many Mansions*, 226.

16. Iobst, *Bloody Sixth*, 304–20. Only 27 of 63 (42.8%) of the soldiers in this unit by January 1865 were residents of Orange County.

17. John G. Barrett, *The Civil War in North Carolina* (Chapel Hill: Univ. of North Carolina Press, 1963), 17. For an excellent study of the process of mobilization, see Richard W. Iobst, "North Carolina Mobilizes: Nine Crucial Months, December 1860–August 1861" (Ph.D. diss. Univ. of North Carolina at Chapel Hill, 1968).

18. From accounts in the *Hillsborough Recorder* I have been able to identify six different ladies' aid societies. Two of these were in Hillsborough and Chapel Hill, and four were in the rural neighborhoods.

19. S.S. Nash to John Roulhac, May 15, 1861, Ruffin, Roulhac, and Hamilton Family Papers, SHC.

20. Helen N. Mickle to Robina Norwood, June 21, 1861, Tillinghast Family Papers, DU.

21. David Thompson to Eliza Thompson, Nov. 25, 1861, Samuel Thompson Papers, SHC.

22. David Thompson to Mary Thompson, Feb. 28, 1862, ibid.

23. *Hillsborough Recorder*, Oct. 31, 1861.

24. Ibid., Nov. 21, 1861.

25. Ibid., May 29, 1861.

26. On North Carolina's ability eventually to clothe her troops, see Bell Wiley, *The Life of Johnny Reb: The Common Soldiers of the Confederacy* (Indianapolis: Bobbs-Merrill, 1943), 113.

27. David Thompson to Eliza Thompson, May 22, 1862, Thompson Papers.

28. David Thompson to Mary Thompson, Aug. 8, 1861, ibid.

29. For announcements of Walter A. Thompson's trips to the troops to carry boxes, see *Hillsborough Recorder*, Dec. 10, 1862; Oct. 14, 1863; Mar. 18, 1864.

30. James A. Graham to Mrs. William A. Graham, June 17, 1861, in Henry M. Wagstaff, ed., "The James A. Graham Papers, 1861–1884," *The James Sprunt Historical Studies* 20 (1928): 105.

31. Ibid.

32. Ibid., Sept. 6, 1861, 107.

33. Ibid., June 17, 1861, 105–6.

34. David Thompson to Eliza Thompson, Nov. 4, 1861, Thompson Papers. For descriptions of the soldiers' diet, see David Thompson to Eliza Thompson, June 9, Aug. 27, 1861; David Thompson to Mary Thompson, Oct. 24, 1861, ibid.

35. David Thompson to Eliza Thompson, Dec. 16, 1861, ibid.

36. James A. Graham to Susan W. Graham, Dec. 17, 1861, in Hamilton and Williams, eds., *Graham Papers*, vol. 5, 346.

37. James A. Graham to Mrs. William A. Graham, Mar. 15, 1861, in Wagstaff, ed., "James A. Graham Papers," 117–18.

38. John P. Lockhart to Dennis Heartt, in *Hillsborough Recorder*, Apr., 1, 1862.

39. Of the 148 soldiers who can be identified as being killed at certain battles, 26 (17.6%) died as a result of the battle of Gettysburg.

40. For example, of the 126 men who died while serving in the Flat River Guards, Orange Grays, and Orange Guards, 67 were the victims of disease; in the 53 of these 67 cases where the disease was specified, 30 were from typhoid and pneumonia. For similar findings, see Wiley, *Life of Johnny Reb*, 244–69.

41. David Thompson to Eliza Thompson, July 4, 1862, Thompson Papers.

42. John Thompson to Mary Thompson, Sept. 27, 1864, ibid.

43. William S. Nichols to Mrs. William F. Strayhorn, July 24, 1863, Mrs. John Berry Papers, SHC.

44. James W. Bacon to Ellen Lockhart, Oct. 20, 1862, Browning Papers; Michael H. Turrentine to "Sister", Apr. 23, 1863, Michael H. Turrentine Papers, DU.

45. Robert Bingham Diary, July 20, Aug. 10, 1863, Robert Bingham Papers, SHC.

46. Robert F. Webb to Lucy Mangum, Apr. 24, 1864, Mangum Family Papers.

47. James W. Bacon to Ellen Lockhart, May 9, 1862, Browning Papers.

48. Adolphus Williamson Mangum to Governor Henry T. Clark, Aug. 19, 1861, Governor Henry T. Clark Papers, NCDAH.

49. *Hillsborough Recorder*, Sept. 25, 1861.

50. David Thompson to Eliza Thompson, Nov. 10, 1862, Thompson Papers.

51. John W. Graham to Susan W. Graham, June 16, 1862, in Hamilton and Williams, eds., *Graham Papers*, vol. 5, 393–94.

52. Samuel A. Craig to "Sister," May 6, 1862, Mary E. Craig Papers, DU.

53. David Thompson to Eliza Thompson, Nov. 29, 1864, Thompson Papers.

54. James A. Graham to Mrs. William A. Graham, Jan. 1, 1864, in Wagstaff, ed., "James A. Graham Papers," 177.

55. David Thompson to Mary Thompson, Aug. 15, 1863, Thompson Papers.

56. Samuel P. Lockhart to Ellen Lockhart, Sept. 11, 1863, Browning Papers.

57. *Hillsborough Recorder*, Aug. 19, 1863.

58. David Thompson to John Thompson, Jan. 7, 1864, Thompson Papers.

59. William R. Clark to Ellen Lockhart, Mar. 18, 1864, Browning Papers.

60. For records of desertion see Appendix 2-A. The 49 men who are listed in the Jordan and Manarin Study (4.6% of the 1061 soldiers listed in this study from Orange County) is clearly an underestimate of the total number of deserters. Further, it does not include men who were listed as A.W.O.L. As evidence that it was an underestimate, I have found men listed as deserters in letters who are not noted in the Jordan and Manarin Study. These other deserters are described in Samuel A. Craig to "Dear Sister Mary," Apr. 25, 1862, Mary E. Craig Papers, DU; John W. Graham to William A. Graham, Mar. 17, 1865, in Hamilton and Williams, eds., *Graham Papers*, vol. 6, 285; Robert D. Graham to William Alexander Graham, Aug. 26, 1864, ibid. 165; John W. Graham to William A. Graham, Feb. 14, 1863, ibid., vol. 5, 462; Robert Y. Walker to Ellen Walker, July 13, 1862, Browning Papers.

Forty-six of the 48 deserters whose year of enlistment was specified entered the army in 1861 or 1862.

61. Seventeen of the 49 deserters (34.7%) were wounded. Of the 722 men noted in the Jordan and Manarin Study who were not killed, 253 (35.0%) were wounded.

62. For a recent study that also points to the role of kinship ties in desertion, see Richard Reid, "A Test Case of the 'Crying Evil': Desertion among North Carolina Troops during the Civil War," *North Carolina Historical Review* 58 (July 1981): 234–62.

63. James A. Graham to "Mother," Feb., 1, 1864, in Wagstaff, ed., "James A. Graham Papers," 178.

64. David Thompson to Mary Thompson, Nov. 20, 1863, Thompson Papers.

65. Elijah G. Faucett to William A. Graham, July 16, 1862, in Hamilton and Williams, eds., *Graham Papers*, vol. 5, 399.

66. *Report of the North Carolina Comptroller of Public Accounts*,

861–64. In 1860 there were 2,224 males ages 15 to 39. At least 1,558 (70.0%) of these males served in the military. When the Jordan and Manarin Study is completed this rate will probably rise. For Paul D. Escott's estimate of the percent of men from North Carolina who served in the army, see *Many Excellent People*, 53–54.

67. More than half of the soldiers fell below the average age at marriage for males, 27.1 years, as indicated in Table 15. Further, the majority of men in their 20s did not head households.

68. Mary C. Jones to Cadwallader Jones, Jr., Apr. 9, 1862, Jan. 13, 1863, Cadwallader Jones, Jr., Papers, SHC. During the 1850s there was an average of 91.2 marriages annually. Between 1862 and 1864 there was only an average of 58.3 marriages annually. For number of marriages, see *Orange County Marriages Bonds to 1868* (Salt Lake City: Genealogical Society of Utah, n.d.), NCDAH.

69. This is calculated by assuming that the average age at marriage for these fathers was about the same as for males during the 1850s, 27.1 years. If the youngest son was 20 to 24 years old when he entered the military and he was born approximately 10 years after his parents' marriage, his father would have been in his late 50s or early 60s. If he was the oldest son, his father would have been about 10 years younger—in his late 40s.

70. Since the overwhelming majority of the soldiers were less than 30 years old, few could have had sons who were more than 12 years old.

71. Orange County Court Minutes, May 27, 1861.

72. William Alexander Graham to Augustus W. Graham, Oct. 10, 1861, in Hamilton and Williams, eds., *Graham Papers*, vol. 5, 304; Josiah Turner, Jr., to Sophie Turner, Jan. 27, 1862, Josiah Turner, Jr., Papers, SHC.

73. L.N. Brassfield to Governor Zebulon Vance, Mar. 27, 1863, Governor Zebulon Vance Papers, NCDAH.

74. Margaret Guess to Governor Zebulon Vance, Aug. 6, 1863, ibid.

75. Louena Cates to Governor Zebulon Vance, July 25, 1863, ibid.

76. Mary Hester to Governor Zebulon Vance, Apr. 24, 1863, ibid.

77. William H. Battle to Richard Battle, Oct. 12, 1863, Battle Papers.

78. Orange County Court Minutes, May 27, 1862.

79. Ibid., Feb. 24, 1863.

80. Ibid., May 27, 1862; Nov. 24, 1863. The benefits were raised from $1.50 for soldiers' wives and $.75 for their children to $6.00 and $3.00.

81. T.S. Neely to John W. Norwood, Feb. 19, 1864, Provisions for Families of Soldiers Folders, Orange County Miscellaneous Papers, NCDAH. For the other types of problems that the grain agent encountered, see T.S. Neely to John W. Norwood, Dec. 11, 29, 1863; Jan. 7, Mar. 10, May 10, June 3, 17, 1864, ibid.

For a recent study of government aid to civilians in North Carolina that specifically discusses conditions in Orange County, see Paul D. Escott, "Poverty and Poor Aid to the Poor in Confederate North Carolina," *North Carolina Historical Review* 61 (Oct. 1984): 462–80.

82. Mary C. Jones to Cadwallader Jones, Jr., June 30, 1862, Jones, Jr., Papers.

83. Caroline Pettigrew to "Minnie," Mar. 24, 1862, Pettigrew Family Papers, SHC.

84. Mrs. Phila Calder to Robert Calder, Mar. 20, May 14, 1863, Calder Papers; Mollie E. Woods to H. Lea McDade, June 30, 1862, John A. McDade Letters and Papers, DU; Mary E. Massey, "Confederate Refugees in North Carolina," *North Carolina Historical Review* 60 (Apr. 1963): 158–82.

85. *Report of the North Carolina Comptroller of Public Accounts*, 1860–63.

86. Paul Cameron to George Mordecai, Nov. 11, 1862, George Mordecai Papers, SHC. On the role played by family and kinship in the refugee situation, see Friedman, *The Enclosed Garden*, 95–97.

87. *Hillsborough Recorder*, Jan. 1, 1863.

88. Paul C. Cameron to Governor Zebulon Vance, Feb. 19, 1863; Henry K. Nash to Governor Zebulon Vance, Feb. 20, 1863; Hugh B. Guthrie to Governor Zebulon Vance, Feb. 21, 1863, Vance Papers.

89. George Laws to Governor Zebulon Vance, Feb. 23, 1863, ibid.; *Hillsborough Recorder*, Feb. 25, Mar. 18, 1863.

90. Henry Armand London to "lil," Feb. 16, 1864, Henry A. London Papers, SHC. For one of the best descriptions of the diverse actions by slaves during the Civil War, see Clarence L. Mohr, *On the Threshold of Freedom: Master and Slaves in Civil War Georgia* (Athens: Univ. of Georgia Press, 1986).

91. For one of the best discussions of the tax-in-kind, particularly in relation to relief for the needy, see Paul D. Escott, *After Secession: Jefferson Davis and the Failure of Confederate Nationalism* (Baton Rouge: Louisiana State Univ. Press, 1978), 68–69, 141–42, 153.

92. "Directions to the Commissioners of the Soldiers Fund in Each Tax Direct," Provisions for Families of Soldiers Folders, Orange County Miscellaneous Papers, NCDAH; Orange County Court Minutes, Feb. 23, 25, Mar. 15, Aug. 23, 29, 1864. For a valuable discussion of the structure of the relief of the poor throughout North Carolina, see William Frank Entrekin, Jr., "Poor Relief in North Carolina in the Confederacy" (M.A. thesis, Duke Univ., 1947).

93. Disbursements for 1864, Provisions for Families of Soldiers Folders, Orange County Miscellaneous Papers. It is impossible to give an exact percentage of the total households which received aid because often more

than one woman lived in the same household. Nevertheless, if each woman who received aid did support a household, it would mean that of the 2125 white households in 1860, 508 (23.9%) received assistance. Paul Escott claims that 19.7% of the adult white women and nearly 35% of the white children received aid in Orange County (*Many Excellent People*, 56–57).

94. Robert F. Morris to John W. Norwood, Apr. 4, 1864, ibid.

95. William Cheek to John W. Norwood, July 4, 1864, ibid.

96. Escott, *After Secession*, 120–21.

97. Only 22 of the 42 planters in 1860 had sons residing in their households between the ages of 15 and 39. Twenty-seven of the total of 39 sons (69.2%) served in the military. The participation rate countywide for males of this age range was 70.0%. Further, since many of the sons of planters were officers, they may have served in regiments not made up primarily of Orange County troops and therefore do not appear as participating in the war effort from the county.

98. John Henry Curtis to Mary Curtis, Oct. 14, 1864, Curtis Papers.

99. Mrs. Emily Nunn to Governor Zebulon B. Vance, Nov. 11, 1862, Vance Papers.

100. Miscellaneous Tax Records, Orange County, June 14, 1864, NCDAH; Orange County Court Minutes, Aug. 28, 1866.

101. Osmond F. Long to William A. Graham, Dec. 28, 1862, in Hamilton and Williams, eds., *Graham Papers*, vol. 5, 435–36, esp. 433–35; Richard Yates, *The Confederacy of Zeb Vance*, (Tuscaloosa, Ala.: Confederate Publishing Company, 1958), 52–53.

102. Paul C. Cameron to Thomas Ruffin, Jan. 5, 1863, in Hamilton, ed., *Ruffin Papers*, vol. 3, 285; Katherine F. Curtis to Elizabeth Creecy, Jan. 4, 1863, Creecy Family Papers, SHC.

103. *Raleigh Standard*, Aug. 26, 1863. For a discussion of unionism along the Cane Creek which evidently also spilled over into neighboring Alamance County, see Escott, *Many Excellent People*, 64.

104. For the gubernatorial election returns, see *Hillsborough Recorder*, Aug. 10, 1864. In Orange County Vance won 85.3% of the vote and a nearly equal share of both the civilian and army electorate.

105. The following discussion of Samuel Phillips is drawn from Robert D. Miller, "Samuel Field Phillips: The Odyssey of a Southern Dissenter," *North Carolina Historical Review* 58 (July 1981): 263–80, esp. 267–68.

106. For the Chapel Hill meeting, see *Hillsborough Recorder*, Feb. 22, 1865; David L. Swain to William A. Graham, Feb. 18, 1865, in Hamilton and Williams, eds., *Graham Papers*, vol. 6, 248–50; John Berry to William A. Graham, Feb. 17, 1865, ibid., 243–44.

107. David L. Swain to William A. Graham, Apr. 16, 1864, ibid., 62–63.

108. David L. Swain to William A. Graham, May 3, 1864, ibid., 85.

109. Paul C. Cameron to Governor Zebulon Vance, Jan. 1, 1864, Vance Papers.

110. William H. Battle to Richard Battle, Jan. 17, 1865, Battle Papers.

111. Martha Mangum to Sally A. Mangum, Jan. 27, 1865, typed copy in Willie Person Mangum Papers, NCDAH.

112. James Phillips to William A. Graham, Apr. 3, 1865, in Hamilton and Williams, eds., *Graham Papers*, vol. 6, 290–91.

113. For evidence that some soldiers had come through the county weeks before and pillaged some farms, see Rawick, ed., *The American Slave*, vol. 14, 304–5, 380–81; David L. Swain to William A. Graham, Mar. 23, 1865, in Hamilton and Williams, eds., *Graham Papers*, vol. 6, 285–86.

114. Cornelia Phillips Spencer Diary, May 4, 1865, Cornelia Phillips Spencer Papers, SHC.

115. John G. Barrett, *Sherman's March through the Carolinas* (Chapel Hill: Univ. of North Carolina Press, 1956), 261–63.

116. Ibid., 226–44; for an interesting examination of the Bennett farmhouse negotiations, see Raoul S. Naroll, "Lincoln and the Sherman Peace Fiasco—Another Fable?" *Journal of Southern History* 20 (Nov. 1954): 483. An insightful description of the Bennett family (whose surname spelling varied) can be found in Arthus C. Menius III, "James Bennitt: Portrait of an Antebellum Yeoman," *North Carolina Historical Review* 58 (Oct. 1981): 305–26.

117. Cornelia Phillips Spencer Diary, Apr. 30, 1865.

Chapter 5

1. If the 409 men noted in Appendix 2-B had not died in the war and had persisted at the antebellum rate for 20- to 39-year-olds (51.2%) in Orange County, the rate of persistence for the 1860s for all males aged 20 and older would have been 50.2%.

The white sex ratio for 1860 to 1880 is shown in table F.

2. The manuscript census does not specify whether a woman was a widow. Nevertheless, by comparing the percentage of all households headed by women in 1870 to that in 1860, we can gain a rough approximation of the increase in widowhood. In 1860, 16.5% of white household heads were women. By 1870, the number had risen to only 20.8%. The only age cohorts that showed a significant increase in the number of households were those in their 30s in 1870. The number of women in this group rose from 39 in 1860 to 77 in 1870.

Table 15 indicates that 60.7% of the soldiers who enlisted were under

TABLE F *Sex Ratio, 1860-80*

Ages	1860		1870		1880	
	Males	Females	Males	Females	Males	Females
20-29	960	1068	683	1086	1211	1256
30-39	592	677	479	800	756	1014
Total	1552	1745	1162	1886	1967	2270
(males per 100 females)	(88.9)		(61.6)		(86.8)	

TABLE G   *Average Age at Marriage for Whites*

	Grooms	Brides	
1850-59	27.1	22.8	years
1860-69	29.5	24.4	years
1870-79	27.3	22.9	years

25 years old. During the 1850s the average white male did not marry until 27.1 years of age (*Orange County Marriage Bonds to 1868*; Orange County Marriage Register, 1868-81, Office of the Register of Deeds, Orange County Courthouse, Hillsborough, N.C.; U.S. Census MS., Orange County, 1850, 1860, 1870, Schedule 1).

The annual number of marriages for whites in 1850-59 was 91.2; 1865-69, 126.8; 1870-79, 103.8. The increase in the number of marriages for the 1870s over the 1850s can be accounted for by the growth during the 1870s of the white population (see table G).

3. This case and the following examples are drawn from U.S. Census MS., Orange County, 1850, 1860, 1870, Schedules 1, 2, 4. For the military records, see Appendix 2.

4. During the 1870s a total of only 178 out of 1321 (13.5%) white men who persisted changed townships. See table F above for the return by 1880 to a more balanced sex ratio.

5. The wills both before and after the war indicate that men might have been inheriting larger estates than they would have if their brothers had survived the war. Specifically, there was a marked decline in the number of sons mentioned in wills left by men from 1865 to 1880 compared to

TABLE H *Sons as Heirs*

	0 sons	1 son	2 sons	3 or more sons	average number	number of wills
1850–April 1861	28.4%	18.9%	27.0%	25.7%	1.81	134
April 1865–80	42.0	18.5	19.8	19.7	1.30	105

those from 1849 to 1861. Of those wills which mention the names of specific children rather than just "children" in general, the number of sons noted as heirs is shown in table H. For the wills, see Orange County Wills, vols. F, G, and H, Office of the Clerk of the Civil Court, Orange County Courthouse, Hillsborough, N.C.

6. U.S. Census MS., Orange County, 1860, 1870, Schedule 1. Newly-weds were returning to the practice of finding their mates from nearby households, despite a 38.5% increase in the number of households between 1860 and 1870. This increase was caused by the creation of independent households by the freedmen.

Because the new township borders sometimes divided the rural neighborhoods and placed the bride's and groom's residences in 1870 in different townships, the false impression is given that the newlyweds resided far apart before marriage. When the households of the bride's and groom's parents are traced back to 1860, before the township lines were drawn, however, the newlyweds can be shown to have lived quite near one another. For example, Morris Lloyd of Chapel Hill Township married Suzanne Lloyd of Bingham Township in 1871. In 1860 their parents lived only 29 households apart in the census. In 1870, however, the drawing of township lines in 1868 makes their parents appear to live 1137 households apart. Because of this difficulty with the township lines, when calculating the distance between households of newlyweds during the 1870s, I omitted newlyweds who resided in different townships in 1870.

7. Cane Creek Baptist Church Membership, 1877, microfilm copy in NCDAH. In the Cane Creek Baptist Church, 42.1% of the surnames of the white male members composed 77.8% of all of the male members.

Addison Mangum Store Ledger, 1871 to 1872, DU; John D. Wilbon Day Book, 1871, John C. Van Hook Papers, DU. At the Mangums' store, 83.6% of the customers were residents of Mangum Township and 98.2% were farmers. Only 33.3% of the customers at John D. Wilbon's store in

Hillsborough were farmers. None of the customers at the Mangums' store made purchases at Wilbon's store.

8. *Hillsborough Recorder*, Dec. 17, 1873; Mar. 25, Sept. 23, Oct. 14, 1874; July 1, Sept. 6, 1876.

9. Ibid., Sept. 23, 1874.

10. For the leadership of the neighborhood lodges, see ibid., Oct. 14, 1874. For an indication that the Grange leaders were affluent men, see Cornelia Phillips Spencer to Judge William Battle, Dec. 12, 1874, Battle Papers. Cornelia Spencer refers to the leaders in the Chapel Hill area as "men of substance" and "some of our best county citizens."

11. For a comparative study, see Jonathan M. Wiener, *Social Origins of the New South: Alabama, 1860–1885* (Baton Rouge: Louisiana State Univ. Press, 1978), 3–34. Unfortunately, because Wiener never compares the rate of persistence for planters to that of nonplanters, he cannot validly compare the impact of the war on the two groups.

The relatively lower rate of persistence of planters compared to all slaveholders and nonslaveholders is the result of the length of time it generally took a man to acquire enough slaves to be a planter. Because planters tended to be older men, they often died between decennial censuses.

For other works which indicate the rate of persistence of planters during the 1870s, but use varying methods for calculating this measurement, see Michael Wayne, *The Reshaping of Plantation Society: The Natchez District, 1860–1880* (Baton Rouge: Louisiana State Univ. Press, 1983), 88–91; Randolph B. Campbell, *A Southern Community in Crisis: Harrison County, Texas, 1850–1880* (Austin: Texas State Historical Association, 1983), 384–86.

12. The value of farms fell during the 1860s from $2,141,690 to $977,308, a decline of 54.4%.

13. The three planters who failed to own enough property to be in the tenth decile of wealth in 1870 owned the following amounts of real estate in 1870: $950, $600, and $0. Because these three men ranged in age from 59 to 80 years, there is reason to believe that they had not become poor but simply had given their property to their children.

14. I have been able to trace the wealth of eleven of the nineteen planters who did not persist. In many of these cases the planter may have died with no surviving descendants in the county, or his property was inherited by a married daughter whose husband's surname makes her impossible to identify as this planter's daughter.

15. Paul C. Cameron to Anne Collins, Dec. 26, 1869, Anne Collins Papers, SHC.

16. Frances Hamilton to Thomas Roulhac, Dec. 12, 1869, Ruffin, Roulhac, Hamilton Papers. For Cameron's estate in 1860, 1870, and 1875,

see U.S. Census MS., Orange County, 1860 and 1870, Schedule 1; "Paul C. Cameron Property List, 1875," June 22, 1875, Cameron Family Papers, SHC.

17. In 1870, of 1445 white farmers who headed households, 495 (34.2%) owned no real estate.

18. In 1870, of 853 black male household heads, only 121 (14.2%) owned real estate. The average number of total acres was 198.5 acres for white farmers and 78.8 acres for black farmers.

19. Robert G. Fitzgerald Diary, Jan. 30, 1868, Fitzgerald Family Papers, microfilm copy in SHC.

20. Ibid., Apr. 15, 16, 17, 20, 21, 25, 1869. In his diary Robert Fitzgerald also notes his purchases of property on Feb. 7, May 7, Sept. 29, Oct. 24, 1868.

21. U.S. Census Office, Eighth Census (1860), *Population of the United States in 1860*, 358; U.S. Census MS., Orange County, 1850, 1860, Schedule 1. Seven of the eight male free Negro household heads in 1850 and four of the five male free Negro household heads in 1860 who owned real estate were mulattoes. Although mulattoes comprised only 14.6% of the total Negro population in 1860, they represented 68.4% of the free Negroes.

On the disproportionate number of mulattoes who were free before the Civil War, see Joel Williamson, *New People: Miscegenation and Mulattoes in the United States* (New York: Free Press, 1980), 24–25.

22. Although they only comprised 25.5% of the Negro men, mulattoes represented 47.9% of the skilled blue collar workers.

23. In 1870, 23.7% of the male mulattoes who headed households owned real estate, but only 11.2% of male blacks who headed households did. In the recent debate over the structure of the postwar economy, all of the participants have failed to note this distinction. By asking why most Negroes did not acquire property, these scholars have not recognized the traditional means by which property was transferred and the unique position held by mulattoes. Therefore, Roger L. Ransom, Richard Sutch, and Jay R. Mandle, who have emphasized the role of discrimination in hindering Negro advancement, have viewed racism in far too monolithic terms. Stephen J. Decanio, Joseph D. Reid, Jr., and Robert Higgs, who have deemphasized the role of discrimination, have failed to identify the competitive advantage mulattoes had over blacks. For a discussion of these works, see Harold Woodman, "Sequel to Slavery: The New History and the Postwar South," *Journal of Southern History* 43 (Nov. 1977): 523–54.

24. This finding significantly differs from that of Roger L. Ransom and Richard Sutch, *One Kind of Freedom: The Economic Consequences of Emancipation* (Cambridge: Cambridge Univ. Press, 1977), 81–105.

Throughout their discussion of the tenure of black farmers in the postwar South, Ransom and Sutch rely solely upon statistics they obtained from the agriculture schedule. By so doing they omit the large number of blacks who labored in agriculture but who were not farm operators, the criteria for being listed in the agriculture schedule. In other words, by relying on the agriculture schedule, Ransom and Sutch have counted farms and not farmers. Their methodology leads them to underestimate the number of blacks who were laboring on farms under the supervision of white farmers.

The difference between their findings and mine can best be understood by identifying the four groups of farmers noted in the population and agriculture schedules of the manuscript census of 1870: 1) those men listed in only the population schedule as farmers who owned real estate; 2) those men listed in only the population schedule as farmers or farm laborers who owned no real estate; 3) those men listed in both the agriculture schedule and the population schedule who owned real estate; 4) those men listed in both the agriculture and the population schedule who owned no real estate. In 1870, in Orange County the 709 black male household heads listed in the manuscript census as farmers and farm laborers were distributed in these four categories as follows: 1) 56, 2) 563, 3) 36, 4) 54.

In order to calculate the total number of farmers who worked on land which they did not own it is necessary to add together 2) and 4). This number divided by the total number of farmers and farm laborers gives the percent of nonlandowning farmers. For 1870, of 709 black farmers, 617 (87.0%) were not independent farmers.

25. Cornelia Phillips Spencer Diary, May 7, 1865.

26. Lizzie DeRosset to Mrs. George Mordecai, Aug. 21, 1865, Cameron Papers.

27. Paul C. Cameron to George Mordecai, Nov. 20, 1869, Mordecai Papers.

28. William A. Graham to David L. Swain, July 3, 1865, in Hamilton and Williams, eds., *Graham Papers*, vol. 6, 315.

29. Selina Thompson to Ellen Hedrick, July 11, 1865, Hedrick Papers, DU. For concern about the shortage of money, see William A. Graham to Mrs. William A. Graham, May 22, 1868, William A. Graham Papers, NCDAH.

30. Ellen Hedrick to Benjamin S. Hedrick, June 7, 1867, Hedrick Papers, SHC.

31. Ellen Hedrick to William C. Thompson, May 18, 1865, ibid.

32. William A. Graham to David L. Swain, May 11, 1865, William A. Graham Papers, NCDAH.

33. Paul C. Cameron to Tod R. Caldwell, Aug. 18, 1865, Caldwell Papers.

34. William H. Battle to Kemp Battle, Dec. 4, 1865, Battle Papers.

35. Cornelia Phillips Spencer Diary, May 7, 1865.

36. Eliza Thompson to Ellen Hedrick, July 4, 1865, Hedrick Papers.

37. Catherine Roulhac to Frances Hamilton, May 21, 1865, Ruffin, Roulhac, Hamilton Papers.

38. James A. Graham to William A. Graham, Dec. 18, 1865, in Hamilton and Williams, eds., *Graham Papers*, vol. 6, 466.

39. Paul C. Cameron to Margaret Mordecai, May 27, 1865, Mordecai Papers.

40. Moses Ashley Curtis to Elizabeth DeRossett, Sept. 28, 1865, Curtis Papers.

41. Cornelia Phillips Spencer to "Miss Eliza," Mar. 3, 1866, Spencer Papers.

42. Ellen Hedrick to William C. Thompson, May 18, 1865, Hedrick Papers, DU.

43. William A. Bingham to Walter W. Lenoir, Feb. 15, 1870, Lenoir Papers.

44. Andrew Mickle to John Kimberly, Aug. 8, 1870, John Kimberly Papers, SHC.

45. William A. Graham to William Graham, Mar. 4, 1870, William A. Graham Papers, SHC.

46. Eliza Thompson to Ellen Hedrick, Nov. 30, 1865, Hedrick Papers, DU.

47. Of the 455 black men who persisted during the 1870s, 100 (22.8%) changed townships.

48. When the black population who resided in different townships is included in the sample in Table 2, the sample size rises to 21 couples and the total percent who resided in the same township equals 57.2%. For two studies which analyze the postwar black family and household patterns in more detail, see Crandall A. Shifflet, *Patronage and Poverty in the Tobacco South: Louisa County, Virginia, 1860-1900* (Knoxville: Univ. of Tennessee Press, 1982), 84-98; Burton, *In My Father's House Are Many Mansions*, 225-313.

49. *Hillsborough Recorder*, Sept. 20, 1865.

50. Minutes of the Orange County Commissioners, Dec. 12, 1868. For a thorough discussion of the freedmen's schools in North Carolina, see Roberta Sue Alexander, *North Carolina Faces the Freedmen: Race Relations during Presidential Reconstruction, 1865-1867* (Durham, N.C.: Duke Univ. Press, 1985), 152-67.

51. For evidence that Negroes made contributions to the freedmen's schools, see Robert G. Fitzgerald Diary, Feb. 8, 1869.

52. W. Roulhac to "Arthur," Jan. 26, 1867, Ruffin, Roulhac, Hamilton Papers.

53. William A. Graham to David L. Swain, Oct. 16, 1865, in Hamilton and Williams, eds., *Graham Papers*, vol. 4, 413–14.

54. Cornelia Phillips Spencer Diary, July 4, 1865; July 4, 1866; Mary J. Curtis to Miss Elizabeth A. DeRosset, July 4, 1865, Curtis Papers; "Handbill: Exercises For Fourth of July Celebration," 1866, Kimberly Papers; Richard S. Webb to "Sister," July 7, 1866, James Webb Papers, SHC; Lucy Battle to William H. Battle, July 4, 1867, Battle Papers.

55. Henry C. Thompson to Benjamin S. Hedrick, July 5, 1867, Hedrick Papers, DU.

56. William A. Graham was another planter who openly asserted his belief that the postwar plantation should vary little from the antebellum plantation. After telling his former slaves the terms under which they could stay on his plantation, Graham specified that his authority was "to remain the same," in William A. Graham to David L. Swain, May 11, 1865, copy in William Alexander Graham Papers, SHC.

57. "Contract for Labor," Apr. 1865, in Hamilton, ed., *Ruffin Papers*, vol. 3, 449–50.

58. Paul C. Cameron to Thomas Ruffin, May 11, 1865, ibid., 451–52.

59. Paul C. Cameron to Thomas Ruffin, Aug. 11, 1865, Ruffin Papers.

60. For other problems that Cameron encountered on his plantation during this six-day period, see Paul C. Cameron to Tod R. Caldwell, Aug. 19, 1865, Caldwell Papers.

61. Samuel Piper to Paul C. Cameron, n.d., Miscellaneous Folder N–Q, #27, 1865, Cameron Papers.

62. Paul C. Cameron to Thomas Ruffin, Oct. 4, 1865, in Hamilton, ed., *Ruffin Papers*, vol. 4, 35–36.

63. Samuel Piper to Paul C. Cameron, Nov., 1865, "Late 1865," Cameron Papers.

64. Paul C. Cameron to Thomas Ruffin, Nov. 27, 1865, in Hamilton, ed., *Ruffin Papers*, vol. 4, 42.

65. Paul C. Cameron to George Mordecai, Oct. 29, 1866, Mordecai Papers. For drafts of Cameron's contracts with his white tenants, see "Labor Contracts," Oct. 22, Nov. 1, 1866, Cameron Papers.

66. Paul C. Cameron to George Mordecai, Sept., 1866, Mordecai Papers.

67. Because the number of acres under cultivation did not fall as sharply as the size of the harvest produced, there is good reason to believe that productivity declined during this period. As a result of the instability in agriculture, the amount of acreage farmed by the planters who persisted from 1860 to 1870 fell from 29,644 to 11,935 acres—a decline of 59.7%.

68. For an excellent discussion of share tenant arrangements, see Ransom and Sutch, *One Kind of Freedom*, 90–94.

69. Most of the white share tenants of 1880 previously had never

owned real estate or slaves. Only 27.9% had owned land in 1870, 20.8% in 1860, and 30.0% in 1850. Only 2.5% of them had owned slaves in 1860 and 15.0% in 1850.

For one of the best descriptions of the changes experienced by landless whites in the postwar years, see Hahn, *The Roots of Southern Populism*, 158–65.

70. Joseph Hubbard Saunders to "Fannie," Feb. 8, 1867, Joseph Hubbard Saunders Papers, SHC; William Bingham to Walter W. Lenoir, Feb. 15, 1870, Lenoir Papers.

71. Where 50.0% of the grooms from landless households married brides from landowning households during the 1850s, only 44.0% did so during the 1870s. For the size of the sample for the 1850s, see Table 12. Because of the need to be sure that the brides and grooms were correctly identified and matched, the size of the sample for the 1870s was only 25 marriages.

72. For the declining price of cotton, see Ransom and Sutch, *One Kind of Freedom*, 188–93.

73. For the records of the New Hope neighborhood store, see Jesse W. Cole Ledger Book, 1867 to 1871, Jesse W. Cole Papers, DU. In August and September of 1869, 9 of the store's 36 customers purchased grain.

74. In 1860 there were 101,354 acres under cultivation. In 1880 there were only 86,401 acres.

75. U.S. Census Office, Tenth Census (1880), *Statistics of the Agriculture of the United States*, (Washington, D.C.: Government Printing Office, 1883), 128, 200, 302; Eugene W. Hilgard, ed., *Report on Cotton Production in the United States*, vol. 3 (Washington, D.C.: Government Printing Office, 1884), 3. In 1880 the yield for cotton was .43 bales per acre and for corn 12.8 bushels per acre. If the same amount of cotton had been produced in 1880 as in 1860, there would have been 2063 more acres that could have been used to grow corn. This acreage would have produced 26,406 additional bushels of corn which, when added to the 366,640 produced in 1880, would have equalled 98.2% of the bushels of corn produced in 1860.

Crop production levels in Orange County from 1860 to 1880 largely paralleled those of North Carolina, except that the decline in corn and wheat was larger and the amount of tobacco grown actually increased (see table I).

For North Carolina's and Orange County's production levels, see Escott, *Many Excellent People*, 175; Robert C. Kenzer, "Portrait of a Southern Community, 1849–1881," 140, 144.

76. U.S. Census MS., Orange County, 1860, Schedules 1 and 2. For the continuity in the ownership of neighborhood general stores, see North Carolina, vol. 19, Orange County, R.G. Dun & Co. Collection, BL–HBS.

TABLE I   *Percentage Change in Production Levels, 1860–80*

Crop	Orange County	North Carolina
corn	−8.4%	−6.8%
wheat	−39.2%	−28.4%
tobacco	+1.6%	−17.9%
cotton	+167.3%	+167.7%

77. *North Carolina Public Laws*, 1874–75, ch. 209, section 1; 1876–77, ch. 283, section 1.

78. For a similar conclusion, see Ransom and Sutch, *One Kind of Freedom*, 146–48. Note that Ransom and Sutch contend (pp. 132–36) that the most efficient spacing of general stores in the Cotton South would have been one store for every 70.3 square miles. Appendix 1-B demonstrates that the average neighborhood was 81.2 square miles in size. Because they focus only on the postbellum mercantile system, Ransom and Sutch are unable to perceive that the postwar territorial monopolies were rooted in the antebellum rural neighborhood.

79. Tilley, *The Bright-Tobacco Industry*, 548; Boyd, *Durham*, 56–59.

80. Boyd, *Durham*, 61; Robert F. Durden, *The Dukes of Durham, 1865–1929* (Durham, N.C.: Duke Univ. Press, 1975), 17.

81. Boyd, *Durham*, 68–70; *Hillsborough Recorder*, May 17, 1871. For the regional impact of the tobacco market in Durham, see Tilley, *Bright-Tobacco*, 206–7.

82. *Hillsborough Recorder*, Dec. 17, 1873.

83. Ibid., Dec. 12, 1873; Feb. 11, 1874.

84. For the best description of the Duke family's rapid rise, see Durden, *The Dukes*, 3–55.

85. Boyd, *Durham*, 97; *Durham Tobacco Plant*, July 13, 1880. The population for 1880 includes Durham's suburbs, which were located just outside of the town's limits.

86. *Chapel Hill Weekly Ledger*, Feb. 8, 1879; U.S. Census MS., Orange County, 1880, Schedules 1 and 2.

87. For the names of the fifteen prominent leaders and information on their backgrounds, see H.V. Paul, *History of the Town of Durham* (Raleigh, N.C.: privately published, 1884), 99–127; U.S. Census MS., Orange County, 1850, 1860, 1870, Schedules 1, 2, 3, and 4.

88. U.S. Census MS., Orange County, 1850, 1860, 1870, 1880, Schedules 1 and 4. Of these 78 men, 71 (91.0%) were natives of North Carolina. I have been able to find 25 of these 78 men in the 1870 manuscript census. Of these 25 men, 13 were residents of Durham in 1870.

TABLE J   *Percent of Population Moving to Durham*
from Other Parts of Orange

	Whites	Blacks
Bingham	0 %	12.5%
Cedar Grove	16.6	23.1
Chapel Hill	34.6	35.3
Hillsborough	30.5	31.2
Little River	25.0	38.9
Mangum	30.4	85.0
Patterson	60.0	100.0
Average	24.7%	41.0%

89. U.S. Census MS., Orange County, 1850, 1860, Schedules 1, 2, and 4. For a recent work that argues that the leaders of the tobacco industry were new men of wealth, see Dwight B. Billings, Jr., *Planters and the Making of a "New South": Class, Politics, and Development in North Carolina, 1865–1900* (Chapel Hill: Univ. of North Carolina Press, 1979), 113–20.

90. U.S. Census MS., Orange County, 1860, Schedule 1, 2, and 4; North Carolina, vol. 19, Orange County, pp. 236-V, 238-D, 282, 283, R.G. Dun and Co. Collection; Paul C. Cameron to Bennehan Cameron, Mar. 31, 1871, Bennehan Cameron Papers, SHC.

91. U.S. Census MS., Orange County, 1860, Schedules 1, 2, and 4.

92. Of the 178 white men who persisted but changed townships, 44 (24.7%) moved to Durham Township. Of the 100 black men who persisted but moved to different townships, 41 (41.0%) moved to Durham Township (see table J).

93. The following examples of whites and blacks who migrated to Durham are drawn from the U.S. Census MS., Orange County, 1870, 1880, Schedule 1.

94. In this analysis I used all employed males above age 10. Of the white males, 71.0% resided with a relative or their family. Of the black males, 60.2% resided with a relative or their family.

95. Of the 358 tobacco factory workers in Durham in 1880, 313 (87.4%) were black.

Of the 297 black male tobacco factory workers in Durham in 1880, 253 (85.2%) were under age 30.

96. Tilley, *Bright-Tobacco*, 515-21.

97. Ibid., 518-19.

98. Ibid., 489-544.

99. Paul, *History of the Town of Durham*, 78.

100. Tilley, *Bright-Tobacco*, 509-75.

101. *Hillsborough Recorder*, Feb. 13, 1878.

102. *Durham Tobacco Plant*, May 18, 1880.

103. N.C. Wilkinson to "Mattie," Jan. 27, 1880, James Southgate Papers, DU.

104. "Durham Tobacco Trade," 1875, Cameron Family Papers; *Durham Tobacco Plant*, Mar. 14, 28, 1877; Nov. 20, 1878; Mar. 9, 1880; "Durham National Bank," Sept. 20, 1878, Cameron Family Papers.

105. *Durham Tobacco Plant*, Dec. 8, 1880; *Durham Herald*, June 14, 1876.

106. Peter Hobbs, "Plantation to Factory: Tradition and Industrialization in Durham, North Carolina, 1880-1890," (M.A. Thesis, Duke Univ., 1971), 23. For Hobbs's calculation of the average distance the tobacco factory owners resided from their factories, see p. 21.

Chapter 6

1. *Hillsborough Recorder*, Aug. 27, 1862; Aug. 10, 1864.

2. Samuel F. Phillips to Kemp P. Battle, Sept. 5, 1865, Battle Papers; Samuel F. Phillips to William A. Graham, Sept. 16, 1865, in Hamilton and Williams, eds., *Graham Papers*, vol. 6, 360-62.

3. Samuel F. Phillips to Kemp P. Battle, Sept. 26, 1865, Battle Papers. For the decline in voting, see *Hillsborough Recorder*, Aug. 8, 1860; Mar. 6, May 15, 1861; P.H. Watson to "Mother," Sept. 24, 1865, Robert W. Winston Papers, SHC.

4. The following narration of North Carolina politics during this period is based primarily upon Joseph G. de Roulhac Hamilton, *Reconstruction in North Carolina* (New York: Columbia Univ. Press, 1914).

5. *Hillsborough Recorder*, Nov. 15, 1865.

6. *Journal of the Constitutional Convention of the State of North Carolina at Its Session, 1868*, 116. In the fall of 1867, 2004 whites registered. This compares to only 953 who voted in the 1866 gubernatorial election.

7. Battle, *History of the University*, vol. 1, 654-57. For the information on Jones, see U.S. Census MS., Orange County, 1870, Schedule 1.

8. Paul C. Cameron to Margaret and Pauline Cameron, Nov. 20, 1867, Cameron Family Papers.

9. *Journal of the Convention, 1868*, 116. It is possible to estimate the percent of whites who voted by subtracting the number of registered black voters (1291) from the total vote (2605). By this calculation whites accounted for a minimum of 1314 votes—65.5 percent of the total number of registered whites. It is doubtful, or course, that every registered black voted.

10. For the vote statewide, see Hamilton, *Reconstruction*, 251.

11. For the best description of the 1868 convention, see Otto H. Olsen, *Carpetbagger's Crusade: The Life of Albion Winegar Tourgée* (Baltimore: Johns Hopkins Univ. Press, 1965), 93–115.

12. The residents of the townships also would elect a constable and a school committee.

13. *Hillsborough Recorder*, Mar. 4, 1868.

14. *North Carolina Standard*, Nov. 18, 1868. In the ratification election, 3187 voters out of a total of 3578 registered voters (89.1%) cast their vote. If we assume that all the blacks who were registered voted, 1805 out of 2197 whites, 82.2% voted.

15. Minutes of the Orange County Board of Commissioners; Orange County Court Minutes, 1850-65. Only 12 of the 15 men who served as commissioners during this period headed households in 1870. Of these 12, 9 commissioners had served as magistrates before the war. One became a magistrate during the war. A contrasting view is expressed by Paul D. Escott who contends that on the local level North Carolina experienced a "political revolution," as demonstrated by the marked change in the composition of the county administrators after the Civil War (in *Many Excellent People*, 144–46, 167). See note 21 below.

16. Ibid. Between 1869 and 1876 the commissioners met on an average of 60.2 days annually.

17. Ten of the eleven commissioners who were either farmers by primary occupation or were listed in the agriculture schedule owned more than $1000 in real estate in 1870. Their average real estate holding was valued at $4763.63. By comparison, despite a similar distribution of real estate values in 1850 and 1870 for male household heads, the average value of real estate owned by an antebellum magistrate was only $2771.08.

18. Eight of the twelve commissioners who headed households in 1870 resided in Hillsborough, Chapel Hill, or Durham townships. Where only 22.9% of the magistrates had a primary occupation outside of farming, 41.7% of the commissioners did.

19. See Table 23 for source revealing Conservative party affiliation.

20. Minutes of The Orange County Board of Commissioners, Sept. 5, 1872.

21. Seventeen of the thirty post-1868 magistrates had been magistrates before the end of the war.

22. *Hillsborough Recorder*, July 28, 1869; Joseph G. de Roulhac Hamilton, "Civil War and Reconstruction in Orange County," in Lefler and Wager, eds., *Orange County*, 116–20.

23. Allen W. Trelease, *White Terror: The Ku Klux Klan Conspiracy and Southern Reconstruction* (New York: Harper and Row, 1971), 189–225.

24. Frenise A. Logan, *The Negro in North Carolina, 1877–1904* (Chapel Hill: Univ. of North Carolina Press, 1964), 48–50; *Laws and Resolutions of the State of North Carolina*, 1877, ch. 141.

25. For Republicans who were elected to township offices, see notes 35, 37, 43 of this chapter.

26. Four of the five commissioners on the previous board were still serving after the new legislation.

27. The coefficient of correlation measures the stability of party identification in election precincts. The coefficient of correlation between the vote for governor in 1872 and 1876 was .89 and between 1872 and 1880 was .94. Between 1876 and 1880 it was .92. For election returns by precinct, see *Hillsborough Recorder*, Aug. 5, 1872; Nov. 15, 1876, Record of Elections by Precincts, Orange County Miscellaneous Papers, Nov. 1880.

28. The coefficient of correlation also can indicate the relationship between race and party identification by comparing the percentage of the registered voters who are either black or white in election precincts and the percentage of the vote cast in these precincts for either the Conservative or Republican party. The coefficient of correlation for 1872–80 between the percentage of black registered voters in a precinct and the percentage of vote cast in that precinct for the Republican party in gubernatorial elections indicates a strong relationship between race and party identification: 1872 = +.90, 1876 = +.86, 1878 = +.96. The coefficient is the same, of course, for the percentage of white registered voters and the percentage of vote cast for the Conservative party.

29. *Durham Tobacco Plant*, May 9, 1876; Jean B. Anderson, "A Genealogy of the Descendants of Nathaniel Harris," (n.d.), a genealogy given to me by the author.

30. There were 2026 white households in 1870. Since there were 52 school districts, there were on average 40.0 white households per district. For reports of the caucus choosing delegates to attend the township meeting, see *Hillsborough Recorder*, Apr. 27, May 4, 1868.

31. C.E. Smith to Orange County Democratic Township Committees, Apr. 17, 1872, William A. Graham Papers, SHC.

32. The turnout for 1880 was calculated by using the ecological regression technique. For an explanation of this methodology, see J. Morgan Kousser, "Ecological Regression and The Analysis of Past Politics," *Journal of Interdisciplinary History* 4 (Autumn 1973): 237–62. For the estimate of

1868 turnout, see note 14 above. The ecological regression methodology indicates that the decline in white turnout occurred quite rapidly, as only 67.0% were voting in 1872.

33. Battle, *History of the University*, vol. 2, 2–12.

34. Cornelia Phillips Spencer to Mrs. D.L. Swain, Dec. 20, 1869, Spencer Papers; Records of the Appointments of Postmaster, 1831–1929, microfilm copy in NCDAH.

35. County Commission Minutes, Aug. 9, 1873.

36. Records of the Appointments of Postmasters, 1831–1929.

37. For evidence of blacks winning township offices in Hillsborough, see Ike R. Strayhorn to A.W. Tourgée, Aug. 11, 1869, Albion Winegar Tourgée Papers, microfilm copy in SHC.

38. *Hillsborough Recorder*, Mar. 6, 1861.

39. For a mention of peace meetings in this area, see Osmond F. Long to William A. Graham, Sept. 3, 1863, in Hamilton and Williams, eds., *Graham Papers*, vol. 5, 527–28. For the vote for Alfred Dockery, see Election Returns by Precincts, Orange County Miscellaneous Papers, 1866, NCDAH. Although Dockery received only 3.9% of the vote in Orange County, he gained 25.6% of the vote in Cates Precinct.

40. *Hillsborough Recorder*, Aug. 5, 1872.

41. In Bingham only 20.1% of the registered voters were black.

42. Eliza Thompson to Benjamin S. Hedrick, Dec. 26, 1871, Hedrick Papers, DU.

43. County Commission Minutes, Aug. 5, 1871.

44. *Hillsborough Recorder*, June 14, 1876.

45. *Durham Tobacco Plant*, Oct. 18, 1876.

46. *Hillsborough Recorder*, Oct. 25, 1876.

47. In calculating this correlation I averaged John W. Graham's vote with that of John Cunningham, the other Conservative who was campaigning, to produce a composite Conservative percent.

48. *Durham Tobacco Plant*, Nov. 6, 1877.

49. *Hillsborough Recorder*, Nov. 7, 1877.

50. Ibid., July 3, 1878.

51. *Chapel Hill Ledger*, July 20, 1878.

52. *Hillsborough Recorder*, Aug. 21, 1878.

53. *Chapel Hill Ledger*, Aug. 28, 1880.

54. Ibid., Sept. 4, 1880.

55. *Orange County Observer*, Oct. 13, 1880.

56. In 1876 Turner received 45.3% of the vote. In 1878, his total rose to 58.2%. In 1880, it declined to 46.3%.

57. See note 15 above.

58. *Hillsborough Recorder*, Apr. 29, 1874.

59. Ibid., May 13, 1874. For the increasing importance of Durham's votes, see *Hillsborough Recorder*, Aug. 5, 1872; Record of Elections by Precincts, Nov., 1880, Orange County Miscellaneous Papers.

60. *Hillsborough Recorder*, Feb. 27, 1878.

61. Ibid., Aug. 14, 1878. In Durham Precinct, Angier won 624, Turner 456, and Hutchins 381 votes.

62. Record of Elections by Precincts, Nov., 1880. Green and Parrish beat Turner countywide by 311 votes. They defeated him in Durham by a 201-vote margin.

63. Boyd, *Durham*, 104–14. For the support of Durham's tobacco manufacturers, see Walter Clark to Augustus W. Graham, February 22, 1881, in Aubrey Lee Brooks and Hugh Talmadge Lefler, eds., *The Papers of Walter Clark*, vol. 1 (Chapel Hill: Univ. of North Carolina Press, 1948–1950), 213.

For the opposition of the Orange County Board of Commissioners and a list of the opponents of the division, see *Orange County Observer*, Jan. 29, 1881; C.E. Parrish to A.W. Graham, Feb. 28, 1881, A.W. Graham Papers, SHC.

64. Walter Clark to A.W. Graham, Feb. 15, 1881, in Brooks and Lefler, eds., *The Papers of Walter Clark*, vol. 1, 213.

65. *Orange County Observer*, Mar. 19, 1881. In 1880 Chapel Hill and Hillsborough gave the Republican gubernatorial candidate 55.2% their votes. Durham gave the Democrat 56.8%. For the vote returns, see note 62.

66. "To the Voters of Durham County," n.d., Hardy Massey Papers, NCDAH. This broadside contains the names of a number of tobacco manufacturers who supported the division including Washington Duke.

Duke and the Republicans were correct in their assessment of the political situation that would result from the division of the county. Although the Democrats of Durham County were able to carry their state house seat at the next election in 1882, the Republicans in Orange County defeated the regular Democrat nominee by 7 votes and elected an Independent to represent the county in the house. Equally important, the Republicans, by a majority of 170 votes, elected Isaac (Ike) Strayhorn, the white Republican leader from Hillsborough, to represent the 20th state senatorial district, which included Orange, Durham, and neighboring Caswell County. For the 1882 election results, see J.S. Tomlinson, *Assembly Sketch Book, Session 1883* (Raleigh, N.C.: Edwards, Broughton, 1883), 14, 43, 61.

67. Ibid.

68. See note 62 above for the number of votes cast by precinct.

69. Bennehan Cameron to Mrs. Anne Cameron, Apr. 6, 1881, Bennehan Cameron Papers.

70. *Orange County Observer*, Apr. 23, 1881; "Proclamation of Gover-

nor Thomas J. Jarvis Establishing the County of Durham," 1881, Durham Miscellaneous Papers, NCDAH.

Epilogue

1. D.L. Rights, "Rural Life Near Chapel Hill," *North Carolina University Magazine* 29 (Apr. 1912): 9–11.
2. Wilmer Harding Clay, "Church Participation in Rural Community Life" (M.A. thesis, Univer. of North Carolina, Chapel Hill, 1947), 52–56.
3. Alfred M. Mirande, "Extended Kinship Ties, Friendship Relations, and Community Size: An Explanatory Inquiry," *Rural Sociology* 35 (June 1970): 261–66.
4. U.S. Census Office, *The Eighteenth Decennial Census of the United States* (1960), *Vol. I: Characteristics of the Population* (Washington, D.C.: Government Printing Office, 1962), part 35, 16, 18, 20; U.S. Census Office, *1980 Census of Population and Housing*, Census Tracts: Raleigh-Durham, N.C. (Washington, D.C.: Government Printing Office, 1983), P. p-1.
5. *Durham Morning Herald*, Apr. 8, 1985. I am grateful to Professor Sydney Nathans of Duke University for bringing this article to my attention.
6. Steven Hahn notes the presence of rural settlements in *The Roots of Southern Populism*, 52–54, but he neither looks at them from as many dimensions as this study nor does he seem to have the genealogical sources to prove kin ties.
For one sociological study which does focus on rural neighborhoods and extensively details family ties in a community during the mid-twentieth century, see Elmora Messer Matthews, *Neighbor and Kin: Life in A Tennessee Ridge Community* (Nashville: Vanderbilt Univ. Press, 1965).
7. John Shelton Reed, *The Enduring South: Subcultural Persistence in Mass Society* (Lexington, Mass.: Heath, 1972), 33–43.
8. Jonathan M. Wiener, *Social Origins of the New South*; Jean E. Friedman, *The Enclosed Garden*; Randolph B. Campbell, *A Southern Community in Crisis*, 395; Paul D. Escott, *Many Excellent People*, xviii; Ransom and Sutch, *One Kind of Freedom*; Hahn, *The Roots of Southern Populism*; Wayne, *The Reshaping of Plantation Society*; C. Vann Woodward, *Thinking Back: The Perils of Writing History* (Baton Rouge: Louisiana State Univ. Press, 1986), ch. 4, esp. 78.

Selected Bibliography

This bibliography includes only those sources cited in notes.

Primary Sources

MANUSCRIPT COLLECTIONS

Southern Historical Collection, Univ. of North Carolina Library, Chapel Hill, N.C.:

Battle Family Papers.
Mrs. John Berry Papers.
Robert Bingham Reminscences.
William Calder Papers.
John Caldwell Papers.
Bennehan Cameron Papers.
Cameron Family Papers.
Anne Collins Papers.
Creecy Family Papers.
Moses Ashley Curtis Papers.
Fitzgerald Papers, microfilm copy.
Thomas Miles Garrett Diary.
William A. Graham Papers.
Heartt and Wilson Family Papers.
Benjamin S. Hedrick Papers.
Cadwallader Jones, Jr., Papers.
John Kimberly Papers.
Lenoir Family Papers.
Henry A. London Papers.
Maddry, Charles Edward. "History of Mount Moriah Church."
Mangum Family Papers.
Mebane Family Papers.
Stephen Moore Papers.
George Mordecai Papers.
Mordecai Family Papers.
North Carolina Mercantile Books.
Parker and Nelson Account Book, 1847–53.
Pettigrew Family Papers.
Thomas Ruffin Papers.
Ruffin, Roulhac, and Hamilton Family Papers.
John Hubbard Saunders Papers.

Cornelia Phillips Spencer Papers.   James Webb Papers.
Samuel Thompson Papers.   Robert W. Winston Papers.

North Carolina Collection, Univ. of North Carolina Library, Chapel Hill, N.C.:

Cameron, Paul C. "An Address before the Orange County Society for the Promotion of Agriculture, the Mechanical Arts, and Manufacturers."

Proceedings of the Grand Royal Arch Chapter, 1860.

Suggs, Eugene. "Sketches of Major General Thomas Lloyd of Orange County."

Manuscript Department, William R. Perkins Library, Duke Univ., Durham, N.C.:

Francis N. Bennett Papers.   Thomas Lloyd Papers.
Hugh Conway Browning Papers.   John A. McDade Papers.
Jesse W. Cole Papers.   Addison Mangum Store Ledger.
Mary E. Craig Papers.   Luther M. Sharpe Papers.
Gill Family Papers.   James Southgate Papers.
Benjamin Sherwood Hedrick   Southgate-Jones Papers.
Papers.   Tillinghast Family Papers.
Leathers, Latta and Co. Day   Michael H. Turrentine Papers.
Book, 1854–56.   John C. Van Hook Papers.

North Carolina Division of Archives and History, Raleigh, N.C.:

Cane Creek Baptist Church Roll, 1829–56, microfilm copy.
Governor Henry T. Clark Papers.
Durham County, Miscellaneous Papers.
Eno Presbyterian Church Session Minutes, 1822–74, microfilm copy.
William A. Graham Papers.
William W. Holden Papers.
McDuffie, D.G. "Map of Durham County, North Carolina, 1881."
Willie Person Mangum Papers.
Hardy Massey Papers.
New Hope Presbyterian Church Register and Session Minutes, 1816–1950, microfilm copy.
Orange County, Court Minutes.
Orange County, Inventories, Sales and Accounts of Estate.
Orange County, Marriage Bonds to 1868.
Orange County, Minutes of the County Board of Commissioners.
Orange County, Miscellaneous Papers.
Orange County, Miscellaneous Tax Records.
Orange County, Negro Cohabitation Certificates, 1866–68.
Orange County, Records of the Wardens of the Poorhouse.
Records of the Appointments of Postmasters, 1831–29, microfilm copy.
St. Matthew's Episcopal Church Records, 1824–60, microfilm copy.

Governor Zebulon Vance Papers.
Richard D. White Collection.
Manuscript Collections used in Orange County Courthouse, Hillsborough,
N.C.:
   Orange County, Marriage Register, 1868–81.
   Orange County, Will Book, volumes F, G, & H.
Baker Library, Harvard Univ., Boston:
   R.G. Dun & Co. Credit Ledgers.

GOVERNMENT DOCUMENTS: NATIONAL

Seventh Census, 1850, Orange County, N.C. Schedule 1 (Free Inhabitants),
   Schedule 2 (Slave Inhabitants), Schedule 4 (Productions of Agriculture),
   Schedule 5 (Products of Industry), and Schedule 6 (Social Statistics).
   National Archives, Washington, D.C., microfilm copy.
Eighth Census, 1860, Orange County, N.C. Schedule 1 (Free Inhabitants),
   Schedule 2 (Slave Inhabitants), Schedule 4 (Productions of Agriculture),
   Schedule 5 (Products of Industry), and Schedule 6 (Social Statistics).
   National Archives, Washington, D.C., microfilm copy.
Ninth Census, 1870, Orange County, N.C. Schedule 1 (Inhabitants),
   Schedule 3 (Productions of Agriculture), Schedule 4 (Products of In-
   dustry), and Schedule 5 (Social Statistics). National Archives, Washing-
   ton, D.C., microfilm copy.
Tenth Census, 1880, Orange County, N.C. Schedule 1 (Inhabitants),
   Schedule 2 (Productions of Agriculture), Schedule 3 (Products of In-
   dustry). National Archives, Washington, D.C., microfilm copy.
U. S. Bureau of Refugees, Freedmen, and Abandoned Lands, 1865–1869.
   Records of the Assistant Commissioner for the State of North Carolina.
   National Archives, Washington, D.C., microfilm copy.
U. S. Bureau of the Census, Eighth Census. *Population of the United
   States in 1860; Compiled from the Original Returns of the Eighth
   Census.* Washington, D.C.: Government Printing Office, 1864
U.S. Bureau of the Census, Eighth Census. *Agriculture of the United States
   in 1860; Compiled from the Original Returns of the Eighth Census.*
   Washington, D.C.: Government Printing Office, 1864.
U.S. Bureau of the Census, Eighth Census. *Manufactures of the United
   States in 1860; Compiled from the Original Returns of the Eighth
   Census.* Washington, D.C.: Government Printing Office, 1865.
U.S. Bureau of the Census, Ninth Census. *The Statistics of the Population
   of the United States; Compiled from the Original Returns of the Ninth
   Census (June 1, 1870).* Washington, D.C.: Government Printing Office,
   1872.
U.S. Bureau of the Census, Ninth Census. *The Statistics of the Wealth and*

*Industry of the United States . . . from the Original Returns of the
Ninth Census, 1870.* Washington, D.C.: Government Printing Office,
1872.

U.S. Bureau of the Census, Tenth Census. *Statistics of the Population of
the United States at the Tenth Census (June 1, 1880).* Washington,
D.C.: Government Printing Office, 1883.

U.S. Bureau of the Census, Tenth Census. *Report on the Productions of
Agriculture as Returned at the Tenth Census, 1880.* Washington, D.C.:
Government Printing Office, 1883.

GOVERNMENT DOCUMENTS: STATE

*Journal of the Constitutional Convention of the State of North Carolina
at Its Session, 1868.*
Laws and Resolutions of the State of North Carolina, 1877.
North Carolina Public Laws, 1874–1875.
*Report of the North Carolina Comptroller of Public Accounts, 1856–
1864.*
Revised Code of North Carolina, 1855.

UNPUBLISHED GENEALOGIES

Anderson, Jean, "The Descendants of Nathaniel Harris"
Browning, Hugh Conway, comp., "Orange County and Hillsborough
Items of History: The Families of Hugh and James Caine"
Ray, William A., and Florence (Ray) Lewis, "The Rays (Raes) Down
through the Years"

NEWSPAPERS

Chapel Hill Ledger   *Durham Morning Herald*
Chapel Hill Weekly Ledger   *Hillsborough Recorder*
Chapel Hill Literary Gazette   *Orange County Observer*
Durham Tobacco Plant   *Raleigh Standard*
Durham Herald

PUBLISHED COLLECTIONS OF PAPERS,
CORRESPONDENCE, DOCUMENTS

Brooks, Aubrey Lee, and Hugh Talmadge Lefler. *The Papers of Walter
Clark.* 2 vols. Chapel Hill: Univ. of North Carolina Press, 1948–50.
Hamilton, J.G. de Roulhac, ed. *The Papers of Thomas Ruffin.* 4 vols.
Raleigh, N.C.: Edwards and Broughton Printing Company, 1918–20.

————, and Max R. Williams, eds. *The Papers of William Alexander Graham*. 7 vols. Raleigh, N.C.: North Carolina Division of Archives and History, 1957–.

Rawick, George P., ed. *The American Slave: A Composite Autobiography*. 19 vols. in Series 1, 12 vols. in Supplement, Series 1. Westport, Conn.: Greenwood Press, 1972 and 1977.

Saunders, William L., ed., *Colonial Records of North Carolina*. 10 vols. Raleigh, N.C.: M.P. Hale, 1866–90.

Shanks, Henry T. *The Papers of Willie Person Mangum*. 5 vols. Raleigh, N.C.: North Carolina Department of Archives and History, 1950–56.

Tolbert, Noble J. ed. *The Papers of John Willis Ellis*. 2 vols. Raleigh, N.C.: North Carolina Division of Archives and History, 1964.

Secondary Sources

BOOKS

Alexander, Roberta Sue. *North Carolina Faces the Freedmen: Race Relations during Presidential Reconstruction, 1865–1867*. Durham, N.C.: Duke Univ. Press, 1985.

Anderson, Jean Bradley. *Piedmont Plantation: The Bennehan-Cameron Family and Lands in North Carolina*. Durham, N.C.: The Historic Preservation Society of Durham, 1985.

Baker, Jean H. *Ambivalent Americans: The Know-Nothing Party in Maryland*. Baltimore: Johns Hopkins Univ. Press, 1977.

Barrett, John G. *The Civil War in North Carolina*. Chapel Hill: Univ. of North Carolina Press, 1963.

————. *Sherman's March through the Carolinas*. Chapel Hill: Univ. of North Carolina Press, 1966.

Barron, Hal S. *Those Who Stayed Behind: Rural Society in Nineteenth-Century New England*. Cambridge: Cambridge Univ. Press, 1984.

Battle, Kemp B. *History of the University of North Carolina*. 2 vols. Raleigh, N.C.: Edwards and Broughton, 1907–12.

Benson, Lee. *The Concept of Jacksonian Democracy: New York as a Test Case*. Princeton, N.J.: Princeton Univ. Press, 1961.

Billings, Dwight B., Jr. *Planters and the Making of a "New South": Class, Politics, and Development in North Carolina, 1865–1900*. Chapel Hill: Univ. of North Carolina Press, 1979.

Blackwelder, Ruth. *The Age of Orange: Political and Intellectual Leadership in North Carolina, 1752–1861*. Charlotte, N.C.: William Loftin, 1961.

Blumin, Stuart M. *The Urban Threshold: Growth and Change in a Nine-teenth Century American Community.* Chicago: Univ. of Chicago Press, 1976.

Boyd, William Kenneth. *The Story of Durham: City of the New South.* Durham, N.C.: Duke Univ. Press, 1925.

Burton, Orville Vernon. *In My Father's House Are Many Mansions: Family and Community in Edgefield, South Carolina.* Chapel Hill: Univ. of North Carolina Press, 1985.

Campbell, Randolph. *A Southern Community in Crisis: Harrison County, Texas, 1850–1880.* Austin: Texas State Historical Association, 1983.

———— and Richard Lowe. *Wealth and Power in Antebellum Texas.* College Station: Texas A & M Univ. Press, 1977.

Craig, David I. *A Historical Sketch of the New Hope Church, in Orange County, North Carolina.* Reidsville, N.C.: S.W. Paisley, 1886.

Curti, Merle. *The Making of an American Community: A Case Study of Democracy in a Frontier County.* Stanford, Calif.: Stanford Univ. Press, 1959.

Dollar, Charles M., and Richard Jensen, *A Historian's Guide to Statistics: Quantitative Analysis and Historical Research.* New York: Holt, Rinehart, and Winston, 1971.

Doyle, Don Harrison. *The Social Order of a Frontier Community: Jacksonville, Illinois, 1825–1870.* Urbana: Univ. of Illinois Press, 1978.

Dula, Lucile Noell, *Hillsborough: Historic Orange County, North Carolina.* Gretna, La.: Pelican, 1979.

Dun, R.G. & Co. (compilers). *The Mercantile Agency Reference Book (and Key) Containing Ratings on the Merchants, Manufacturers, and Traders Generally, Throughout the United States and Canada.* 15 vols. New York: R.G. Dun, 1867–81 (bound volumes in Library of Congress).

Durden, Robert F. *The Dukes of Durham, 1865–1929.* Durham, N.C.: Duke Univ. Press, 1975.

Escott, Paul D. *After Secession: Jefferson Davis and the Failure of Confederate Nationalism.* Baton Rouge: Louisiana State Univ. Press, 1979.

————. *Many Excellent People: Power and Privilege in North Carolina, 1850–1900.* Chapel Hill: Univ. of North Carolina Press, 1985.

Friedman, Jean E. *The Enclosed Garden: Women and the Evangelical South, 1830–1900.* Chapel Hill: Univ. of North Carolina Press, 1984.

Gutman, Herbert G. *The Black Family in Slavery and Freedom, 1750–1925.* New York: Pantheon, 1976.

Hahn, Steven. *The Roots of Southern Populism: Yeoman Farmers and the Transformation of the Georgia Upcountry, 1850–1890.* New York: Oxford Univ. Press, 1983.

Hamilton, J.G. de Roulhac. *Reconstruction in North Carolina*. New York: Columbia Univ. Press, 1914.

Harris, J. William. *Plain Folk and Gentry in a Slave Society: White Liberty and Black Slavery in Augusta's Hinterlands*. Middletown, Conn.: Wesleyan Univ. Press, 1985.

Hilliard, Sam Bowers. *Hog Meat and Hoecake: Food Supply in the Old South, 1840–1860*. Carbondale: Southern Illinois Univ. Press, 1972.

Holt, Michael F. *The Political Crisis of the 1850s*. New York: Wiley, 1978.

Iobst, Richard W. *The Bloody Sixth: The Sixth North Carolina Regiment, Confederate States of America*. Raleigh, N.C.: North Carolina Confederate Centennial Commission, 1965.

Johnson, Guion Griffis. *Ante-Bellum North Carolina*. Chapel Hill: Univ. of North Carolina Press, 1937.

Johnston, Henry Poellnitz. *The Gentle Johnstons and Their Kin*. Birmingham, Ala.: Featon Press, 1966.

Jones, Cadwallader. *A Genealogical History*. Columbia, S.C.: Ye Bryan Printing Company, 1899.

Jordan, Weymouth T., and Louis H. Manarin, eds., *The North Carolina Troops, 1861–1865: A Roster*. Vols. 1-9. Raleigh: North Carolina Department of Archives and History, 1961.

Katz, Michael B. *The People of Hamilton Canada West: Family and Class in a Mid-Nineteenth Century City*. Cambridge: Harvard Univ. Press, 1975.

Knights, Peter R. *The Plain People of Boston, 1830–1860*. New York: Oxford Univ. Press, 1971.

Kruman, Marc. *Parties and Politics in North Carolina, 1836–1865*. Baton Rouge: Louisiana State Univ. Press, 1983.

Lefler, Hugh Talmadge, and Albert Ray Newsome. *A History of A Southern State: North Carolina*. 3rd edition. Chapel Hill: Univ. of North Carolina Press, 1954.

Lefler, Hugh Talmadge, and Paul Wager. *Orange County, 1752–1952*. Chapel Hill: Orange Printshop, 1953.

Lloyd, Allen Alexander, and Pauline O. Lloyd. *History of the Town of Hillsborough, 1754–1966*. N.p.: privately published, n.d.

Logan, Frenise A. *The Negro in North Carolina, 1877–1904*. Chapel Hill: Univ. of North Carolina Press, 1964.

Mathews, Donald G. *Religion in the Old South*. Chicago: Univ. of Chicago Press, 1977.

Matthews, Elmora Messer. *Neighbor and Kin: Life in a Tennessee Ridge Community*. Nashville: Vanderbilt Univ. Press, 1965.

Merrens, Harry Roy. *Colonial North Carolina in the Eighteenth Century:*

A Study in Historical Geography. Chapel Hill: Univ. of North Carolina Press, 1964.

Mohr, Clarence L. *On the Threshold of Freedom: Masters and Slaves in Civil War Georgia*. Athens: Univ. of Georgia Press, 1986.

Monahan, Thomas P. *Pattern of Age at Marriage in the United States*. Vols. 1–2. Philadelphia: privately published, 1951.

Moore, John W., ed. *Register of North Carolina Troops in the War between the States*. Vols. 1–4. Raleigh, N.C.: North Carolina State Publisher, 1882.

Norton, Clarence Clifford. *The Democratic Party in Ante-Bellum North Carolina, 1835–1861*. Chapel Hill: Univ. of North Carolina Press, 1930.

Oakes, James. *The Ruling Race: A History of American Slaveholders*. New York: Knopf, 1982.

Olsen, Otto H. *Carpetbagger's Crusade: The Life of Albion Winegar Tourgée*. Baltimore: Johns Hopkins Univ. Press, 1965.

Owsley, Frank Lawrence. *Plain Folk of the Old South*. Baton Rouge: Louisiana State Univ. Press, 1949.

Paul, H.V. *History of the Town of Durham*. Raleigh, N.C.: privately published, 1884.

Pegg, Herbert Dale. *The Whig Party in North Carolina*. Chapel Hill: Colonial Press, n.d.

Perkins, S.O. et al. *Soil Map of Durham County*. Washington, D.C.: U.S. Department of Agriculture, 1920.

Ramsey, Robert W. *Carolina Cradle: Settlement of the Northwest Carolina Frontier, 1747–1762*. Chapel Hill: Univ. of North Carolina Press, 1964.

Ransom, Roger L. and Richard Sutch. *One Kind of Freedom: The Economic Consequences of Emancipation*. New York: Cambridge Univ. Press, 1977.

Reed, John Shelton. *The Enduring South: Subcultural Persistence in Mass Society*. Lexington, Mass.: Heath, 1972.

Robert, Joseph Clarke. *The Tobacco Kingdom*. Durham, N.C.: Duke Univ. Press, 1938.

Rutman, Darrett B., and Anita H. *A Place in Time: Middlesex County, Virginia, 1650–1750*. New York: Norton, 1984.

Ryan, Mary P. *Cradle of the Middle Class: The Family in Onieda County, New York, 1790–1865*. Cambridge: Cambridge Univ. Press, 1981.

Sanders, Charles Richard. *The Cameron Plantation of Central North Carolina, 1776–1973*. Durham, N.C.: privately published, 1974.

Shields, Ruth Herndon et al., comps. *A Study of the Barbee Families of Chatham, Orange, and Wake Counties in North Carolina*. Boulder, Colo.: privately published, 1971.

Shifflett, Crandall A. *Patronage and Poverty in the Tobacco South: Louisa County, Virginia, 1860–1900.* Knoxville: Univ. of Tennessee Press, 1982.

Sitterson, Joseph Carlyle. *The Secession Movement in North Carolina.* Chapel Hill: Univ. of North Carolina Press, 1939.

Soltow, Lee. *Men and Wealth in the United States, 1850–1870.* Lexington, Mass.: Heath, 1973.

Sydnor, Charles S. *Gentlemen Freeholders: Political Parties in Washington's Virginia.* Chapel Hill: Univ. of North Carolina Press, 1952.

Tilley, Nannie Mae. *The Bright-Tobacco Industry, 1860–1929.* Chapel Hill: Univ. of North Carolina Press, 1948.

Tomlinson, J.S. *Assembly Sketch Book, Session 1883.* Raleigh, N.C.: Edwards, Broughton, 1883.

Trelease, Allen W. *White Terror: The Ku Klux Klan Conspiracy and Southern Reconstruction.* New York: Harper and Row, 1971.

Turner, Frederick Jackson. *The Frontier in American History.* New York: Henry Holt, 1920.

Turner, Herbert Snipes. *Church in the Old Fields: Hawfields Presbyterian Church and Community in North Carolina.* Chapel Hill: Univ. of North Carolina Press, 1962.

Vanatta, E.S. et al. *Soil Survey of Orange County.* Washington, D.C.: U.S. Department of Agriculture, 1921.

Watson, Henry Legare II. *Jacksonian Politics and Community Conflict: The Emergence of the Second American Party System in Cumberland County, North Carolina.* Baton Rouge: Louisiana State Univ. Press, 1981.

Wayne, Michael. *The Reshaping of Plantation Society: The Natchez District, 1860–1880.* Baton Rouge: Louisiana State Univ. Press, 1983.

Wiener, Jonathan M. *Social Origins of the New South: Alabama, 1860–1885.* Baton Rouge: Louisiana State Univ. Press, 1978.

Wiley, Bell. *The Life of Johnny Reb: The Common Soldiers of the Confederacy.* Indianapolis: Bobbs-Merrill, 1943.

Williamson, Joel R. *New People: Miscegenation and Mulattoes in the United States.* New York: Free Press, 1980.

Woodward, C, Vann. *Thinking Back: The Perils of Writing History.* Baton Rouge: Louisiana State Univ. Press, 1986.

Wooster, Ralph. *Politicians, Planters, and Plain Folk: Courthouse and Statehouse in the Upper South, 1850–1860.* Knoxville: Univ. of Tennessee Press, 1975.

Wright, Gavin. *The Political Economy of the Cotton South: Households, Markets, and Wealth in the Nineteenth Century.* New York: Norton, 1978.

Yates, Richard. *The Confederacy of Zeb Vance.* Tuscaloosa, Ala.: Confederate, 1958.

ARTICLES

"Autobiography of Col. William Few of Georgia." *Magazine of American History* 7 (Nov. 1881): 340–58.

Barney, William L. "Patterns of Crisis: Alabama White Families and Social Change, 1850–1870." *Sociology and Social Research: An International Journal* 63 (Apr. 1979): 524–43.

Escott, Paul D. "Poverty and Governmental Aid for the Poor in Confederate North Carolina." *North Carolina Historical Review* 61 (Oct. 1984): 462–80.

Gatling, Eva Ingersoll. "John Berry of Hillsboro, North Carolina." *Journal of Architecture Historians"* 10 (1951): 18–22.

Isaac, Rhys. "Dramatizing the Ideology of the Revolution: Popular Nobilization in Virginia, 1774–1776." *William and Mary Quarterly* 33, no. 3 (1976): 357–85.

Katz, Michael B. et al. "Migration and the Social Order in Erie County, New York: 1855." *Journal of Interdisciplinary History* 8 (Spring 1978): 669–701.

Kousser, J. Morgan. "Ecological Regression and the Analysis of Past Politics." *Journal of Interdisciplinary History* 4 (Autumn 1973): 237–62.

Linden, Fabian. "Economic Democracy in the Slave South: An Appraisal of Some Recent Views." *Journal of Negro History* 31 (Apr. 1946): 140–89.

McCormick, Richard P. "Suffrage, Classes and Party Alignments: A Study in Voter Alignments." *Mississippi Valley Historical Review* 46 (Dec. 1959): 397–403.

Massey, Mary E. "Confederate Refugees in North Carolina." *North Carolina Historical Review* 40 (Apr. 1963): 158–82.

Menius, Arthur C. III. "James Bennitt: Portrait of an Antebellum Yeoman." *North Carolina Historical Review* 58 (Oct. 1981): 305–26.

Miller, Robert D. "Samuel Field Phillips: The Odyssey of a Southern Dissenter." *North Carolina Historical Review* 58 (July 1981): 263–80.

Mirande, Alfred M. "Extended Kinship Ties, Friendship Relations, and Community Size: An Explanatory Inquiry." *Rural Sociology* 35 (June 1970): 261–66.

Naroll, Raoul S. "Lincoln and the Sherman Peace Fiasco—Another Fable?" *Journal of Southern History* 20 (Nov. 1954): 459–83.

Nash, Francis. "The History of Orange County—Part I." *North Carolina Booklet* 11 (Oct. 1916): 63–68.

Pole, J.R. "Election Statistics in North Carolina to 1861." *Journal of Southern History* 24 (May 1958): 225–28.

Pressly, Thomas J. "Bullets and Ballots: Lincoln and the 'Right of Revolution.'" *American Historical Review* 67 (Apr. 1962): 647–62.

Reid, Richard. "A Test Case of the 'Crying Evil': Desertion among North Carolina Troops during the Civil War." *North Carolina Historical Review* 58 (July 1981): 234–62.

Rights, D.L. "Rural Life near Chapel Hill." *North Carolina University Magazine* 29 (Apr. 1912): 9–11.

Throne, Mildred. "A Population Study of an Iowa County in 1850." *Iowa Journal of History* 27 (Oct. 1959): 305–30.

Wagstaff, Henry M. "The James A. Graham Papers, 1861–1885." *James Sprunt Historical Studies* 20 (1928): 1–324.

Woodman, Harold. "Sequel to Slavery: The New History of the Postwar South." *Journal of Southern History* 43 (Nov. 1977): 523–54.

Wyatt-Brown, Bertram. "The Ideal Typology and Antebellum Southern History: A Testing of a New Approach." *Societas* 5 (Winter 1975): 1–30.

DISSERTATIONS AND THESES

Butts, Donald C. "A Challenge to Planter Rule: The Controversy over the Ad Valorem Taxation of Slaves in North Carolina, 1858–1862." Ph.D., Duke Univ., 1978.

Clay, Wilmer Harding. "Church Participation in Rural Community Life." M.A., Univ. of North Carolina, 1947.

Entrekin, William Frank, Jr. "Poor Relief in North Carolina in the Confederacy." M.A., Duke Univ., 1947.

Heath, Raymond, Jr. "The North Carolina Militia on the Eve of the Civil War." M.A., Univ. of North Carolina, 1974.

Hobbs, Peter. "Plantation to Factory: Tradition and Industrialization in Durham, North Carolina, 1880–1890." M.A., Duke Univ., 1971.

Huffman, Frank J., Jr. "Old South, New South: Continuity and Change in a Georgia County, 1850–1880." Ph.D., Yale Univ., 1974.

Iobst, Richard W. "North Carolina Mobilizes: Nine Crucial Months, December 1860–August 1861." Ph.D., Univ. of North Carolina, 1968.

Jeffrey, Thomas Edward. "The Second Party System in North Carolina, 1836–1860." Ph.D., Catholic Univ. of America, 1979.

Kenzer, Robert C. "Portrait of a Southern Community, 1849–1881: Family, Kinship, and Neighborhood in Orange County, North Carolina." Ph.D., Harvard Univ., 1982.

Schlotterbeck, John T. "Plantation and Farm: Social and Economic Change in Orange and Greene Counties, Virginia, 1716 to 1860." Ph.D. Johns Hopkins Univ., 1980.

Smith, Cortland Victor. "Church Organization as an Agency of Social Control: Church Discipline in North Carolina, 1800–1860." Ph.D., Univ. of North Carolina, 1966.

Index

Smith, Hiram M., 123
Snipes, Adeline, 99
Snipes, James, 99
Snipes, John B., 99
soil types. *See* geography
soldiers. *See* Civil War
Sons of Temperance, 60, 201–2, 204. *See*
    politics
Southerland, Fendal, 35
Southgate, James, 126
Sparrow, George, 82
Sparrow, Houston, 82
Stanford, Susan, 99
Stanford, Sauvin, 99
Stephens, John W., 133
Strayhorn family, 7
Strayhorn, Bryant, 22
Strayhorn, Gilbert, 7
Strayhorn, Harriet, 138
Strayhorn, Isaac, 138, 231
Strayhorn, Mary Jane, 14
Strowd, H.M. Cave, 41
Strudwick, Frederick, 65
Sutch, Richard, 152, 220–21, 225
Swain, David L., 91

taxes, 53, 89, 203
Tew, Charles C., 33
Thompson family, 139
Thompson, David, 75, 76, 78, 81,
    82–83
Thompson, Eliza, 108
Thompson, Walter A., 76
Thompson, William E., 139
Tilley family, 56
tobacco, 35–36, 111, 113, 196, 225
tobacco manufacturers, 114–18, 227,
    231
tobacco manufacturing, 30–31, 114–19,
    122–23
transportation, 11; *see also* North Caro-
    lina Central Railroad
treating. *See* politics
Turner, Josiah, Jr., 58, 61, 139–42, 143,
    144
typicality of Orange County. *See* Orange
    County

Umstead, Alvis K., 120, 134
Umstead, James N., 120
Umstead, John W., 134
unionism. *See* Civil War
University of North Carolina, 32, 33, 44,
    91, 93, 137, 138, 150

Vance, Zebulon, 85, 86, 90–91, 129, 142
voluntary associations, 46–50, 101–2,
    200–1, 219. *See* Grange; Masons;
    militia; neighborhoods; Orange
    County Agricultural Society; slave
    ownership; Sons of Temperance
voter turnout: antebellum, 58, 61,
    204–5; postbellum, 129, 130–31,
    136, 227, 228, 229–30; *see also*
    politics
voting, continuity in party support,
    65–66, 206, 229

Ward, Sally, 98
Ward, Sutton, 98
Watson, Henry Legare II, 205–6
Watson, William S., 82
Webb family, 114
Webb, James, 118
Webb, Robert F., 73, 79, 119, 120, 134
"Webb and Whitted Tobacco Factory,"
    30
Webb, Roulhac, and Company, 118
wheat, 35, 111, 225
Whigs: and Know-Nothings, 65; meet in
    courthouse, 203–4; profile of antebel-
    lum active participants, 63
White Cross neighborhood, 9, 15–17,
    34, 35, 56, 66, 74, 90, 99, 114, 150
widowhood. *See* Civil War; kinship.
Wiener, Jonathan, 152, 219
Wilkins, James, 98
Wilkins, Malinda, 98
Wilkins, William, 98
Woods family, 12
Woods, Henderson, 41
Woods, William, 41
Woodward, C. Vann, 152
Wooster, Ralph, 202
Worth, Jonathan, 129